MASTERING THE ASSESSMENT
CENTER PROCESS

ABOUT THE AUTHOR

Dr. Linsey Willis, with more than thirty-nine years of Human Resources and management experience, is currently president of L.J. CRAIG & Associates Inc., a management and organizational consulting firm. Her firm's clients represent a diverse mix of organizations from the public, private and not-for-profit sectors in the U.S., the Caribbean, Canada, Thailand and Dubai, U.A.E. Linsey serves as an expert witness for attorneys in the employment law and personal industry disciplines. Dr. Willis is also a full-time instructor for Florida Atlantic University's College of Business. She is on the faculty of its Management Department and teaches management and human resources undergraduate and graduate courses. She also teaches for the university's Executive Education department, for the HR and Advanced HR programs awarding students certificates of completion. Dr. Willis holds a doctorate in Public Administration from Nova Southeastern University, a master's degree in forensic studies from Indiana University, a master's degree in public administration from Florida Atlantic University, and a B.A. in political science from the University of Kentucky. She has also earned certification in human resources from the Human Resources Certification Institute which has certified her as a Senior Human Resources Professional (SPHR).

Second Edition

MASTERING THE ASSESSMENT CENTER PROCESS

The Fast Track to Promotion

By

LINSEY C. WILLIS, DPA, SPHR

President, L. J. Craig & Associates, Inc.
Boca Raton, Florida

Instructor
Florida Atlantic University
College of Business – Management Department
Boca Raton, Florida

CHARLES C THOMAS · PUBLISHER, LTD.
Springfield · Illinois · U.S.A.

Published and Distributed Throughout the World by

CHARLES C THOMAS • PUBLISHER, LTD.
2600 South First Street
Springfield, Illinois 62704

© 2021 by CHARLES C THOMAS • PUBLISHER, LTD.

ISBN 978-0-398-09370-9 (paper)
ISBN 978-0-398-09371-6 (ebook)

First Edition, 2017
Second Edition, 2021

Library of Congress Catalog Card Number: 2021014731 (print)
2021014732 (ebook)

With THOMAS BOOKS *careful attention is given to all details of manufacturing and design. It is the Publisher's desire to present books that are satisfactory as to their physical qualities and artistic possibilities and appropriate for their particular use.* THOMAS BOOKS *will be true to those laws of quality that assure a good name and good will.*

Printed in the United States of America
MM-C-1

Library of Congress Cataloging-in-Publication Data

Names: Willis, Linsey, author.
Title: Mastering the assessment center process : the fast track to promotion / by Linsey C. Willis, DPA, SPHR.
Description: Second edition. | Springfield, Illinois : Charles C Thomas, Publisher, Ltd., [2021] | Includes bibliographical references and index.
Identifiers: LCCN 2021014731 (print) | LCCN 2021014732 (ebook) | ISBN 9780398093709 (paperback) | ISBN 9780398093716 (ebook)
Subjects: LCSH: Police—United States—Examinations, questions, etc. | Police—Promotions—United States. | Police administration—United States. | Police—Vocational guidance—United States.
Classification: LCC HV8143 .W54 2021 (print) | LCC HV8143 (ebook) | DDC 363.2/2076—dc23
LC record available at https://lccn.loc.gov/2021014731
LC ebook record available at https://lccn.loc.gov/2021014732

*This book is dedicated to all the members of the
Thin Blue Line that protect all of us each day, and
do it without fame, without fortune, and without fail.*

*A special dedication is made to the members of the
line that have fallen in service, and to their families.
Their memories of their loved ones, and the mission
of the Thin Blue Line, live on in all of us.*

PREFACE

Thank you for purchasing this book. It was written because I know that you need and want what this book offers. After reading the sample exercises and commentary contained herein, you will be convinced that your time and money have been well spent. Why? Because you will have practiced the exercises herein, and beyond just reading about the assessment center (AC) process, you will have learned about many of the most important components of the process. For example, you will know what assessor notes look like and how they should be taken. You will know what a comprehensive Assessor Guide looks like and why an assessor's notes are so important.

I have read most of the books about the AC process, its skill dimensions, descriptions of the AC process, tips for preparing for an AC evaluation, and much more. Of course, a number of those books provide some sample in-basket items, but most are missing many of the essential sample exercises and components included in this book. Law enforcement officers preparing for promotion evaluations understand and can prepare for a paper-and-pencil 100-item multiple-choice test, but they have shared with me that often they are confused, afraid, nervous or just plain curious about what they will experience when they go through the AC process.

And, the AC process is the "Cadillac" of systems used to identify management potential I know of and the best method for testing whether a candidate can demonstrate a talent for planning and organizing and possesses the necessary judgment, communication skills, and decision-making ability to move up the ranks. Many candidates do possess these abilities but have not learned how to apply them. This book will teach you how to use all your potential. Just possessing certain innate abilities or really wanting a job is not enough. You must be prepared to show that you can do that job, and you must learn how to do that. In addition, it is almost impossible for an individual to fake his/her way through an AC process, although many candidates who have failed, perceive that their "buddies" did in fact do just that. But, as you probably already know, the assessors are sitting in the back of the room taking notes or will take notes later while listening to an audio or video recording of the process. If candidates are trying to fake their way through it, the assessors will note that they peppered their answers with a lot of "uhs" or "ums," repeated phrases, or made statements that had nothing to do with what the exercise is really about, or wrote things unrelated to the exercise. If the situation occurs where one or more candidates are able to obtain high scores even though they were not prepared, then the process as conducted was not valid.

Here are some examples of invalid processes:

- No job analysis was conducted.
- The exercises are based on vague job descriptions.
- Some of the exercise components may never occur in the agency.
- The exercise response standards are severely lacking in content.
- There is no evidence of a linkage between the job tasks and the abilities required to successfully complete the tasks.
- If no job analysis exists the weight given each skill dimension will not be available.
- There is no record of critical incident job analysis notes obtained during assessment process conducted by the consultant.
- Because the assessors indicate they were trained by another vendor, they may not be trained for the specific agency's AC process.
- Candidates who participate in a process for their city or agency helped a vendor develop the exercises and then the vendor was hired by their city to administer the process they will be competing in.
- The chief or assistant chief develops material that gives the impression of internal bias or suggests that the process will not be strictly confidential.
- Some assessors take few or no notes and the test administrators do nothing about this because no one will be auditing the final score sheets.
- There are problems during the administration of the process which provide an unfair disadvantage to the candidates who experienced these problems. Sometimes there are mechanical problems such as printer breaking down. Perhaps some candidates have long wait times between exercises and others do not; or candidates are not sequestered and morning candidates share information with their friends whose process starts later.

All of the sample exercises included in this book have been used in past AC processes or in customized coaching exercises. The names of the individuals and agencies have been excluded for confidentiality purposes. Read on, and learn at a pace comfortable for you and treasure your new insights.

What also makes our knowledge and experience so relevant for you is that all of the other consultants in the United States whose work and reputations I am familiar with, do not have the 360-degree experience with the AC process. The 360-degree feedback process involves obtaining feedback from a circle of personnel who extend beyond direct reports. I am not minimizing or denigrating the knowledge they add to the topic at hand, because I have read their books and many of the books are very well written and comprehensive. The consultants who provide group training on the AC process do not have the knowledge and training on how to design, develop, implement, administer and score AC exercises. They have only taken their knowledge and experience with AC processes they have participated in and turned this experience into a consulting enterprise.

Consulting firms make considerable money when 25–30 people pay anywhere from $500–$1,500 for one or two days of group training. This is an excellent way to learn what you will be experiencing after you pass the written examination. My firm (L.J. Craig & Associates) has a totally different business model. We provide our clients with a return on their investment; approximately 98 percent of the law enforcement officers we have coached over the past several years have been promoted. Their ranks range from sergeant up through and including chief of police, from all across the United States, from small agencies to large city departments, and including state highway patrol officers and sheriff's deputies and some federal agencies.

The design, development, administration and scoring of any AC process takes anywhere from 300 to 600 work hours—for smaller agencies with fewer than a dozen candidates. At a minimal cost of $20 per hour, that would represent a minimum cost of $6,000 to $12,000 for such an assessment center. A good AC process is extremely labor intensive.

I have always breathed a sigh of relief once a process is completed. This is because of the rigorous nature of the design and administration of the process which includes writing candidate feedback reports (this process is too time consuming and difficult for assessors). Other consultants I know from other firms have been relieved at completion, too—because no lawsuit had been filed. That has happened many times all over the United States since the 1970s, especially with large urban departments. We have never had a lawsuit filed against our firm nor has anyone threatened to file one. Nonetheless, it is always a concern.

With coaching, I have never had a sigh-of-relief moment after that process is over. In fact, after every coaching assignment, I have felt elated, proud and delighted because I knew I helped someone to best utilize their innate abilities. As a professional and a human being, I love the face-to-face contact most (of the time via Zoom) after the promotion process is complete.

L.C.W.

ACKNOWLEDGMENTS

In June 2015 during the annual meeting I have with my two affiliates, Bill Reilly, Assistant Police Chief (ret,) and Lt. Paul Patti (ret), we discussed our goals for the coming year. We meet at the same place each year and dine on seafood in Melbourne, FL. During our lunch, great ideas are generated and my affiliates had a great idea which was presented to me more like a police command: "Linsey, you have to write a book on AC's and use an experiential approach." This book fulfills their command in less time than I anticipated. Therefore, I first want to acknowledge Bill and Paul for their collaboration, inspiration, support, and friendship.

I also want to acknowledge my husband, J. Frank Willis, without whose support, love, nurturing, interest, and admiration, I would not be doing what I am doing at this stage of my career.

My appreciation and admiration are also owed to Dr. Pat Maher, a retired police lieutenant, with whom I have been friends since 1982. We met at a conference on the assessment center process and thereafter have worked together on various projects including conference presentations. Additionally, the help of Rick Michelson, also a retired police lieutenant, is also acknowledged. I also want to thank Andy Scott, a former police chief, whom I have also known for more than 20 years. He has been a supportive colleague, former client and friend. Finally, I want to acknowledge Alan Chertok, a lawyer and retired police chief, whose national and international law enforcement experience makes him exceptionally well qualified to have reviewed my book.

Others who read and gave invaluable input on this book include: Dr. Melinda Holmes; Craig Roegner, RAC, federal ATF; and Michael Annese, a fire department battalion chief, author of *The Victory Cycle* (2015), and a successful candidate in past assessment center processes.

Last but not least, I want to thank Dr. David Herst a colleague at Florida Atlantic University's College of Business.

One additional and very important person I want to acknowledge is Dr. Robert S. Sloat, one of my associates helped edit my book.

Thank you all so much.

CONTENTS

EXHIBITS

MASTERING THE ASSESSMENT CENTER PROCESS

Chapter 1

INTRODUCTION

This book has been written for all police officers who want to be promoted, whether to sergeant, lieutenant, captain, deputy or assistant chief or chief or any person from a state or federal law enforcement agency. And anyone interested in learning more about the assessment center process of candidate evaluation, to include practitioners working in human resource departments or Industrial Organizational psychologists and the like may also find this book useful. This book is not designed to teach HR professionals how to design an assessment center process, nor is it to be considered a comprehensive textbook on the subject.

The majority of the chapters in this book contain sample exercises which you can complete, and then later review with the Assessor Guides, role player scripts and other material contained in the Exhibits Appendix. Sample candidate reports may be found in Chapter 16.

It is not necessary to read the chapters consecutively because each chapter is written to stand alone. If you choose to start reading in the middle or near the end of the book, you will not feel that what you just learned is disconnected from another chapter. I do, however, recommend that if you have little or no understanding of the assessment center (AC) process, that you read the book from cover to cover.

Chapter 2

YOUR CANDIDATE TRAINING SCRIPT

OVERVIEW

Throughout my career designing AC processes one of the important components is the candidate orientation. Orienting candidates somewhere between one and two weeks before the process is relatively standard. Candidate orientation should never be excluded from any process because of budgetary or time constraints, nor should it be done just a day or so before the process. However, some agencies do not give candidates much advance notice. Nevertheless, candidates should know quite fully what they are going to be experiencing, which includes not only an overview of what an AC process is about, but how they will be scored, etc.

Most of this chapter is designed so that you will learn much of what assessors are taught in their training. The material was prepared initially for one of my clients. I decided that because the agency had never before used AC methodology, I wanted them to use the best process my firm could provide, so I created an abbreviated assessor-training manual.

You might envision yourself sitting in the training room of your department. Then:

- Clear your desk or work space of instructional materials and distracting objects;
- Pretend that I am in the room making a formal presentation to you using the following material;
- Prepare to read very carefully.

THE ASSESSMENT CENTER PROCESS

Pretend you are one rank above the position you currently hold. Assume that you are participating in an assessor training program for your department. Pretend also that this section of the book is part of the trainer's script. What you will read starts out very broadly, then goes into great detail, and then repeats some concepts to reinforce your learning.

The term "AC" refers to a standardized system used for identifying an individual's strengths and weaknesses for a predetermined purpose, such as a promotion or employee development. An AC is a process not a place. The AC is a testing methodology. The term "assessment" usually refers to a comprehensive, multi-faceted view of an individual in which information gleaned from a variety of measurements is brought together. The information that is derived is related to the critical job dimensions for the target position and is designed to predict who will be successful in that position.

The usual assessment center program lasts from one to two days and may last longer depending on the number of exercises used. That duration depends on the complexity of the target position. The participants go through four to six exercises specifically designed to elicit behaviors which have been identified as important to effective performance in the position. These key behaviors are identified through a comprehensive job analysis of the position. This job analysis is one key factor which supports the legal defensibility of the assessment process. As the candidates go through each exercise, the trained assessors observe and record the behaviors demonstrated in each candidate's performance. After all the behavioral simulations are completed by the candidates, the assessors prepare an assessor integration discussion with other assessors who have observed the same participants.

Each assessor evaluates each skill dimension based on the evidence presented from all the exercises, and a numerical rating for each dimension is determined independently by each assessor. The numerical ratings assigned by the assessors are compared, and an integration discussion ensues until a group consensus on a single numerical rating for each dimension is reached. This discussion is vital to the success of the assessment process in that the assessors must discuss all the behavioral data collected and agree upon standards in reaching the consensus rating assigned. After a consensus is reached on each of the dimensions, the final profile of the candidate is achieved. This final profile provides each candidate with their scores from all assessors across all exercises and skill dimensions.

A Brief History

The first major documented use of AC procedures in American industry was a monumental study called the Management Progress Study which was conducted at AT&T beginning in 1956 (Bray, 1964; Bray & Grant, 1966; Bray, Campbell & Grant, 1974). The study involved four-hundred and twenty-two recently hired males whose progress had been followed to determine their range of professional growth and the characteristics which led to their success in management. The results of the initial eight-year "predictive validity study" were quite positive. Eighty-five percent of the individuals who successfully reached the middle management level had been correctly identified by the assessment process (Bray & Grant, 1966; Thornton & Byham, 1982).

Over the approximately sixty years since the AC method was used in the private sector including such companies as AT&T and JC Penny, the method which was used to study adult development has expanded to a great many countries (Lievens & Thornton, 2005). After its use became common in the U.S. it gained acceptance in the United Kingdom and then was adopted by Germany, Japan, South Africa and then other country participants, who attended one of the International Congress conferences on the AC method, including Sweden, South Korea, India, Indonesia, Kuwait, Brazil, Venezuela, Russia, China, Singapore, and Malaysia (Thornton & Krause, 2009). Based on research by Thornton and Rupp (2006), the method has gained acceptance in other fields during the last fifty years, including developmental planning and advanced training. And soon after the AT&T Management Progress Study (Howard & Bray, 1988) was completed, other large corporations found that the AC method was able to identify those who had managerial talent (Thornton & Byham, 1982; Thornton & Krause, 2009).

With that background, let's go back to the years before AC was widely adopted by private industry. The use of AC assessment and selection methods had been evolving and accelerating since its first use in this country by the Office of Strategic Services, which later became the Central Intelligence Agency. That agency assessed 5,391 persons in the United States between December 1943 and August 1945 (Mackinnon, 1977, Office of Strategic Services, 1948).

During the first year of the OSS in 1942, a large number of recruits whose performance was later deemed questionable were hired, since selection was not based upon any professional or uniform screening process. In later years, an AC methodology was utilized to predict an applicant's likelihood of success as a spy. The actual techniques and exercises used included varied and the process and methods used by the OSS involved identifying behaviors related to successful performance.

The same methods are currently being used. Moreover, a multitude of scholarly journal articles and books have been written on the methodology. Among them, Thornton, and Rupp (2006) wrote *Assessment Centers in Human Resource Management: Strategies for Prediction, Diagnosis, and Development* and Thornton and Gibbons (2009) published Validity of Assessment Centers for Personnel Selection in the *Human Resource Management Review.*

In 1970, an article by William C. Byham, appeared in the Harvard Business Review. The article based upon his experiences, as well as others, in the implementation of the AC process for JC Penney, captured and communicated to the general business community the enthusiasm for the evolving AC concept and the validity evidence obtained up to that point. Bray et al. (1974) have also succinctly explained why it is that ACs make sense. These authors formulated the requirements of management into two basic categories. One category relates to the technical aspects of a job and to the procedural and informational foundation of effective performance. The second category encompasses various features of a managerial skill nature, including communications, motivation, influence, and leadership. Each position in a managerial hierarchy represents some blend of the two categories i.e., technical skill and managerial skill. Specific technical competencies are not measured because the Assessors are required to concentrate upon the more universal aspects of effective management performance working with and through other people.

AC Process Specifics

The AC method integrates different kinds of information in a testing setting. In this context, an AC can be thought of as both a place and a process. It is a place where individuals participate in a variety of measurement techniques. It is also a process designed to provide standardized and objective conditions for evaluation.

The AC method has two major strengths. First, it uses techniques designed to simulate critical behaviors related to success on the job. It then facilitates the integration of information by pooling data from a variety of assessment sources.

Another strength of the AC method is that candidates participate in different types of simulation exercises which are designed to reflect, as close to reality as possible, the actual job they are testing for. The best exercises are those designed so the candidate feels as though they are actually on the job, regardless of the length of the simulation, perhaps ten minutes to make a presentation, twenty minutes to interact with a role-playing "irate citizen," etc. Each exercise or measurement technique is designed to assess a predetermined skill, certain abilities or competencies. These techniques include group exercises, "in-basket" exercises, pencil-and-paper tests, and assessment process. The techniques may also include specifically designed role-playing problems, telephone calls, or simulated assessment process.

Reports are prepared describing the assessment's outcome. Depending on the intent of the process, these reports can contain diagnostic information concerning a participant's strengths and weaknesses, or simply a statement predicting the candidate's potential for success in the management position.

Performance by participants in the AC process is observed by a trained team of assessors from one to two ranks above the position being tested for. These evaluators receive special training and participate as members of the assessment team. Over the years I have trained several hundred persons to serve as assessors. The number of days required for their training has always been a difficult issue to deal with. There are many reasons for this. The assessors have three main roles: observation, documentation and evaluation.

When I first received training on the AC process in the early 1980s, the program lasted five days. I later participated in a training for assessors session. At a minimum, one day of training should be provided for each exercise. However, the training is determined by a number of factors to include; whether or not the assessors have been previously trained; how many exercises are being used; how many exercises each assessor will be responsible for each day; and, budgetary constraints.

Overall, the longer the assessor training period runs, the costlier the whole process becomes and the less willing many HR departments or police staffers involved in HR issues are to spend more money. It is fairly typical for these personnel to emphasize that they will have difficulty obtaining assessors from neighboring agencies to serve for more than a few days, cannot afford to add two more days to the schedule or to note that they have assessors on staff who have already been trained by other vendors. Nonetheless, my position is that anything less than one full day of training misses the mark. As you read through this book and practice the exercises you will understand why assessor training is so important.

Each assessor has several key functions to perform. They will follow the schedule provided by the test administrators and observe or read the assigned candidate's interactions and documents throughout the day. At the end of each day, the assessors report on what behaviors they observed with other members of the assessment team, and the effectiveness of the behaviors noted. While the length of training varies from center to center, all assessors receive special instructions concerning each aspect of the process.

An AC can also be defined as a sophisticated rating process which is designed to minimize as many forms of rater bias as possible. Each candidate is given the same opportunity to demonstrate his/her abilities in standardized situations.

There must be a sufficient number of assessors so that each candidate is observed by more than one judge. The process requires that independent judgments of behaviors and effectiveness are made. Multiple observers, multiple sources of information and specifically defined objective dimensions of performance all add to the objectivity of the process. In summary, an AC has the following characteristics:

- Multiple assessment techniques are used.
- Multiple assessors are used.
- Assessors receive training prior to participating in a center.
- Judgments resulting in an outcome (i.e., recommendations for promotion, specific training or development) are based on pooled information from all assessors.
- An overall evaluation of behavior is made by the assessors at a separate time from their observations.
- Simulation exercises are used.

- Those simulation exercises are developed to tap a variety of pre-determined behaviors and have been pretested prior to use to ensure that the techniques provide reliable, objective and relevant determinations for the sponsoring organization.

WHY ASSESSMENT CENTER MEASUREMENTS ARE ACCURATE

Overall Assessment Ratings

One of the reasons well-designed AC measurements are accurate is because the Overall Assessment Rating (OAR) is based on average ratings drawn from all of the exercises and skill dimensions as evaluated by each assessor (see Exhibits Appendix). The success of their predictions depends on assessor's identifying a candidate's effective and ineffective performance in each exercise across the skill dimensions.

Why are AC process categorizations valid? Because the assessors have taken notes about what they observed for each candidate—including statements made by the candidate and the candidate's written communication. In the following paragraphs, some of the more important factors affecting AC measurements are outlined.

The assessor has carefully observed and documented each candidate's behavior, and can therefore make some valid inferences. What is relevant to that process is the assessor's note-taking skills and dealing with a great deal of relevant information. Also, an assessor is observing a candidate's behavior for only the length of the exercise in the formal testing setting. Below are examples of notes I took during a coaching session for one of my clients from which I was able to infer from the notes I took during the coaching session what skill dimension was being tapped into.

- **"I would ask him why he has had performance problems"**
- **"Provide employee assistance counseling"**
- **"Give him a chance to take responsibility"**
- **"Ask him for his feedback"**

Given these notes, can you infer that the candidate made some decisions? Also, were the decisions appropriate based on the context? Regardless of what you (the reader) think, the notes are documented evidence of the candidate's behavior (i.e., the words came directly from his mouth based on the notes he took when preparing the exercise).

The notes derived from AC exercises are evidence of a candidate's ability to plan and organize and make decisions. All of the data assembled for each candidate includes a final assessment of their overall AC ratings, and final written predictions about how they should perform in the job. But, assessors must suppress their natural tendency to be either too harsh or too kind in their many observations which will of necessity lead to final conclusions. For example, care must be taken not to infer that a person was silent for ten minutes in a group discussion because they felt intimidated, but rather that the person was just silent or perhaps mentally evaluating comments made by other participants in the group discussion exercise. Period. The candidate may be silent for many reasons, which include both situational and personal factors. During a period of silence, assessors can learn much from the body language of the silent candidate. Such behaviors could include eye contact, nods of agreement, note-taking, writing, or any number of other examples, all of which should be documented.

Advantage of Working in Groups

Working in groups does more than provide accuracy or safety in numbers. The more individual scores there are, the more likely it is that each candidate will be measured objectively. Assessors independently and without consulting one another, determine which score each candidate should receive for each skill dimension. Since assessors must depend on each other for reliable, observational information, each assessor is motivated to remain highly attentive to each candidate's performance. The integrity of the process is maintained by the fact that anything reported is open to challenge by another assessor and must be defensible. The assessor must cite or read the behavioral observations backed by their notes to the other assessors. In other words, there must be evidence in the assessor's notes or the candidate's own writings to support any given score. Without such supporting evidence you have nothing.

Practice is Beneficial

If you practice something the proper way, that practice is beneficial. In AC evaluations, the proper way is determined in large part by the controlled sequence of exercise and procedures. With standardized procedures, each repetition amounts to practice and improved ability to perform assessments. Assessors develop a frame of reference with experience that enables them to sort the behaviors observed.

The more opportunities a person has to serve as an assessor, the better they will become in the three major assessor responsibilities: observation, documentation, and evaluation.

Observation—Use of Behavioral Data

Assessment ratings which become part of a candidate feedback report are based on observable behavior rather than conjecture. Observable behaviors can always be described by a verb and an adverb, "The individual spoke well." If several repetitions of "speaking well" are observed, we might reasonably use an adjective and noun as part of a characterization, "The person is a good speaker." Ultimately, we might wish to use a generalized noun "speaking ability" in referring to a quality possessed by a person.

The assessors can usually agree that an individual spoke, or decided, or summarized. They can also agree somewhat less often whether an individual spoke, decided, or summarized well or poorly and to what degree. Therefore, specific behaviors should be noted. Direct quotations or as much of the essence of statements made are essential. However, assessors are not expected to transcribe conversation verbatim.

The conclusions drawn from several observations that an individual is a "good decision-maker" logically involve steps to get there: the application of verbs and adverbs to actions which are conceptualized from on-going behavior (e.g., decisions being made well or poorly) and the use of adjectives and nouns as a means of generalizing from the observed behaviors to the more enduring characteristics of the individual (e.g., "This person is a good decision-maker" or "The individual has lots of decision-making ability"). The assessor is *not* to write down the latter statement, but attempt to record what the candidate actually said that substantiates his/her conclusion. But remember, even though these sound decisions made are based on only one testing session, they are predictors of how the candidate is likely to make decisions on the job.

Below is another example from one of my coaching clients whose written statements are about how he would coach a problem employee whose job performance may be adversely affected by an impending divorce:

- **"Once the meeting takes place, be empathetic with situation"**
- **"First thing I would do is tell him I know he can do the job"**
- **"Review his past performance appraisals"**
- **"Ask him about the incident"**

If you are familiar with psychological assessment, or if you have ever taken a psychological test, you likely understand that different tests measure different things in different ways. The emphasis on verbs, adverbs and behavioral statements and observations in AC discussions ensures that the categorization of the behavioral statements in the various skill dimensions—such as planning and organization—are based on factual evidence. During the testing process, assessors take ownership of their behavioral information and again, they defend the ratings they assign. I also always remind them that their evaluations are impacting a candidate's career.

Assessors are usually line managers who can be counted upon to see how responses relate to the work environment. This is especially the case where the exercises provide a representative sample of the current work environment. You will learn how to take notes that are actual observations of the candidate's behavior as opposed to conclusive statements. Then you will review the Assessor Guides at which point you will be able to match your notes with the behaviors and actions listed in the checklists. The next section covers the categorization process in more detail.

Categorization of Behavioral Observations

One of the critical outcomes of an AC is accurate categorization (i.e., the behavioral statements made by the candidate). The act of categorizing, with some justification, can be performed by some assessor after five minutes' exposure to a candidate. Below is an example of my notes for another client's written sample which I categorized as planning and organizing behaviors:

- **"As a sergeant in charge of this operation, I will first gather information by holding a community meeting . . ."**
- **"Meet with my squad of eight officers"**
- **"Meeting with the bar owner"**

These statements are also examples of decision making, and the client received credit in the Assessor Guide for making the planning statements.

One way to decrease errors is to increase the number of chances of being right. As the number of behavioral dimensions and situations observed increases, the chance of overlooking an important fact of a candidate's qualifications decrease. Many duplications exist in an AC process to serve as a form of "checks and balances." For example, the members of the assessor team may jot down the exact same notes give or take a few different words, in different sections of the assessment. These provide the assessors with multiple inputs decreasing the likelihood a behavior might be missed in less extensive evaluations.

Good assessment categorizations can be accomplished if the behavioral dimensions have been carefully chosen and if behaviors relevant to these dimensions are elicited by the exercises. Another example of categorization for a written report for planning and organization is: scheduled follow-up meetings and included dates and times. It is, after all, the individual's behavior, not the work environment, which is being assessed. The validity of behavioral categorization depends, in large part, on making sure that the type of exercises being used actually measure behaviors relevant to the skill sets which actually relate to the work environment for the position.

Validity and Reliability

Two important characteristics of perception are used advantageously by the AC process. First, much of what we observe is relative, or determined by relationships among things seen. AC assessments are powerful because they are based upon undeniable facts about an individual and are therefore predictive of a person's managerial skills.

One of the reasons that the AC methodology has stood the test of time is that it has repeatedly demonstrated validity and reliability when subjected to controlled research studies. Validity refers to an assessment's ability to measure what it was intended to measure, while reliability is the consistency of the measurement instrument and the assurance that it does measure what it is supposed to measure. Content validity requires that the tasks (or simulations) covered by the testing procedure reflect actual job content—or, ensuring the exercise simulations are job-related. The successful prediction of a candidate's future job performance is boosted the more the assessment exercises resemble the actual job. To recap, the issues or concerns which are paramount in the development of a valid and reliable AC process include:

- A thorough job analysis of the target position and the resultant identification of the critical job dimensions.
- The development of exercises that accurately reflect the tasks associated with the position.
- Standardized and thorough training of the assessors.
- Standardization of the methodology which ensures that all candidates are treated the same way, with the same exercises, the same assessors, same Assessor Guides, same length of time for each exercise, the same instructions.

THE JOB ANALYSIS

The principles which should guide the design of AC exercises and Assessor Guides are the same as those used in the development of any written examinations and structured assessment process. To establish the validity of an AC process, the exercises must be chosen or created on the basis of a job analysis. Job analysis is the systematic process of collecting information and data about all the functions specific to the nature of a particular employment classification.

For the sake of brevity, there are basically three parts to a job analysis:

- Identify the job completely and accurately.
- Describe all tasks of the particular job accurately.
- Indicate the requirements the job places upon the individual for successful performance.

Job analysis data has many very important purposes in human resource management systems. A job analysis can be used to determine what kinds of selection tests will be used. The job analysis can aid in placement decisions and what training needs to be conducted based on a training needs assessment. There are several ways to conduct a job analysis. Any complete job analysis is one that discloses the critical knowledges, skills, abilities and other personal characteristics that are essential components of the specific position. The skill dimensions measured in an AC process serve as common labels such as leadership, interpersonal relations, decision making, organizing and planning, and flexibility.

Once the requirements of the target job are established, they must be evaluated and screened in order to derive a final set of assessment dimensions. The list below summarizes some information about skill dimensions.

- The assessment skill dimensions should be defined in behavioral terms. For example, oral communication can be defined in terms of eye contact, enunciation, voice modulation, and gestures.
- The assessment dimensions should exclude skills which can more easily be observed outside of a simulation context, such as technical competence.
- A final list of anywhere from six to no more than nine dimensions will be measured in an AC process.
- Since the AC process may align with an existing performance appraisal system it may be a good idea for the consultant to make sure that the performance dimensions evaluated in each are similar. However, AC exercises should not be developed to align exclusively with the current performance appraisal system.

Once the final assessment dimensions are determined and agreed to by the job incumbents who are referred to as subject matter experts (SMEs), the designer of the AC is in a position to select or construct the measurement instruments. At this stage, there is no substitute for experience and professional judgment. The designer must decide whether each dimension is most effectively measured, for example, by a standardized paper-and-pencil test, a commercially available simulation exercise or a new exercise tailor-made for the organization.

Exhibit 1 (see Exhibits Appendix) depicts actual skill dimensions, their definitions and final weightings based on a one-hundred percent scale, taken from a police department sergeant process designed by my firm. The SMEs were asked to distribute the percentages across all of the dimensions. The weight given each dimension was the last part of the job analysis process. Then all of the data was presented, discussed, tabulated and averaged across all the SMEs. Exhibit 2 (see Exhibits Appendix) depicts actual skill dimensions, their definitions and final weightings for the AM and PM shifts also based on a 100 percent scale, taken from a police detective process for the same police department.

In summary, a careful job analysis will not only establish the validity and reliability of an AC process, but it will also enhance the designer's ability to select appropriate exercises for the process. However, the exercises are useless without the assessors, who should be well trained so they are objective and proficient in observing, documenting, and evaluating behavior.

An Assessor's Roles and Responsibilities

This section about an assessor's major responsibilities has been included to provide you with some insight about what assessors around the country are expected to learn during their training. The more you know about this process, the more comfortable you should feel when going through an AC process yourself. Of course, the latter statements assume that the assessors who will be evaluating you are well trained, which I sadly say, is not always the case.

One of the most critical components of the whole AC process is the team of assessors. The assessors are responsible for collecting, recording and evaluating the participants' behavior as observed in the job task simulations. Specialized and highly concentrated training is necessary to provide the assessor with the essential competencies to effectively and accurately complete their responsibilities during the AC. As a result, assessor training is structured around the development of specific competencies so that the assessor can reliably record and evaluate the observed behaviors.

The assessor must have a thorough understanding of each of the behavioral simulations used during the AC process. Each assessor will complete the exercises first, to have a feel for what a candidate will experience. Completing the exercises will also give the assessor knowledge of the different aspects, key points and major problems involved in a simulation.

Assessors must be able to record as many behaviors as they can, and as rapidly as they can. They should also ensure that the behaviors they document on paper are the most relevant comments made by the candidates. Overall, without enough training, an assessor will be unable to make objective evaluations. Once the assessors have observed and recorded the behaviors, they observe, their next task will be to categorize those behaviors under the appropriate dimensions.

Purpose of Evaluating Behavior

By evaluating participants in an AC process relative to their skill in each dimension, one can produce a profile of each candidate which should capture their strengths and weaknesses. A caveat is that if assessors have not received sufficient training on how to fairly observe, document and evaluate candidates' skills, then they will be unable to prepare a final report which accurately sketches their strengths and weaknesses. Two reports may be found in Chapter 17.

Once the assessors have observed and recorded behavior, their next task will be to categorize that behavior under the appropriate skill dimensions. After an assessor has classified the behavior under a particular dimension, the next step is to decide how good the candidate was in exhibiting that dimension. It is at this point that the assessor can start to evaluate the positive or negative aspects of the behaviors. To accomplish this, the assessor must have a thorough understanding of the five or seven-point rating scale and of the standards for determining where on the scale the candidate demonstrated a particular dimension.

Participants are not compared with other participants, but are compared against an absolute standard as required for success in the target-level position. This process takes practice, particularly in reaching agreement on what the standards are and reliably applying those standards to the behaviors observed.

Sample Rating Scales

A five-point rating scale may be used to evaluate candidate's performance in each exercise, to rate the candidate's performance in each dimension. Other scales (1–7, 1–10) may also be used. A five-point scale is most commonly used unless the agency specifically wants its own scale used. Two different versions of five-point rating scales are depicted in **Exhibits 4 and 5** in the Exhibits Appendix.

5 **Highly desirable**
4 **Desirable**
3 **Somewhat desirable**
2 **Would consider**
1 **Would not consider**

It is important to remember that each point relates to a distinct level of performance. That is, the difference between a 5 or a 4 is not merely one point, but, rather, it is more like an academic grade of an A or a B. The assessors must arrive at a numerical rating. While it is sometimes difficult to rate candidate performance, it must be done, based on the observed behaviors. Taking good notes results in more clarity and makes this much easier.

DISTRIBUTION OF SCORES

There is often a tendency to avoid the highest and lowest ratings (1 and 5). But it is critical to use the full range of scores, if they clearly apply. If any of the scores are eliminated simply because they represent the extremes, then the scale is reduced from five levels to four or three. This, in turn, causes an artificially foreshortened range that results in a test that poorly differentiates performance levels among participants.

There is no specified distribution of how scores should be assigned, but past experience gives us an indication of expected frequency:

5 **5 to 15 percent of the total scores**
4 **15 to 25 percent of the total scores**
3 **35 to 50 percent of the total scores**
2 **15 to 25 percent of the total scores**
1 **Less than 5 percent of the total scores**

A score of 1 is not encountered too frequently, largely because of the evaluation processes that are a part of most assessment procedures. Potential participants who feel that they are not qualified for the position will usually screen themselves out. In most promotion systems, there are one or more screening steps (e.g., a written examination) that participants must pass in order to continue on to the AC process. This screening process enhances the likelihood that participants are minimally qualified in most rating categories.

The Assessor Integration Discussion

The assessor integration discussion is held after all the exercises have been completed and all assessor tabulation forms (this is my word for a matrix) have been completed. During the discussion, the assessors discuss the performance of one candidate in at least one of the assessment exercises. Each assessor reads their notes of the participant's behavior in the exercise to the other assessors. Notes can be abbreviated, and only key examples of behavior need to be recorded. Generally, only extremely good or bad behavior needs to be recorded. The notes aid each listening assessor to develop their own overall rating for each dimension and defend that rating. No assessor should be allowed to dominate the integration process which includes a discussion. Assessors have a responsibility to call it as they see it and to objectively discuss the behaviors observed relative to the standards established to reach consensus on the final evaluation for each dimension. Each assessor's independently determined rating is not intended to influence the other assessors, but rather as a contribution to a consensus that will be reached after they have paid close attention to the other assessors' appraisals.

The observations reported from the assessor tabulation form for each exercise become part of the large pool of observations on which final judgments on the participant's performance are based. The final scores for all assessors for all dimensions across all exercises are recorded on what is referred to as a master matrix form.

Determining the Final Overall Rating

Assessors evaluate the data and then determine a rating for each dimension for the candidate. They weigh the behavioral observations according to the importance or weight of the exercise compared to other exercises, if applicable. For example, several obvious examples of poor judgment displayed in an in-basket exercise may be far more significant than two moderate examples of good judgment seen in a group discussion exercise. If there are conflicting observations by the assessors where the point spread is more than two points, then they should review their notes and discuss why they are more than two points apart. Although a two-point spread can be defended—say three assessors score it, 4,4,2—it is much better if the assessor who gave the candidate a two raises his/her score, if it seems reasonable. Once the assessors have determined their ratings, they list them on what is known as the assessor master matrix.

The test administrator then asks the assessors who have assigned ratings markedly different from the other assessors to explain their reasoning. The group discusses the differences and arrives at a consensus rating for each dimension. After the discussion, each assessor determines the final overall ratings for each skill dimension for each candidate.

The Candidate Feedback Report

At the conclusion of the AC process for all candidates, the assessors start to prepare a written report for each candidate which comprehensively describes, by dimension, the performance of the candidate. If, however, the consulting firm is writing the reports after all the files have been compiled, the report writing process supervised/facilitated by the consultant commences. Regardless of who is responsible for writing the candidate feedback reports, the writers must have a complete understanding of each dimension as well as the categorization process. Again, sample candidate feedback reports may be found in Chapter 17.

Chapter 3

THE ASSESSOR GUIDES

OVERVIEW

When candidates are assessed during an AC process or any multi-component testing process, their innate abilities are what is being measured. A person's relative strengths and weaknesses are measured in the simulations and written exercises. There are hundreds of universal abilities, which means abilities that are relevant to most jobs. During a job analysis process, the knowledges, skills and abilities are identified and recorded by the job analyst or consultant. Given that many abilities are somewhat universal to most jobs, like the ability to communicate orally, the job analyst does not have to totally "reinvent the wheel," because there is a great deal of information and standing definitions of skill dimensions in the public domain. However, the final descriptions of the skill dimensions for a particular job title should be agreed upon by the job analyst and the SMEs.

The Dictionary of Occupational Titles has been replaced with the more ability-based Occupational Information Network (O*NET; Peterson et al., 2001). If you want more information about some of the universal competencies for law enforcement job titles you should go to O*Net online. Using this information as a baseline for any job description largely eliminates the need to reinvent the wheel.

DIFFERENCE BETWEEN AN ABILITY, SKILL AND COMPETENCY

Academics have stated that more abstract inferences are required when making ability judgments compared with task judgments (Harvey, 1991; Morgeson & Campion, 2000). Task statements are different than

22

ability statements but the abilities are necessary in order an employee to perform the tasks correctly. For example, in order to prepare reports an employee must be able to write or type.

Abilities are also referred to as skill dimensions or competencies de pending on the purpose for which each is being used. Competency modeling has emerged as somewhat of a major discipline in HR practice in the last fifteen years. Shippmann et al. (2000) noted that between 75% and 80% of surveyed companies has some form of competency-related applications in place. Although there is much confusion associated with the practice of competency modeling, perhaps one of the most confusing issues involves actually defining a competency. The same applies somewhat to defining an ability.

What does the aforementioned have to do with the AC process and your innate abilities? To recap, you should know and understand that an ability can also be referred to as a skill dimension (which is very common in the AC process) and may also be referred to as a competency by your HR Department.

According to many researchers (Ulrich, Brockbank, Yeung & Lake, 1995; Fleishman, Wetrogan, Uhlman & Marshall-Mies, 1995; Boyatzis, 1982; Barrett & Depinet, 1991; Shippmann et al., 2000) there are numerous ways to define what is considered to be a competency. An excellent example of competencies is one I used to design, develop, and administer a management assessment center process for a former client. The competency categories and individual competencies follow over the next few pages.

COMPETENCY MODEL FOR MANAGEMENT SELECTION IN A LARGE PUBLIC SECTOR ORGANIZATION

Relationship Building

- **Negotiation:** Negotiates win-win outcomes by being well prepared, gaining trust, searching for creative and mutually beneficial solutions, and being willing to compromise when appropriate.
- **Peer Relationships:** Can quickly find common ground and solve problems for the good of all; is seen as a team player and is cooperative; encourages collaboration; can be candid with peers. Cultivates trusting relationships that are maintained over time.

Management

- **Judgment and Reasoning:** Effectively diagnoses problems; identifies core issues; exercises common sense; sees critical connections and ramifications and analyzes alternatives.
- **Decisiveness:** Makes clear-cut decisions without unnecessary delay, even in tough situations.
- **Dependability:** Can be counted on to meet commitments and deadlines.
- **Planning and Organizing:** Establishes short-term goals; clarifies roles and responsibilities; sets priorities and milestones, and is not distracted by unimportant details or activities.

Environmental Awareness

- **Organizational Awareness:** Is alert to events and trends within the organization and considers how they might influence the long-term performance of the organization. Can maneuver through complex political situations effectively and quietly. Keeps up on developments outside the organization that may have an impact on the business, such as trends in the industry, new technologies, and events in the larger economic and political environments.

Compelling Vision

- **Strategic Focus:** Thinks strategically, creates an ongoing, dynamic strategic process, and communicates the organization's long-term direction to staff.
- **Creativity and Innovation:** Personally generates new ideas or improved approaches, products and solutions.
- **Coaching:** Facilitates career development of subordinates by providing regular coaching. Helps change behavior, improve performance and sustain commitment through encouragement, support, collaborative problem-solving, goal-setting, and feedback.

Leading Change

- **Delegation and Empowerment:** Places trust in others by moving decision-making close to the level at which the work is done and by giving others the responsibility, authority, independence and support they need to succeed.

- **Creating Buy-In:** Effectively builds commitment and wins support for initiatives through personal and professional credibility, trustworthiness, persuasive, stakeholder involvement.
- **Culture Management:** Proactively aligns the organization's/ workgroup's culture to support its strategy and core values.
- **Handling Resistance to Change:** Identifies sources of resistance to change and effectively deals with them before they can undermine change initiatives.

Communication

- **Oral Communication:** Ability to speak and/or signal people to convey or exchange information; gives clear assignments or directions to subordinates and receives assignments or directions from others; speaks with others with poise, voice control, and confidence. Ability to deliver information, explain procedures, to follow and give oral instructions; ability to communicate effectively and efficiently with persons of varying educational backgrounds with a variety of technical or professional vocabularies.

The examples that follow in the next section include demonstrated knowledge, skills, or abilities; a blend of knowledge, skills, abilities, motivations, beliefs, values, and interests; a motive, trait, skill, aspect of one's self-image or social role, or a body of knowledge. Please recall that the evidence of their abilities is "the words they wrote and spoke" during an AC process.

Again, what is most important is how the abilities are defined. Each skill dimension should be clearly defined in terms of the behaviors or actions an employee must demonstrate in order to successfully complete various tasks. The clearer the definitions and sub-dimensions are, the easier it is for the testing professionals to ensure that the behaviors and actions are measured well in the various exercises.

You will notice in the next section that some of the definitions are more detailed than others even though the different and sometimes, overlapping definitions were validated by the different agencies in the course of working on the job analysis process. What follows are some of the skill dimensions I have compiled. Note that they are in the form of actual notes I took during client-coaching sessions.

LIST OF MANY UNIVERSAL ABILITIES

The next several pages list many universal abilities which my firm has used for past AC processes.

Management/Supervision: Leads through example; identifies and resolves subordinate performance problems through appropriate means; maintains order and discipline; delegates responsibility and authority commensurate with subordinates' competence and tasks assigned; maintains balance between management and employee concerns and issues; effectively guides employees toward task accomplishment; displays initiative, confidence, and patience; maintains comosure in the face of criticism or dangerous situations; solicits information and feedback from subordinates; uses persuasion and negotiation to reach objectives.

Coaching and Mentoring: Provides opportunity and guidance to develop subordinates; counsels and mediates conflicts among subordinates; favorably influences others to gain cooperation and compliance; monitors employee performance in order to analyze strengths and weaknesses and takes corrective action.

Coaching: Facilitates career development of subordinates by providing regular coaching. Helps change behavior, improve performance and sustain commitment through encouragement, support of collaborative problem-solving, goal setting, and feedback.

Below are some notes I took from a client coaching process which are coaching behaviors:

- **"I am a teacher"**
- **"I passed on what I learned to them to inspire people to be better"**
- **"I redirected their daily duties"**
- **"I allowed them to fail. . . . I evaluated everything"**

An Assessor Guide for the coaching dimension may be found in **Exhibit 3** in the Exhibits Appendix.

SKILL DIMENSIONS AND DEFINITIONS

More universal skill dimensions and their definitions continue over the next few pages and sample behavioral observation notes from some of my past clients are also included. Below are three different ways of defining leadership.

1. **Leadership:** Provides a work environment which encourages clear and open communications. Provides adequate feedback to personnel under charge concerning their performance and takes timely and appropriate disciplinary actions as necessary. Exercises enthusiasm in influencing and guiding others toward achievement of established goals and objectives. Personally directs the development and training of personnel under charge, ensuring their proper induction, orientation and training.

2. **Leadership:** Provides a work environment which encourages clear and open communications. Has a clear and comprehensive understanding of the principles of effective leadership and how such principles are to be applied. Provides adequate feedback to staff so they know whether their performance levels are satisfactory. Commends and rewards employees for outstanding performance yet does not hesitate to take disciplinary action when necessary. Exercises enthusiasm in influencing and guiding others.

3. **Leadership (Leading/Staffing):** Provides a work environment which encourages clear and open communication; applies effective leadership principles; provides adequate feedback to personnel under charge concerning their performance, and takes timely and appropriate disciplinary actions as necessary; exercises enthusiasm in influencing and guiding others toward achievement of established goals and objectives; regularly seeks new and improved methodologies, policies and procedures for enhancing the effectiveness of those under charge; employs imagination and creativity in the application of duties and responsibilities; is open to change and supports achievement of goals and objectives; works with upper management, where appropriate to select and recommend employment of qualified personnel; personally directs the development and training of personnel under charge, ensuring their proper induction, orientation and training.

Below are some of my notes for a client that reflect leadership behaviors:

- **"Can't break confidences"**
- **"The leader sets the tone"**
- **"If you want to improve the standard, you have to set the standard"**
- **"Communication and involving people"**
- **"Set the groundwork"**

Exhibit 4 in the Exhibits Appendix depicts different leadership behaviors for a particular exercise. Leadership can be measured as a single distinct ability if it is well defined, but in reality, planning and organizing, judgment and decision making are sub-components of a person's ability to manage people. But we must not forget that there is a difference between someone who is a just a good manager and not really an effective leader. As you have already learned, the AC process predicts who will be successful in management positions, and as a person moves up the management hierarchy it is important that they also possess the innate abilities to go a step further and lead an organization.

Dr. John Kotter, who is now retired, was a professor of organizational behavior at Harvard Business School in Boston. His seminal 1990 article, "What Leaders Really Do," has been used in many management and leadership training programs. Here are a few quotes from the article, which was reprinted in the Harvard Business Review in 2001:

> Leadership is different from management, but not for the reasons most people think. Leadership isn't mystical and mysterious. It has nothing to do with having "charisma" or other exotic personality traits. It is not the province of a chosen few. Nor is leadership necessarily better than management or a replacement for it. Rather, leadership and management are two distinctive and complementary systems of action. Each has its own function and characteristic activities. Both are necessary for success in an increasingly complex and volatile business environment. (p. 85.)

> Management is about coping with complexity. Its practices and procedures are largely a response to one of the most significant developments of the twentieth century: the emergence of large organizations. Without good management, complex enterprises tend to become chaotic in ways that threaten their very existence. Good

management brings a degree of order and consistency to key dimensions like the quality and profitability of products. Leadership, by contrast, is about coping with change. (p. 86.)

Perception and Analysis: To identify, assimilate and comprehend the critical elements of a situation; to interpret the implications of alternative courses of action; to evaluate factors essential to a problem's solution; to separate relevant from irrelevant information.

Problem Analysis: Ability to coordinate, manage, strategize, and correlate data and other information. Includes the exercise of discretion in determining actual or probable consequences, and in referencing such evaluation to identify and select alternatives.

Below are my notes for a client exercise which reflect problem analysis behaviors.

- **"Constant process of improving people observation process"**
- **"Need to measure the effects and our success"**
- **"Do not want to duplicate efforts"**

Judgment: Exercises analytical judgment in areas of responsibility. Identifies issues or situations as they occur and specifies decision objectives. Identifies or assists in identifying alternative solutions to issues or situations. Implements decisions in accordance with prescribed and effective policies and procedures and with a minimum of errors. Seeks expert or experienced advice where appropriate and researches issues, situations and alternatives before exercising judgment.

Below are my notes which are examples of judgment behaviors for a client for a subordinate counseling exercise.

- **"I'd approve his request for time off"**
- **"Give him a memo about the vehicle accident"**
- **"Document his time"**
- **"Document and follow-up"**

Below are two different definitions of *judgment* and *decision* making.

1. **Judgment/Decision Making:** Ability in exercising analytical discretion in areas of responsibility by identifying issues or situations as they occur; researching issues, situations, and alternatives before

exercising and specifying decision objectives; identifying or assisting in identifying alternative solutions to issues or situations; recognizing when a particular policy, procedure or strategy does not foster the desired result and moving decisively and explicitly to develop and implement alternatives; implementing decisions in accordance with prescribed and effective policies and procedures, and with a minimum of errors; and seeking expert or experienced advice where appropriate.

2. **Judgment/Decision Making:** Exercises discretion in areas of responsibility and in developing and implementing courses of action affecting functions under charge. Identifies issues or situations as they occur and specifies decision objectives and alternative solutions to issues or situations. Implements decisions in accordance with prescribed and effective policies and procedures and with a minimum of errors. Where appropriate, seeks expert or experienced advice and researches issues, situations and alternatives before exercising judgment. Recognizes when a particular policy, procedure or strategy does not foster the desired result, and moves decisively and explicitly to develop and implement alternatives.

Below are my notes from a client's exercise which reflect statements suggesting judgment behaviors.

- **"Have administrative Lt. gather statistics"**
- **"Hold intelligence meetings with all sources"**
- **"Maintain contact with the media"**
- **"Use COPs unit"**
- **"Make sure officer collects reports timely basis"**

Planning and Organizing: Plans and organizes daily work routine. Establishes priorities for the completion of work in accordance with sound time-management methodology. Efficiently organizes own work and that of subordinate staff. Ensures that personnel understand what results are expected of them and that each is regularly and appropriately informed of all matters of concern to them. Avoids duplication of effort. Estimates expected time of completion of work elements and establishes a personal schedule accordingly. Attends on time, required meetings, planning sessions and discussions. Implements work activity in accordance with priorities and estimated schedules. Plans, coordinates and uses information effectively to enhance activities and production. Knows and understands expectations regarding such activities and works to ensure such expectations are met. Develops and formulates ways, means, and timing to achieve established goals and objectives. Effectively and efficiently organizes, arranges and allocates manpower, financial and other designated resources to achieve such goals and objectives.

Below are the notes my associate Dr. Robert Sloat provided for one client based on a report she wrote:

- **"What you wrote is quite good as a general essay, as related to making an oral presentation. However, this is not a specific plan of action. For example, on page three you list a dozen or so community components."**
- **"How are the committees organized? What are their tasks? How do they relate to strategic planning?"**
- **"In writing such an essay, you begin with the general ideas/ information and then in your body you focus on specifics, and then in your conclusion you complete the essay with the general. . . ."**

Below are my notes for another exercise which are different examples of planning and organizing behaviors:

- **"Sergeant Mandall will follow-up"**
- **"Refer to Lt. to obtain his personnel file"**
- **"Will have a discussion and agree on an action plan"**
- **"Will add two extra cars"**
- **"Follow with updates"**

Relationships With Others/Human Relations: Ability in striving to develop and maintain excellent rapport with personnel under charge and listening to and considering their suggestions and complaints and responding appropriately; sharing knowledge with managers, supervisors and co-workers for mutual benefit; contributing to maintaining high morale among all employees; dealing with people beyond giving and receiving instruction; adhering to policies in the discharge of duties and responsibilities, and ensuring the same from personnel under charge; developing and maintaining cooperative and courteous relationships inter- and intra-departmentally, and with external entities; tactfully and effectively handling requests, suggestions and complaints in order to establish and maintain good will; and emphasizing the importance of maintaining a positive image.

Interpersonal (Dealing with Employees and the Public): Develops and maintains cooperative and courteous relationships with employees and the public so as to maintain good will toward the agency to project a positive city image. Tactfully and effectively handles requests, suggestions, and complaints in order to maintain good will within the city. Emphasizes the importance of maintaining a positive image of the agency and the city. Interacts effectively with the public. Adaptable to performing under stress when confronted with emergency situations or tight deadlines.

Adaptability: Ability to remain flexible and patient in the face of constantly changing needs, and to influence events and to execute the actions required to complete cases.

The following nine **adaptability** behaviors from a written exercise used in a past process.

1. Be patient and realize and accept that some cases are never solved.
2. Break each case into small pieces and approach one piece at a time.
3. Engage in stress management exercises: deep breathing, short breaks from work, exercise, drinking plenty of fluids etc.
4. Get away from my desk and go outside or down the hall when it gets too stressful.
5. Be open to changes in each case.
6. Work a bit on each case every week, if possible.
7. Remember that flexibility is needed when dealing with people's (detectives) ideas.
8. Recognize the need to respect other people's ideas.
9. Document other behaviors or actions not listed above.

Below are my notes for two different clients for an exercise concerning dealing with people behaviors:

- **"Want to be there for him"**
- **"He will meet with me in face-to-face meetings"**
- **"I'll fight for you"**
- **"Thank him"**
- **"Commend him for his 16 years of service"**

- **"Show confidence in him"**
- **"We can work together"**
- **"Capable of doing good work"**
- **"He will see that I support him"**

As part of an in-basket exercise, below are my notes taken from the Assessor Guide regarding a client's memos written to people in the police department.

- **"We can get to know each other"**
- **"Look forward to working with you"**
- **"Thank you for sharing your concerns"**
- **"We take your concerns seriously"**

Exhibit 5 (see Exhibits Appendix) depicts the interpersonal behaviors a candidate should demonstrate when responding to a component of an exercise which taps into interpersonal skills.

Strategic Thinking/Innovation: Ability to operate from a strategic perspective in own area of department; recognize the broad implications of issues; show openness to new ideas and perspectives; see the relationship between citizens, community groups, other city departments, subordinates and governmental processes; consider strategic issues affecting own area when making decisions; create strategies that balance long–term and short–term goals. Ability to approach problems with curiosity and open-mindedness; generate innovative ideas and solutions; stimulate creativity and innovation in others; challenge the way it has always been done; champion new ideas and initiatives; support those who initiate change and take risks.

Oral Communication: Ability to speak and or signal people to convey or exchange information; give assignments or directions to subordinates and receive assignments or directions from others; speak with others with poise, voice control and confidence. Ability to record and deliver information, explain procedures, follow and give verbal and written instructions; counsel and teach employees; and communicate effectively and efficiently with persons of varying educational and ethnic backgrounds.

Written Communication (General): Ability to effectively communicate in writing by using proper grammar, punctuation, spelling, sentence and paragraph structure, word usage, and legibility.

Written Communication (Language Ability): Ability to prepare reports, correspondence, forms, records, etc., with proper format, punctuation, spelling, and grammar.

In my research for this book I reviewed a list of skill dimensions and their definitions from an article by Vasilopoulos, Reilly, & Leaman (2000). One of the studies the authors conducted included 249 applicants for the job of U.S. Border Patrol agent. All of the applicants completed a battery of three tests administered on computers. They were from different cities in the US. The applicants completed tests that assessed their cognitive ability and personal characteristics. The skills and definitions below are direct quotes, not my paraphrasing.

Conscientiousness

"Includes behavior that is organized and thoughtful, with a great attention to detail and follow through. It can be contrasted with behavior that is careless and negligent."

Cooperativeness

"Includes behavior that helps to meet the goals of the work group and the Immigration and Naturalization Service (INS) by following the chain of command, collaborating with others both inside and outside of INS, assisting citizens or aliens in need, sensitivity to other cultures, and genuine concern for the well-being of others. It can be contrasted with behavior that is disruptive to the work group, such as insubordination or uncooperative actions, and shows a lack of concern for others."

Emotional Maturity

"Includes behavior that involves maintaining self-control, remaining calm in potentially volatile situations, acting in a professional manner, and using the minimum amount of force needed to apprehend an illegal alien or smuggler. It can be contrasted with behavior that is immature, irrational, shows a lack of self-control, and involves the use of excessive force without having to be told. It can be contrasted with behavior that involves failing to do what it takes to do the job successfully because of laziness or lack of interest."

Integrity/Honesty

"Includes behavior that involves following agency policy and the letter and spirit of the law, and avoiding even the appearance of impropriety. It can be contrasted with behavior that involves breaking the law and deviating from agency policy."

Judgment

"Includes behavior that involves making sound decisions in situations when multiple options are available and using common sense to avoid putting oneself or others in danger. It can be contrasted with behavior that indicates a lack of judicious decision-making skills."

Initiative

"Includes behavior that involves perseverance in performing the duties of the job, going beyond expectations to accomplish a task, and performing" (Vasilopoulos, Reilly, & Leaman, 2000, p. 64).

You should note that there are a few different dimensions used for the agent position that are different from the ones I previously mentioned. Integrity and honesty can be measured somewhat in an AC. But the best way to measure this is via a personality paper-and-pencil self-report test. The same applies to emotional maturity. A simulation exercise could be developed to tap into emotional maturity but its development would be rigorous and a role player would probably be needed.

BEHAVIORALLY ANCHORED RATING SCALE (BARS)

A BARS can be used to evaluate candidate's performance in AC exercises. BARs are very time-consuming to develop because each anchor—1, 3 and 5 are the anchors on a five-point scale—needs to be clearly defined. I have only used a BARS for a few AC processes because I favor the assessor checklist format, and have provided many samples in this book. Like assessor checklists, a BARS helps to ensure that the assessors have observed the listed behaviors, as reflected in their notes and memos written a candidate. The following question was given to the candidate to write or speak a response. The question can be used for any management job.

Please review the organizational chart. During your first 60-90 days on the job, what strategies would you employ to get to know your staff? What would you do to ensure an open line of communication between you and your direct reports and their employees and why?

Question with Organizational Chart: For this question the candidate is given a copy of the agency's organizational chart and is then asked the question below.

Skill Dimensions Measured in This Question: quality of work, specifically the quality of communication; initiative and enthusiasm; relationships with others; planning and organizing; staffing, leadership, judgment and decision making.

Exhibit 6 (see Exhibits Appendix) is a very detailed depiction of a BARS that is used by assessors to evaluate the candidate's response to the question.

Chapter 4

HOW PRACTICING CRITICAL INCIDENTS CAN HELP DEVELOP YOUR SKILLS

OVERVIEW

So far you have learned about skill dimensions, how some are defined and what some of the sub-dimensions are. Important components of job analysis were also covered. Given that the critical incident method has always been a part of all job analysis, I want you to better understand how data from the critical incident job analysis process can be used to develop simulation exercises or be turned into items in an in-basket exercise.

This chapter contains many critical incidents from different subject matter experts from different ranks and agencies across the U.S. The names of the agencies, subject matter experts and dates of the assessment process were removed for confidentiality purposes.

STUDYING AND PRACTICING YOUR SKILLS WITH CRITICAL INCIDENTS

While reading the different incidents and how the SME handled the situation, try to think how you would handle the same or a similar incident for your department. Also, imagine how the incident could be part of an assessment process. You can also create your own critical incidents and write down how you would handle each one.

The subject matter experts provide as much information as they can but are not always able to recall every detail of an event. Obviously, the best incidents are those that do have a great deal of specific details, particularly the best and worst ways to handle the situation. Regardless of the richness of the critical incident, not all incidents can be used for an assessment. One of the reasons for this is having to rewrite the incident for a testing format and to ensure that none of the contents of the incident favor any candidates taking the test, who may have direct knowledge of the incident.

A critical incident job analysis assessment process typically takes between one and two hours depending upon how well-spoken the subject matter expert is. Some are very comfortable with their recollection and provide a great deal of detail; others have trouble thinking of an incident to describe. Some subject matter experts like to talk about their work; others do not. To get their brains working I usually suggest that they think of tactical, HR, general management, and ethical issues with which they have recently dealt. This often helps because it helped them focus. I am always lucky enough to elicit about six good incidents. Many are usable for a variety of reasons, but especially useful are those in which:

- The incident can easily be rewritten and used as an item in an in-basket exercise.
- Several effective actions taken are listed.
- Specific details of the incident can be altered to avoid favoring any test-taker who might have knowledge of the incident.

During each critical incident assessment process, I bring my laptop computer and ask each subject matter expert if it is okay if I type their responses. No one has ever refused. The incident in this chapter represents the exact data I collected and saved within each agency's file. However, I bold faced each title to make your reading easier. Given that the data reflects the notes I was able to type while the subject matter expert was talking, many sentences are incomplete and there may be some typos. The idea is to collect as much of what the subject matter expert says and not to be worried about perfect transcription. Even with typos, the information is rich nonetheless.

A CRITICAL INCIDENT, QUESTION AND ASSESSOR GUIDE

The next section includes a sample critical incident I obtained from a sergeant.

Shots Fired Call: "In neighborhood with a lot of problems, officers arrive on scene. I put myself on the call too—alert tones go out to indicate something more serious is to be dispatched. When officers arrive, my concern as a sergeant is where is shooter at, what confirmation do we have regarding where it took place—inside or outside—which gives us more direction re: how we will proceed. Dispatch could not provide any further information. One officer got there, and another arrived a few seconds later. I want officers to be together for safety issues. They made contact with complainant. A bullet went through bathroom and set on windowsill. Two kids inside with mom. Bullet went through glass. Got an idea of where bullets came from, got casings."

"We did not have any victims and it was a random act—they left—so investigation did not turn into much that we could do much with. We had someone photograph the woman's apartment window. Maintain the evidence, before moving it. Bullet hole in window. You should not collect it or pick it up—photograph before moving it for consistency's sake. Sergeant needs to remind the officers to get photos first. On that scene, most important thing is officers getting there and being there together for safety purposes so they can watch each other's backs. Do we have a victim, a crime scene, a shooter, a need for backup, etc.? Wait for backup before going out on foot. If we had a victim on the road, this would change the whole complexity: lock down whole area for vehicles etc."

Below is the actual question. The subject matter of the question is always noted and each candidate receives a printed copy of the questions which the assessor reads aloud.

Shots Fired and Officer Witness: You are the sergeant and are in your office listening to the radio when you hear a newly hired officer advise dispatch, "Shots fired." A man shot at another man in a parking lot. The suspect abandoned the vehicle and fled on foot. Another person drove off in another car. Other shots were fired at people in the parking lot. A crowd is gathering. The officer is pursuing on foot. Based on his tone of voice, he appears to be very stressed. What actions do you take? What are some of the important issues to consider?

The Assessor Guide for the competency-based structured situational assessment question above evokes the judgment/reasoning and interpersonal behaviors listed below.

Most Appropriate Judgment/Reasoning Behaviors/Actions

1. Find out if reporting officer is with any other officers.
2. Go to scene as a supervisor is definitely needed here.
3. Request additional resources as needed; should include have fire department come in or stage the equipment depending upon further details.
4. Determine exact number of scenes going.
5. Attempt to identify witnesses.
6. Attempt to isolate witnesses from one another.
7. Find out if officer is still pursuing alone.
8. Continue to listen to radio while on route to scene.
9. Contact the OIC (after baseline facts are obtained).
10. Make sure an officer has contacted Fire Rescue; ambulance is on way.
11. Continue to monitor and manage other scenes as needed.
12. Consider switching all involved units to separate channel.
13. Make sure someone protects crime scene.
14. Make sure all evidence is secured, an investigator is contacted to photograph and collect evidence.
15. Make sure someone sets up a perimeter.
16. Find out if a canine unit is available to search for man who fled.
17. Make sure someone controls crowds.
18. Start preparing macro tactical plan for managing entire scene: finding perpetrator, assessment processing witnesses, preparing reports, etc.
19. Further advise the OIC.
20. Ensure staging area for media is set up; consider having PIO
21. Document other behaviors/actions not listed above.

Most Appropriate Actions Dealing with People/Interpersonal Behaviors

1. Talk to probationary officer and provide praise and moral support given nature of this scene.
2. Make sure someone is attending to the injured party.
3. Make sure witnesses are okay.
4. Make sure people in crowd are not injured.
5. Consider a formal debriefing if appropriate.
6. Document other behaviors or actions not listed above.

WHY AND HOW YOU CAN USE CRITICAL INCIDENTS TO DEVELOP YOUR INNATE ABILITIES

You are an expert or have great familiarity with what an After Action Report is. It is also highly likely that you have attended training on how to deal with critical incidents. Correct rapid response to critical situations is an essential ability for any officers—especially those in supervisory roles.

You can develop the skills you already have (i.e., planning and organizing, judgment, decision making) by **reviewing, discussing, reading, analyzing, practicing and assessing** your own strengths and weaknesses. Here's how you can use critical incidents to build on your strengths and shore up on your weaknesses. You can use the ones I have shared with you and others you can make up or some you have discussed or experienced with your colleagues.

Here are some steps you can take:

- Realize the importance of trying to best remember what happened when you were handling or involved in a critical incident.
- Learn and remember after discussion with other colleagues, what the best and worst ways of handling the incident might have been. For example, what should have Officer John Doe done differently to handle the situation? What did he do that was effective or ineffective? What did the officer do that was, or could have been, problematic?
- Review in your mind, out loud to yourself, or in a group discussion, what skills were being used by the supervisors to handle the situation. To reiterate: examples of skills again, are planning and organizing, dealing with people, judgment, decision-making, and problem analysis.
- Analyze the entire incident and write down or speak aloud while looking at yourself in a mirror, what the major issues are, which of those issues is the most critical and why, and then write down or speak aloud and record how you would handle each issue.
- Reread your department's standard operating procedures (SOPs), directives, administrative orders and other documents that outline how different situations are supposed to be handled. Compare your actions to them.

- Use your own judgment and decision-making skills when responding to assessment exercises, not how your colleagues tell you to act just because they have previously participated in an AC process.

I cannot emphasize enough the importance of ***reading, rereading*** and then ***rereading again*** your department's SOPs, directives, administrative orders and other guiding documents, or those of the agency to which you are applying. Know your state's laws, local codes, and be aware of the United States Supreme Court's decisions, especially regarding the Fourth and Sixth Amendments to the Constitution of the United States.

Chapter 5

PRACTICE, PRACTICE, PRACTICE

PRACTICE INSTRUCTIONS FOR ALL EXERCISES

If you want the opportunity to practice your strengths and improve in areas of weakness, you will have several opportunities to do so by practicing the exercises contained in the coming chapters. For any exercise in an AC, candidates are provided with clear and detailed instructions. So as not to be repetitive, the instructions for the exercises are *only* included in this chapter. Some of the exercises have separate test administrator instructions, whereas others do not. The following practice instructions are labeled by exercise type. For all exercises you should:

✓ Find a quiet room where you will not be interrupted.
✓ Get a stopwatch.
✓ Get a pad of paper, pens or pencils, and a few highlighter pens and sticky notes.
✓ Set up your laptop and printer as you will need to use this when writing memos, reports and/or preparing other documents.
✓ Remove the exercise from the book or make copies of it.
✓ Sit back and get a sense of what the most important issues are to someone of the rank for which you are testing.
✓ Read the instructions out loud to yourself and then start the stopwatch.
✓ You may want to visualize what those important issues are.
✓ Start working on completing the exercise. I have not provided you with any other instructions because you *must* utilize your innate abilities to complete the exercise.

43

✓ *Do not* go over time.

✓ For the IB exercises, read every item and if this is what you would normally do, make notes on the item(s) or on a separate piece of paper.

✓ *Do not* make any assumptions and *do not* make up things that are not indicated in the items.

✓ If you are practicing the oral presentation or any of the other exercises, also follow those instructions verbatim.

✓ Once you have completed the exercise, if you have time, review what you have done and make any necessary revisions. If time has expired, relax; take a break and then move to the Assessor Guide for the particular exercise in the Exhibits Appendix.

✓ The Assessor Guide includes a checklist with the most important behaviors/actions the assessor(s) will consider in evaluating your performance and determine your score.

✓ My firm has always used a five-point rating scale. You can refer to other different rating scales, if relevant, which are **Exhibits 7–9** in the Exhibits Appendix.

LAYOUT OF IN-BASKET (IB) ITEMS

In a typical in-basket, your exercise packet contains numbered items which are not in subject/topic/issue order. In other words, the item numbers which appear on the bottom of each page are not in alphabetical or numerical order. For the sake of brevity, many of the items in the IB exercises in this chapter are presented with more than one per page. When you practice each IB you can prioritize the items by writing them down on a sheet of paper or removing the pages from the test booklet.

PRACTICE GUIDE FOR EXERCISES WITH A ROLE-PLAYER

There are several points you need to consider when practicing any of the exercises in this book with a role-player, as follows:

- If you read the role-play script (see **Exhibit 17** in the Exhibits Appendix) before you practice the exercise, you are cheating yourself.

- If you were really participating in this exercise, the instructions may be read to you by a test administrator face-to-face, or a person on a television screen or computer screen.
- While the instructions are being read, or if you have just read the instructions silently or aloud to yourself, visualize yourself on the scene.
- Note the amount of time you are allotted to prepare your presentation.
- When your stopwatch dings, stop.
- *Do not* go over time.
- Once you have completed your presentation, if you have time, review the actions you indicated should be taken and the behaviors you demonstrated.
- Take a short break and pick up the Assessor Guide (see **Exhibit 16** in the Exhibits Appendix).
- The Assessor Guide, which includes a checklist, cites the most important behaviors/actions a candidate should demonstrate in writing in a written exercise or a written exercise that is then presented orally.
- If you used a video recorder to observe your mannerisms, watch it carefully. Listen to your pauses (uhs and ums). See if you were tense, repeated the same words or phrases more than once, etc.
- If you are ambitious, do the whole exercise again and tape it again.
- You may also consider inviting one or two trusted friends or relatives to come to your home and review the first recording with you and note your behavior. Then review the second recording and do the same. Note any changes.
- Given that you will not have a role player in front of you when you start the timer, you should pretend you are talking to the role player.
- Visualize someone in front of you. Verbalize (out loud) what you would say to them to the fullest extent possible. Also consider how they may respond.
- You can record your performance on an audio or video-recorder. Make sure you set the audio or video to the time listed in the instructions for each exercise. When the time is up, stop.

- Now you can look at the role-play script. Read it thoroughly and go back and recall or listen to what you said to the imaginary role player.
- Then go the Assessor Guide (see **Exhibit 16** in Exhibits Appendix) and read it over thoroughly. Recall or listen to what you said and how you behaved in practice and try to determine what check marks the assessors would have given you.

Remember, if you were really participating in an actual AC process, the assessors would be in the room taking notes. They would only take notes on what you said not what the role player says. After the exercise is over and before the next candidate enters the room, the assessors will use some of that time to review their notes. At the end of the day they complete the scoring process. They will independently use the Assessor Guide to check the behaviors you demonstrated. The behaviors are the words you spoke which they wrote down. The statements you make and how you use your body language (which is an important part of effective oral communication) are what will appear in the assessors' notes. Their verbatim quotes or short abbreviated summaries are the evidence of your behaviors. The assessors should not be writing conclusions.

To recap, assessors are trained to take down verbatim quotes and the essence of a candidate's behavior, and their notes are the factual evidence of a candidate's performance. Many agencies now make video recordings of all exercises to ensure that every word is on record. The videos are later reviewed by the assessors who take notes from the recordings. Then they begin the rating process without speaking to one another. The final thing the assessors do is discuss the positive and negative behaviors and actions and consider reinforcing the positives and eliminating the negatives.

USING THE ASSESSOR GUIDES TO DEVELOP YOUR INNATE ABILITIES

As you practice the exercises and then review the Assessor Guides all of which are found in the Exhibits Appendix, you will notice the format is the same. There is no absolute standard format or layout for an Assessor Guide. The most commonly used format uses a checklist which lists the most appropriate behaviors or actions a candidate should demonstrate. The *other behaviors/actions demonstrated* but not listed statement is a very important component of any assessor checklist, because there are many behaviors or actions a candidate can demonstrate or state that are acceptable but not listed. Remember, the behaviors listed in the Assessor Guides are those considered normal and expected given the particular scenario. However, every human has unique abilities and sometimes we are unpredictable. Therefore, one will respond with an acceptable behavior that was not expected by the human beings who wrote the Assessor Guide. A creative response which is a "wow" behavior must be noted and credit given in the candidate's evaluation.

Whenever I have conducted assessor training, I always tell the trainees:

- It not necessary to include every possible behavior because the most appropriate behaviors are listed.
- If Assessor Guides were several pages long, it would make their jobs very difficult.
- Copy your notes onto the checklists that are appropriate including any notes that are not listed on the Assessor Guide.
- The notes and check marks are the evidence of the candidate's observed behavior.
- The Assessor Guides my firm develops are probably more detailed than others they have seen because I would rather provide you with more rather than less information.

Chapter 6

THE INFAMOUS IN-BASKET (IB) EXERCISE

INSTRUCTIONAL OVERVIEW

The following text are my instructions to you about IB exercises so read the contents as if you were listening to me giving you advice. The majority of my coaching clients have completed an IB exercise even if they are not sure one will be part of their AC process. Many of them just want to have the experience of having completed one. Others are lucky enough to have been provided with a candidate orientation guide which notifies them in advance that an IB will be part of their assessment process and/or the types of exercises are listed in the testing announcement. Moreover, when candidates complete one of my firm's in-basket exercises, they actually learn how to better plan and organize, and make decisions after carefully analyzing all of the items. They also learn why interpersonal skills are relevant even when responding in writing to e-mail messages, citizen complaint letters, etc.

During this exercise, candidates are typically provided with documents often found in the in-basket of a supervisor at the level for which they are testing. It might include memos, e-mails with or without attached reports, letters, and a calendar. They are given a specified amount of time to complete the entire in-basket exercise and indicate the action(s) they would take as a result of receiving each item. The most appropriate responses for each item are listed in the Assessor Guide and usually include a determination of which items should receive immediate attention, or none at all. After prioritizing, the supervisor might look for scheduling inconsistencies; find mistakes in stated policies, procedures or reports; delegate responding correspondence and other activities to a subordinate, and make decisions about how a problem employee should be handled.

The IB is a commonly used exercise starting at the rank of sergeant. However, an IB exercise should not be used to test a candidate's planning and organizing, judgment and decision-making or written communication abilities unless the position sought involves reviewing, analyzing and processing a lot of different types of paperwork. Also, this should be documented in the job task analysis and in a validation report. The types of items commonly found in-basket exercises should be those actually found in the in-baskets of those currently working at that supervisory level.

The exercise in this chapter has two parts. The first part is an item description guide and is listed as such on the next few pages. The in-basket exercise appears as **Exercise 6-1** with a title and the instructions which you must read to yourself before you start work on the exercise. Remember to adhere to the time requirements.

IN-BASKET ITEM DESCRIPTION GUIDE

The Assessor item description guide is typically given to the Assessors, not the candidates. It is a short summary of each item in the exercise. The Assessor Guide for this exercise is Exhibit 10 in the Appendix.

ITEM 1

E-mail from Ashley to Brite.
Summary: Police misconduct in park (Shift III).
Issues: Need to conduct an internal investigation. To Chief through Deputy Chief Pesky marked confidential, and sealed in some fashion. High priority. Memo to Ashley saying he received it and to keep info confidential.

ITEM 2

E-mail from Killian to Brite.
Summary: Asking for more than a week off.
Issues: Must deny or pass on to DC Pesky because of shortage of personnel as noted in **Item 15**. Must be sure that Killian has a response of his decision/actions and an explanation based on info in Item 15.

ITEM 3

E-mail from Snoke to Brite.
Summary: Report of complaint re: Slyck alleged harassment and attitude (e.g., surly and antagonistic).
Issues: Citizen making a general allegation, but is highly desirous of action resulting in discipline. Must be forwarded to Chief through DC Pesky recommending investigation. Also, he needs to note Snoke's inappropriate reference to the complainant in official records and must address issue with Snoke. Must be sure some notification is made to citizen that matter is being addressed.

ITEM 4

E-mail from Pesky to Brite.
Explanation of why Pesky won't be available and appreciation for his efforts.
Issues: Helps to understand lack of people to contact but not of much other value. A note of appreciation/understanding to new boss is appropriate. Also advises him of weekly staff meeting—should place on his calendar.

ITEM 5, PAGE 1

E-mail from Maxwell to Brite.
Summary: Welcome memo from secretary with organizational information attached
Issues: Attached is helpful in understanding who the key staff are and the size and structure of the department, but not vital. Should thank secretary for her efforts, but has to note in some fashion that he will deal with her "who to trust/not trust" comment as inappropriate.

ITEM 5, PAGES 2–3

Organizational chart
Staffing of Patrol Shifts I, II, III.
Summary: Chart is for informational purposes only. Staffing complement can be used to delegate work to staff, other.
Issues: Same as above.

ITEM 6

E-mail from Carter (911) to Brite.
Summary: Need for training re: communications protocol/procedures/supervision.
Issues: Specific radio communications problems and their extent need to be identified before specific corrective action can be taken. Needs to obtain further details. Needs to let Carter know he is concerned about his absence, and that he will follow-up on his return. Can start gathering info now via Carter and his sergeants to get a full perspective.

ITEM 7

Letter from PTA commending Slyck.
Summary: Letter from PTA President of DeQuency Elementary School commending the PR with children by Officer Slyck.
Issues: Normally an easy issue to dispose of with a commendation of some sort. However, such action is complicated because of the other complaints and needed internal investigations of Slyck. Note or copy of letter to Slyck and filing in personnel file is appropriate, but overly effusive praise is not a good idea. Would be inconsistent to commend and discipline at same time. Letter of thanks to writer for taking time to write is important.

ITEM 8

E-mail from Bollen to Gage.
Summary: Sergeant's memo is "unofficial" and points to possible problems with officer Pace perhaps requiring counseling and may involve misconduct.
Issues: Could jump to conclusion that he is an officer involved in misconduct referenced in Item 1, but there is insufficient info to do so. Establishment of a positive link is insufficient at this point. Issue is of high priority because if he is an alcoholic or is having major emotional problems, his promotion to sergeant could spell serious problems. Needs to investigate ASAP informally as there is no formal charge or evidence of misconduct, only rumors. Also, must be sure that the sergeant understands that there is no way to keep a potential

issue as serious as is indicated "unofficial" once he passes it on formally in writing.

ITEM 9

Letter from citizens to Commanding Officer.
Summary: Letter commending Slyck for saving drowning child.
Issues: See Item 7. Should also prepare thank you response to citizens. May/should write commendation letter to Slyck despite his other problems.

ITEM 10

E-mail from Pesky to Gage.
Summary: Requests input on transfer of Slyck to Burglary Suppression.
Issues: Slyck has an equal amount of commendations and complaints of misconduct that are/should be referred to internal affairs for investigation. No reassignment should be made while the investigations are pending and the complaints are unresolved. Pesky should be so notified.

ITEM 11

E-mail from Bollen to Gage.
Summary: Complaint from Meagher re: his performance evaluation.
Issues: There is insufficient information to make a decision. The performance evaluation must be reviewed, discussed with the rater, and then discussed with the officer. Action will depend on those outcomes. Must make sure Meagher is aware that matter is being handled.

ITEM 12

E-mail from Grace to Pesky delegated to Gage.
Summary: Complaints from City Council, City Manager and Parks Department about juveniles hanging out in the park, dumping trash, smoking dope and drinking.
Issues: Needs to develop a remedial plan that can/should be delegated to a sergeant to initiate. Needs to inform Pesky and Grace of action

taken. Also, could be that some of the problems are potentially caused by officers in Item 1 and any remedial plan could affect internal affairs investigation for those problems.

ITEM 13

Letter from citizen Neal Jones to Chief.
Summary: Citizen complaint re: crime increase and invitation to community gathering.
Issues: Will be absent during the meeting. Needs to assign a representative to attend, gather specific complaints, obtain crime data, and prepare a draft response. Needs to notify citizen indicating a PD representative will attend and must advise Pesky and Grace of his actions.

ITEM 14

E-mail from Gage to Pesky.
Summary: His shift is short staffed; has only 17 officers, notes reasons why this is so.
Issues: This should be addressed in some way by the candidate (e.g., utilize other staff, respond to e-mail, other). Related to Item 2 re: Killian asking for time off.

ITEM 15

E-mail from Snoke to Gage.
Summary: Contact made with Robert Murray about Slyck's interaction with his son. Citizen complaint about Slyck.
Issues: Related to item 3. This issue needs to be addressed with Slyck; schedule meeting with Slyck, counsel him, follow-up with citizen by Gage because Murray wants to pursue the matter.

ITEM 16

Letter from citizen Denis Menis passed to Gage by Pesky.
Summary: Letter of complaint about conduct and attitude and language used by Slyck in issuing traffic summons.
Issues: Must be investigated either in combination with other complaints of Slyck or by itself. Can't make any decisions, but there is a

pattern of complaints emerging at this point. Must let citizen know matter is being investigated.

ITEM 17

E-mail from Grace to Brite.

Summary: He congratulates Brite on his promotion, acknowledges that he is going out of town but asks him to provide his suggestions about how the district system is doing before he leaves town.

Issues: Some suggestions must/should be provided even if it entails only writing a few notes on the item.

EXERCISE 6-1
ABC POLICE DEPARTMENT
ORAL, WITH NOTES IN-BASKET EXERCISE LIEUTENANT

Candidate Instructions

This test is commonly known as an In-Basket Exercise. Although the situation in this exercise is artificial, with some unrealistic restrictions on the time allowed you and the methods and activities employed in communicating with others, the problems you will deal with are real, having been obtained from actual situations lieutenants in law enforcement encounter in their jobs.

The purpose of this exercise is to evaluate your ability to perform certain critical management functions and to display your style and approach to handling common situations police lieutenants encounter. You are of course, not able to actually get in contact with anyone else. You must decide what action to take and follow through on your own. Your information is limited to what is provided in the exercise, but it should be sufficient to allow you to make informed decisions and suggest appropriate responses. You can suggest immediate action of a certain kind—drafting a letter or memorandum, say, or choose to delay action for various reasons, or delegate a response to a subordinate.

Your decision may not be assisted by "learning" something not in the exercise, or to state that you have obtained some sort of agreement that allows you to avoid taking any action. That is, you cannot make up things that allow you to ignore, avoid or delay choosing some form of action.

A scenario, staff complement, and necessary information to handle all items are contained in the In-Basket materials.

This exercise is set in a hypothetical police department. It is not intended to replicate your agency, and you are not being tested on your knowledge of your agency's policy, procedures, or practices. This exercise has an organizational structure that is smaller in scope than that of your agency. This is done to limit your areas of concern to those necessary to complete the exercise and not distract you or lead you into an erroneous course of action.

Do not assume that just because you would do something in your agency that it is the "right" or the only way to do something in this exercise. By the same token, just because you would not do something that is done in the fictional ABC Police Department, do not assume that it is "wrong" to do it in this exercise. You are expected to use *your own best judgment* in handling the items. This exercise is designed to test your management and supervisory abilities in certain defined areas and not your knowledge of the procedures or operations of any agency.

There are a total of seventeen items in the basket, some of which are more than one page in length. Review each document carefully to make sure that you have read it completely and understand it. All of the items have an item number at the top of each page. You must handle every item in the exercise in some manner. "Handling" an item may mean nothing more than reviewing it and holding it for future action, or it may require some immediate action of some sort. You should dispose of each item according to your best judgment. In an actual situation, you could seek out more information before deciding on a course of action. But in this case, you are of course limited solely to the information at hand. This is not unlike many actual circumstances where you are forced to take action under less than ideal circumstances.

We recommend that before starting to complete the in-basket that you first review all items and make sure that you are familiar with the entire contents.

You may handle related or similar items by combining them in some manner and disposing of them with a single memo, if that seems appropriate. So that we know how you handle the material, *write down everything* that you decide to do. Write memos to yourself about things you want to do when you report to your new assignment. If you are going to do something, do it. If you would write a letter, *write it—exactly as you would write it were you at your desk in your new job.* If you would hold something until a later date, indicate that fact on the item or by attaching a memo to it also tell what you would do with that item on that later date. If you would not do anything with an item, then indicate that on the item. Make sure that *every item that you handle has some indication that you have handled it, and what you did with it.* Assessors will assume that any item not having a disposition on it has not been handled.

When writing a letter or memo in response to an in-basket item, write the item number on that document so that it can be matched up if it becomes separated. Attach any documents that you prepare to the original item with a paper clip.

A supply of paper, paper clips, memos, scratch pads, etc. is available to you. Additional supplies are available if needed. An organizational chart and other items are provided to assist you in determining where certain items might be sent.

You may write on any items or mark them up in any manner you see fit. If you want to, you may write on the item any comments, directions, etc. that you want to make in lieu of making such comments on a separate piece of paper.

You have exactly two hours to handle all seventeen items. You will only be given a five-minute warning, therefore, budget your time and keep track of it carefully.

After you complete the in-basket exercise, or when time is called, place all items, supplies, materials, instructions into the envelope provided. Make sure the items are in the exact order you want the assessor to review them.

Scenario

You have recently been promoted to the position of lieutenant in the police department of the City of Palm Island. You were formally offered the position, and you accepted effective February 15, 20XX. On January 28, 20XX, you were contacted by the chief and told that the person whose retirement was creating the vacancy died suddenly and unexpectedly. The chief strongly urged you take the post immediately so that the department could continue to operate with a minimum of disruption. You agreed to assume the position ASAP, but indicated that you would be unable to report to work until February 15, 20XX.

From January 30 through February 14, 20XX, you will be on a special assignment with your military reserve unit in the Middle East. Therefore, you cannot report to work in City of Palm Island until after this assignment is completed. Because of the nature of your assignment and your location, you will not be available by telephone or e-mail to anyone in that city while you are on this assignment.

In order to get a grasp of things prior to reporting to your new job, you agreed with the chief to stop by the office and review any materials in your predecessor's in-basket. You also told the chief that you would make sure that any compelling matters would be disposed of.

You stop by the office on Saturday afternoon, January 30, 20XX. Because it is Saturday, no one else is available in the office. All of the administrative and non-critical line staff is off-duty. All files and records are locked up, and since you do not know the filing system, you would have a difficult time finding anything in any event. You have to leave in exactly two hours in order to be able to report to your reserve unit on time.

In disposing of the items in the in-basket, your *sole* means of communicating with anyone is in writing. Therefore, any messages, direction, or information that you relay must be clear, concise, and complete. No one can contact you during your military assignment, so if questions arise, they cannot be answered during your absence. You will not have an opportunity to follow-up on anything until your return. You cannot take any materials with you, because you will be too busy to handle it while on assignment, and if anyone needs any of it, it wouldn't be available to them.

You want to impress your new boss and your new subordinates with your ability to take charge and your decisiveness. Therefore, you will want to handle everything in the in-basket and take any action that you deem appropriate to make sure that the department runs smoothly in your absence.

Remember, this is Saturday afternoon, January 30, 20XX.

- YOU ARE I. M. BRITE.
- THIS IS NOT THE POLICE DEPARTMENT YOU WORK FOR.
- YOU ARE FILLING A POSITION MOST RECENTLY HELD BY LIEUTENANT M.T. GAGE.
- YOU CANNOT REACH ANYONE BY TELEPHONE OR IN PERSON.
- FILES, COMPUTERS, AND RECORDS ARE NOT AVAILABLE TO YOU. YOU MUST WORK ALONE WITH THE INFORMATION AT HAND.
- YOU HAVE TWO HOURS AND THEN YOU MUST LEAVE TO REPORT TO YOUR RESERVE ASSIGNMENT.
- YOU CANNOT TAKE ANY OF THESE MATERIALS WITH YOU, SO THEY MUST BE HANDLED PRIOR TO LEAVING.
- YOU WILL BE COMPLETELY OUT OF CONTACT WITH ANYONE IN THE CITY UNTIL YOU RETURN TO WORK ON FEBRUARY 15, 20XX.
- YOU WANT TO DISPOSE OF EVERYTHING IN THE IN-BASKET.
- YOU SHOULD TAKE ANY ACTION TO SET UP ACTIVITIES FOR YOUR RETURN PRIOR TO LEAVING THE OFFICE, EVEN IF SUCH ACTIVITIES ARE NOT A SPECIFIC IN-BASKET ITEM. YOU WANT THE OFFICE TO RUN AS SMOOTHLY AS POSSIBLE IN YOUR ABSENCE.
- BE SURE TO MAKE IT CLEAR WHAT YOU DID FOR EACH OF THE ITEMS IN THE EXERCISE.

ITEM 1

E-MAIL MESSAGE

Date: January 26, 20XX
To: Lt. Gage

Reply Wanted:
From: Sergeant. Ashley
No Reply Necessary:

There are rumors that several of the Shift III officers are hanging out in Meadows Park late at night. They are boozing it up and leaving a mess. The information that I have is that some of the younger ones are smoking pot and some are having intercourse with underage girls. I wanted you to know about this so that you could take action as soon as possible.

ITEM 2

E-MAIL MESSAGE

Date: January 29, 20XX
To: Lt. Brite

Reply Wanted: Absolutely
From: Officer Killian
No Reply Necessary:

Congratulations on your promotion. We have heard a lot of good things about you and all of the guys are looking forward to having you on the shift. It is unfortunate that you have to assume your command so early because of the unfortunate and untimely death of Lt. Gage, but this family matter for me is a time—certain situation.

I hate to do this to you when you're just coming on, but I just got the information at the last minute. Our daughter is a stewardess for United. She has a friend with a condominium in Hawaii which she can get for free for almost a week. We can also fly for almost nothing. The only hitch is that we have to leave Monday night and will return next Sunday late in the evening. I realize this is short notice, but we won't have the opportunity for a free vacation like this for a long time, if ever. I would really appreciate anything that you could do to help out in this matter, as would the "little woman."

Sergeant. Snoke said that you had to approve it because it was such short notice. I heard you were coming in in the morning, so I thought that I would take a chance and drop this in your box. You can leave a note in my mailbox and I'll pick it up when I come in. Thanks ever so much.

ITEM 3

E-MAIL MESSAGE

Date: January 25, 20XX
To: Lt. Gage

Reply Wanted:
From: Sergeant. Snoke
No Reply Necessary:

I received a complaint from Hector Hernandez, 1352 West St. City of Palm Island, p/n 827-1780. Mr. Hernandez stated that he is being harassed by Officer Slyck. He claims that Officer Slyck constantly stops him and others in the neighborhood and gives them tickets. He believes that Slyck is prejudiced against Spanish persons and is harassing them. He says that Slyck's attitude is surly and antagonistic, but couldn't be more specific.

Mr. Hernandez is very desirous of disciplinary action being taken against Slyck. He states that he will push this all the way if we try to cover up. Slyck has cited Mr. Hernandez 3 times in 4 weeks, once for expired registration; once for no taillight; and once for an expired driver's license. I told Mr. Hernandez that we would let him know what we were going to do by February 2. In my opinion, Slyck is a good officer and Hernandez is just a dirt bag who's trying to stir up the community.

ITEM 4

E-MAIL MESSAGE

Date: January 30, 20XX
To: Lt. Brite

Reply Wanted:
From: Assistant Chief Pesky
No Reply Necessary:

I was looking forward to meeting you. I had planned to stop in for a while Monday morning to chat with you, but I received a last minute invitation to play golf with the Chief.

It is my practice to hold staff meetings every Wednesday. All lieutenants are expected to attend unless they receive a prior excuse from me. We meet at 1900 hours for about 2 hours.

I appreciate you coming in and cleaning out Gage's in-basket. He was a good man, respected by the troops, and will be missed by all. I'm sure that you will find that most important matters have been disposed of.

ITEM 5

E-MAIL MESSAGE

Date: January 30, 20XX
To: Lt. Brite

Reply Wanted:
From: Arvilla Maxwell, Secretary
No Reply Necessary:

I was glad to hear that you were coming to work for us. I look forwrd to meeting you when you report to work. Assistant Chief Pesky told me that you would be coming in to review items in Lt. Gage's in basket, so I got some information together for you.

I would normally make it a point come in on Saturday and help you out, but I have to visit my dear mother who is taking care of my ill sister's children.

When you finally report to work, I will fill you in on all details and tell you who to trust and not to trust.

ITEM 5, PAGE 2

CITY OF PALM ISLAND POLICE DEPARTMENT

The Police Department is divided into 2 bureaus. Field Operations is commanded by the assistant chief, and Administrative Services is commanded by the director. Both report directly to the chief of police. The chief has an executive secretary and an administrative assistant, and Internal Affairs reports directly to the chief.

Field Operations is responsible for the primary police functions of patrol, investigations, and special operations, and community policing. Patrol is divided into 3 shifts, each commanded by a lieutenant. The city has three districts. A sergeant commands the Traffic Section, and Lieutenants command each of the remaining sections.

Administrative Services is responsible for support operations for the department, including most administrative functions, and is divided into the Communications Division, Information and Records Services Division, and Administrative Support Division. The department also has a Family Services Bureau.

The department has a total of 235 personnel distributed as follows:

1	Chief of Police
1	Assistant Chief
1	Director
4	Lieutenants
18	Sergeants
150	Police Officers
60	Non-sworn Personnel
235	Total Personnel

ITEM 5, PAGE 3

STAFFING OF PATROL DIVISION

Assistant Chief Pesky

Shift I (2300-0700) (1500-2300)	Shift II (0700-1500)	Shift III
Lieutenant Howard	Lieutenant Sac	Lieutenant Gage
Sergeant Bonham	Sergeant Fielder	Sergeant Ashley
Sergeant Runner	Sergeant Queen	Sergeant Snoke

Traffic Section
Sergeant Queen

ITEM 6

E-MAIL MESSAGE

Date: January 29, 20XX
To: Lt. Brite

Reply Wanted:
From: J. Carter, 911 Shift Supervisor
No Reply Necessary:

Congratulations on your new position. I am sorry about the sudden death of Lt. Gage.

I am the evening Shift Supervisor of the 911 Dispatch Center. At your earliest convenience I need to talk to you about some problems in communications. The officers assigned to your area, especially the new ones, are using the radios improperly and giving the dispatchers a hard time. You are aware, I am sure, of our past problems in this area. We need to make sure that both sides cooperate.

ITEM 7

1098 Sunny Crest Drive
City of Palm Island, FL 32101

January 28, 20XX

E. Grace, Chief of Police
City of Palm Island Police Department
386 Palm Island Blvd
Palm Island, FL 32105

Dear Chief Grace,

As President of the DeQuency Elementary School PTA, I want to take this opportunity to bring to your attention the fine job that Officer Gary Slyck is doing with our children.

Office Slyck spends a lot of this time in the school area when the children are coming home after school activities. He stops to talk to them and tells them to be aware of strangers, enforces speeding laws and watches out for strangers hanging out around the school.

At our meeting today, all of the mothers were saying how much better they felt knowing that Officer Slyck is watching out for their children. We think you should know what a good officer this man is.

Sincerely,

Jane Howell

Jane Howell
President, PTA

Gage.
We need more like Slyck!
Pesky

ITEM 8

UNOFFICIAL NOTE

Date: January 25, 20XX
To: Lt. Gage

Reply Wanted:
From: Sergeant Bollen
No Reply Necessary:

Please consider this an unofficial note. I am concerned about Officer Pace. He is generally an open, affable person. Of late, he has been extremely quiet, morose, uptight, and defensive. The grapevine says he is drinking heavily off-duty. His work has fallen off, and 3 different officers working with him have asked to be reassigned to different partners.

When I try to open the door for discussion, he acts very disrespectful. It might be a matter of personal problems at home, or something more serious. Pace has an excellent record and will probably make sergeant off the next promotional list. I do not wnt, in any way, to jeopardize his career, but I thought that you ought to know.

ITEM 9

5842 Crocus Circle
City of Palm Island, FL 32101 January 26, 20XX

Commanding Officer
City of Palm Island Police Department 386 Palm Island Boulevard
City of Palm Island, FL 32105

Dear Sir:

Yesterday at a party, our three-year-old son, James, fell into the swimming pool. It was several seconds before anyone noticed him and by the time we got him out, he wasn't breathing. We called your Police Department and Officer Gary Slyck came in seconds with red lights on and siren screaming. He grabbed James and started mouth-to-mouth breathing and kept at it until the paramedics arrived and James could be transported to the hospital.

The doctors said that the only thing that kept our precious son from dying or suffering permanent brain damage was the quick action by Officer Slyck.

We just wanted you to know how grateful we are to Officer Slyck and the entire City of Palm Island Police Department.

Gratefully yours,
Mr and Mrs. George Dugg

Gage,
Looks like a commendation is in order!
Pesky

CONTENTS
GRACE
NOTED

ITEM 10

E-MAIL MESSAGE

Date: January 25, 20XX
To: Lt. Gage

Reply Wanted:
From: Assistant Chief Pesky
No Reply Necessary:

Officer Gary Slyck has applied for transfer to the Burglary Suppression Team. I would appreciate any information on his performance and the recommendations of his supervisors. Please advise me by January 29 so I can work out assignments with the new personnel coming to work on February 8.

ITEM 11

E-MAIL MESSAGE

Date: January 22, 20XX
To: Lt. Gage

Reply Wanted:
From: Sergeant Bollen
No Reply Necessary:

Officer Meagher stopped into the office today to see you about his recent performance evaluation. Although it was satisfactory, he takes exception to a comment in the narrative section that says that "Officer Meagher's performance has improved lately," and is considering filing a formal grievance.

The performance evaluation was put into his file without him having seen it or signing it and he just saw it today. Sergeant Ashely prepared the evaluation. I told Meagher to get in contact with you when you return to see what could be done about it.

ITEM 12

E-MAIL MESSAGE

Date: January 23, 20XX
To: Assistant Chief Pesky

Reply Wanted:
From: Chief Grace
No Reply Necessary:

The City Manager, City Council, Parks Director, and I are receiving numerous complaints from citizens residing in the area of Meadows Park. As you know, Meadows Part is the area where most juvenile activities are centered. In addition to the scheduled activities, it is also becoming a hangout late at night for juveniles using dope and drinking.

Most of the complaints concern malicious mischief to surrounding property, dumping of trash on nearby lawns, and drag racing up side streets. In addition to the use of narcotics, there appears to be some sales of narcotics.

Gage —
Please develop a plan of action to remedy the sitution ASAP. I have informed the Chief that you will be handling. I need your plan by January 29.
Pesky

ITEM 13

3740 Canyon Crest Road
City of Palm Island, FL 32101 January 22, 20XX

Chief of Police:

For the past 3 years I have lived at the above address with my wife Ann, and children, Benjamin and Jeanine.

As you may be aware, the past few months have brought to our neighborhood a sharp increase in the rate of residential crime, up from an already high level. Having been twice the victim, the crime rate has become very personal to us.

I have talked to many of my neighbors about this problem and our strong feeling is that we want to do something about the situation now. I have read a lot about the community banding together to fight crime. I have invited 20 neighbors to my home at 3:00 pm, February 2, 20XX to consider ways and means for protecting ourselves from the juvenile delinquents responsible for these crimes. If you are concerned, as we are, and wish to help, we would be pleased if you or your representative would attend and explain how you propose to assist us in cutting crime in our neighborhood.

Sincerely

Neal R. Jones

Neal R. Jones

Gage, please handle this and let me know what happens. I need to brief the Chief on the results of your meeting.
                                              Pesky

ITEM 14

E-MAIL MESSAGE

Date: January 15, 20XX
To: Assistant Chief Pesky

Reply Wanted:
From: Lt. Gage
No Reply Necessary:

Patrol Shift III is becoming critically short of personnel. We have only 17 officers actively assigned to the shift and we should have 20. In addition, Gallo is on military leave until February.

Jones is in the hospital with a gall bladder operation and will be off for a month; Cheffin, Gilbert, and Laffoon start vacation on January 23rd. Mack took off last night for 2 weeks with an on-duty injury; and O'Donnell is resigning effective January 29th.

We're operating short up to 2 cars per shift. Some of the officers are starting to complain. Even with running short of cars, we are spending 16 man-hours per shift of vacancy overtime.

At this rate, our overtime budget will be expended by mid-February.

Gage — I talked to Grace about this. We won't
get any relief until the new recruits report on
February 8. and then it will only be partial.
We will just have to do the best we can.

Pesky 1/18/XX

ITEM 15

E-MAIL MESSAGE

Date: January 12, 20XX
To: Lt. Gage

Reply Wanted:
From: Sergeant. Snoke
No Reply Necessary:

Per your instructions, I contacted Mr. Robert Murray. He said that his 16-year-old son was home alone last night and that officer Slyck kicked in the front door of his house for no reason, grabbed his son, and beat him up with a flashlight and left him in the house without medical treatment. Mr. Murray said that his son has some cuts and that he was taking him to the hospital for x-rays. He wants you to call him at his office, 827-2889. He seems highly desirous of pursuing this matter, although I think he can be placated if we act quickly on this matter.

ITEM 16

E-MAIL MESSAGE

826 Rose Street
City of Palm Island
X State, 32102

Dere Sir,

I got a ticket today that I didn't deserve from Officer Slyck, I know that I can't do anything about it except to pay it the ticket because it's just my word against his, and the judge always believes them.

I don't think I should be treated that way though. He knows that I was going to have to pay money and on top of that he was discourtesy to me! He called me dumb son of a bitch. Mr. Watch Commander, I an note dumb, I thght officers supposed to respect the public. I think something ougt to be done about this. Yours in offiense.

Dennis Menis.

Gage,
What this all about?
Pesky

ITEM 17

E-MAIL MESSAGE

Date: January 25, 20XX
To: Lt. Brite

Reply Wanted:
From: Chief A.E. Grace
No Reply Necessary:

Congratulations on your promotion. As you know we have had our three district system for several years.

I know that this is before you officially assume your new position, but I am asking all of our Lieutenants to give me their personal thoughts and suggestions as to how they think the system is working, with respect to geographic accountability, staffing, etc.

I know you are going out of town from January 30 and will be back on the February 15th. However, I need this memo before you leave town. Thanks.

INSTRUCTIONAL SUMMARY

Analysis and Discussion About the In-Basket Exercise

The following are my summary instructions to you about IB exercises so read the contents as if you were listening to me giving you advice.

If you took the time to complete the exercise which included a review of the Assessor Guide you were probably surprised how many actions/behaviors, you did not include in your written responses. Do not be surprised or dismayed that your evaluation of how you did was not good. Do not forget that if you really completed the in-basket, two or three trained assessors would evaluate or score your responses. Having completed a practice exercise, you are one step ahead of your competitors. To recap what you should have learned, the following points—although not all are included here—are important to remember when completing this or any IB exercise:

- Carefully read the exercise instructions.
- Read through the entire IB before you start working on completing any items.
- Prioritize the items into a rank order list but do not waste too much time doing this. No one group of SMEs will ever totally agree to the exact order of the items.
- Many of the items in the exercise were interrelated.
- You should have been or be able to identify and sort the related items into one pile.
- You can write several memos if the topic is not one where you would normally copy to other individuals in your police department.
- You can write one memo, as an e-mail, to cover many topics.
- Do not forget to consider what interpersonal behaviors/actions are necessary.
- Many items are designed to elicit your judgment and decision making, planning and organizing skills, etc.
- No one is going to receive a perfect score.
- Do not think that the exercise was structured to trick you.
- Remember that more than one assessor and preferably three assessors will be scoring each IB.

Now that you have finished the exercise you can go to the Assessor Guide (see **Exhibit 10** in the Appendix).

Chapter 7

OTHER FORMATS FOR
IN-BASKET (IB) EXERCISES

INSTRUCTIONAL OVERVIEW

The following are my instructions to you about different formats for IB exercises so read the contents as if you were listening to me giving you advice.

When I completed my first one-week training program on AC methodology, the training included learning how to write IB feedback reports. Part of the hands-on training involved being provided with a template and some sample reports. I was not trained on how to develop an oral, IB with notes exercise. It was not until many years later that I devised a different type of an IB exercise. One of my former clients asked me if I could write an IB exercise designed such that the candidates would orally present to an assessor panel how they would handle each item. The client also wanted the candidates to be able to refer to their notes during their oral presentation.

When conducting a job analysis for another client and then discussing the number and different types of exercises I would likely recommend, the client wanted four exercises. Given the large number of candidates and looking for a way to streamline the process, I created an IB exercise wherein the skill dimensions would be measured differently. The new method which I had used for the client who asked for an oral IB exercise, accomplished several things. It reduced the hours the assessors had to work, accomplished the same result in fewer days, and gave the candidates an opportunity to inform the assessors why they handled the items the way they did.

The Oral, With Notes In-Basket exercise entails the same components as a standard exercise but differs in a few ways. First, the candidate is asked a few questions that they must answer when meeting with the assessors. Second, the candidate does not actually write memos or reports that are turned in to the assessors and evaluated for the effectiveness of their written communication. And, third, the assessors take notes on what the candidate says and then they use the Assessor Guide to check off what the candidate covered.

An oral IB exercise is tapping into the same skill dimensions but it is an easier exercise than a standard IB. It is a streamlined process which saves time and costs for the agency. However, I have only used this type of IB when the police department HR staffers request the use of an oral format rather than one involving a lot of documents.

Just like all of the exercises provided in this book, you can prepare the exercises. The instructions and exercises follow.

There are two different IB exercises in this chapter. The two exercises appear as **Exercise 7-1** and **Exercise 7-2** with titles and the instructions which you must read to yourself before you start work on the exercise. Remember to adhere to the time requirements.

EXERCISE 7-1
ABC POLICE DEPARTMENT
ORAL, WITH NOTES IN-BASKET EXERCISE SERGEANT

Candidate Instructions

This test is an in-basket exercise with an oral component. Although the situations in this exercise are artificial, the problems you will deal with are real, having been obtained from actual situations police sergeants at your department encounter in their jobs.

This exercise is designed to test your management and supervisory abilities in certain defined areas and not your knowledge of the procedures or operations of the fictitious ABC Police Department. You will be evaluated on the following skill dimensions: **Problem Analysis, Judgment/Reasoning, Planning and Organizing, Management/Supervision and Oral Communication**.

Your information is limited to that actually provided in the exercise material. Sufficient information is provided to allow you to take an appropriate action of some type ranging from deciding that the matter is unimportant and need not be dealt with, or can be postponed until a later time, can be delegated to someone else to handle, or you can handle it yourself immediately.

You are not able, however, to actually contact anyone else. You must decide what action you would take without discussing the issue with anyone.

A scenario and necessary information to handle all the items are contained in the in-basket.

This exercise is set in a hypothetical police department. The addresses, phone numbers and street addresses are also hypothetical.

There is a total of ten individual items, some of which are more than one page in length, others are just noted in a numbered list. Be sure to review each document carefully to make sure that you have read it completely and understand it. All of the items have an item number at the top of each page.

You *must* note how you would handle every item in the exercise in some manner. "Handling" an item may mean nothing more than reviewing it and holding it for future action, or it may require immediate action of some sort. You decide on the action to take for each item according to your best judgment. In an actual situation, you may desire more information before deciding on a course of action, but in this case you are limited to the information at hand and must make a decision based only on the available information.

You may write on the item or type your actions on a separate piece of paper. You may use your written notes when you meet with Dr. Willis or one of her associates. However, your notes will not be used to score this exercise.

During your fifteen-minute ZOOM meeting with Dr. Willis do the following:

Orally tell her how you have prioritized the items. Dr. Willis will also have your written material to review. Tell her everything that you would do to handle the item. If you would write a letter, *indicate exactly what you would say in the letter if it were an actual situation*. If you would hold something until a later date or delegate it, indicate this—as well as what you would do with that item on that date. If you would not do anything with an item, then tell her why you would not do anything. Make sure that you identify every item you plan to take action on.

You have forty-five minutes to review the ten items. It is up to you to budget your time and keep track of it carefully. Use a stopwatch, your wristwatch or a cell phone's timer and stop when the time is up. If you were actually completing this exercise in an assessment center process you would be given a signal when five minutes are left to complete the exercise. After you complete the exercise or when time is called, a test administrator would collect all of your materials.

Scenario

You are Sergeant, James/June Axelrod. Today is Sunday, February 21, 20XX, and you are going on vacation tomorrow for two weeks. You work in the west district of the city.

No one else is available in the office. All of the administrative and non-critical line staffers are off-duty. All officers are out on the streets handling critical calls. All files and records are locked up, and since you do not know the filing system, you would have a difficult time finding anything in any event. In addition, over this weekend the entire computer network has been taken off-line for upgrades. So, you must handle all of this paperwork without calling anyone. As usual, all telephones are working to receive calls. However, you need only be concerned with your telephone.

To reiterate, you have forty-five minutes to review the items in the packet on your desk. If you were actually going through the assessment center process, upon completion of the exercise you would be escorted into another room for another exercise.

ITEM 1

E-MAIL MESSAGE

To: Sergeant Axelrod
From: Lieutenant Smith

Date: February 17, 20XX
Subject: Neighborhood Association Meeting

Could you please attend a meeting at the Emedy East and Elder Park Neighborhood Association meeting on February 26, 20XX at the Emedy East neighborhood Community Center.

They want to discuss the problems with people walking around the neighborhoods drunk. They rae also very concerned about the drug sales.

The address and phone number are: 1136 Meadows Drive, X State, 33982 (839) 243-5258.

Thanks.

ITEM 2

NOTE

To: Axelrod, Sergeant

Date: (Saturday Night, February 20)

From: OIC

Officer Stupor and I are currently handling a domestic at someone's home. Officer Stupor appears to be off balance and appears to be drunk. This same issue occurred a week ago.

ITEM 3

X City
Police Department
Routing & Transmittal Slip
❑ Priority
❑ Routine

Date: February 20, 20XX

To: Sergeant Axelrod

From: Lieutenant Smith

Subject: Probationary Employee Jamie Ryan

❑ For your   ❑ Take Appropriate Action & Reply   ❑ Reply
information

❑ Other

Officer Stupor and I are currently handling a domestic at someone's home. Officer Stupor appears to be off balance and appears to be drunk. This same issue occurred a week ago.

ITEM 4

E-MAIL MESSAGE

To: Sergeant Axelrod
From: Lieutenant Smith

Date: February 19, 20XX
Subject: Damaged Vehicle

I do not have the report yet regarding the damage to Officer Mayham's vehicle that occurred on your last shift. Please take care of this. Thanks.

ITEM 5

X City
Police Department
Routing & Transmittal Slip
❏ Priority
❏ Routine

Date: February 19, 20XX

To: Sergeant Axelrod

From: Lieutenant Smith

Subject: Complaint Letter

❏ For your information   ❏ Take Appropriate Action & Reply   ❏ Reply

❏ Other

Please review the attached and write a response. Captain Combs asked me to do this but I think you might have better details to provide to the neighborhood association on how they can help us and what we've been doing to stop the burglaries. Thanks.

ITEM 5a

Snow Drift Homeowner's Association
23 Narrow Rd.
X State 33982

February 17, 20XX

John Combs, Captain
ABC Police Department
200 Center of City
X State 33981

Dear Captain Combs:

Our neighborhood Association has received several complaints about poor service from your District.

There are delayed responses for emergencies, particularly burglaries. Also, based on the last newsletter we read, there were over 102 burglaries in our district. There are way too many of these occurring. We had several in our complex. Many of us are fearful of going out, particularly at night.

A lack of information is also given out over the telephone, with citizens being told to come to the District station, only to find out that the information could have easily been given over the phone. To make matters worse, some of us traveled in the ice and snow.

On behalf of our association, I would appreciate it if you would look into these matters and report back to me as soon as possible on what actions you have taken to remedy the problems.

Sincerely,

Ed Haines

Ed Haines, President
Snow Drift Homeowner's Association

ITEM 6

X City
Police Department
Routing & Transmittal Slip
❏ Priority
❏ Routine

Date: February 16, 20XX

To: Sergeant Axelrod

From: Lieutenant Smith

Subject: Probationary Employee Jamie Ryan

❏ For your   ❏ Take Appropriate Action & Reply   ❏ Reply
information

❏ Other

Please talk to Officer Reston about the attached letter and report back to me. Thanks.

ITEM 6a

**X City
Sun Times**

100 Stoughton
X State 33982

February 15, 20XX

Police Captain
ABC Police Department
200 Winding Rock Rd.
X State 33981

Dear Captain Coombs:

As you know, the X Sun Times has long enjoyed a good working relationship with the Police Department and the West District. Last night, however, we experienced a problem. While our photographer was trying to get photographs at the scene of a bar brawl and shooting on February 14, 20XX, Officer Reston said to him, "You idiot, get out of here or I will arrest you." He then told him that he was interfering with the department's ability to handle the scene and asked him to leave. Then he physically removed him from the scene. During this encounter which turned physical, he was rude and abrasive!

The photographer was Mr. Ansel, one of our most experienced photographers. We are formally requesting that you investigate this matter and take appropriate action to prevent this from happening again.

Sincerely,

Raymond Roundtree

Raymond Roundtree
President and Publisher

ITEM 7

E-MAIL MESSAGE

From: Officer Smith
To: Sergeant Axelrod

Date: 02/20/20XX
Subject: Officer Bentley

Why is officer Bentley sick again on my Friday? This has happened three times over the last few weeks. This is not fair.

ITEM 8

X City
Police Department
Routing & Transmittal Slip
❏ Priority
❏ Routine

Date: February 19, 20XX

To: Sergeant Axelrod

From: Lieutenant Smith

Subject: Complaint Letter

❏ For your information   ❏ Take Appropriate Action & Reply   ❏ Reply

❏ Other

As you can see the attached letter was written to the Chief. Mr. Duckheimer has now called and wants to file a formal complaint over the phone regarding his traffic citation. I need you to call him back and take the complaint.

ITEM 8a

X CITY
HILLS WHOLESALERS, INC.
5842 Snow Circle
X State 33982
(829) 555-4367

Police Chief
ABC Police Department
200 Center of City
X State 33981

February 18, 20XX

Dear Chief Scofield:

On February 18, 20XX, a police officer stopped me and gave me a traffic citation. He said I was speeding. He said I was going 40 in a 25-mile zone. I was not, and he did not have a speed gun. Is he trying to fill a quota?

I am big supporter of your department and have never had a ticket.   I am going to file a formal complaint.

Sincerely,

Richard Duckheimer

Richard Duckheimer, President
Hills Wholesalers

ITEM 9

TELEPHONE MESSAGE

From: Steno Clerk, Jones
Date: February 19, 20XX

Time: 4:00 pm
Subject: Sarah Williams—Car Accident

Please call back Sarah Williams. She is requesting an update on the car accident she had on December 16, 20XX. Her number is (829) 291-5896.

ITEM 10

E-MAIL MESSAGE

From: McMaster, Lieutenant Patrol
To: Sergeant Axelrod

Date: February 18, 20XX
Subject: Problem-Solving Initiative

Please develop a problem-solving initiative to deal with the drug dealing on King Street. Please have it completed in one week. Thanks.

ORAL, WITH WRITTEN SCENARIOS IB EXERCISE

Instructional Overview

The following are my instructions to you about oral with written scenarios IB exercises so read the contents as if you were listening to me giving you advice.

For this type of IB exercise the candidate is given a set of instructions and told that they have forty-five minutes to review the items and write down how they would handle them. At the end of the preparation time, the candidate is escorted into a room where they will have up to fifteen minutes to present these intended actions orally to the assessors. The candidate is allowed to take their notes into the room but the notes would not be used by the assessors to score his/her performance.

This is a difficult exercise because the candidate is not writing memos, letters or reports. Moreover, the candidate must utilize their time to the fullest, by:

- Being well organized when making the presentation, and does not repeat the same items (which wastes time).
- Telling the assessors what they will be covering, cover the items and summarize what's been covered.
- Identifying the related items and covering them during the informal oral presentation.
- Being very specific about how they will handle each item.
- Recognizing that they cannot cover every single item in fifteen minutes and should therefore, cover only the most important items.

In Exercise 7-2 you will find the Assessor Guide for the Oral, with Written Scenarios IB exercise for the Sergeant rank. In this type of exercise, the candidate is asked to respond to four different scenarios. The presentation is informal because they do not need to stand up, use an easel and paper or a projector to show slides.

EXERCISE 7-2
ABC POLICE DEPARTMENT
ORAL, WITH WRITTEN SCENARIOS IN-BASKET EXERCISE SERGEANT

Candidate Instructions

This test is commonly known as an In-Basket Exercise. Although the situations in this exercise are hypothetical, with some artificial restrictions on your time and the methods and activities you may employ to communicating with others, the problems you will deal with are real.

You will be assessed on four of the skill dimensions listed in the sheet provided to you during the Candidate Orientation session: **Decision Making/Judgment, Planning and Organizing, Interpersonal (Dealing with Employees and the Public), Oral and Written Communication**.

This exercise is also set in the ABC Police Department and it uses hypothetical persons.

A scenario and necessary information to handle all items are contained in the exercise. You have been supplied with paper, paper clips, etc., to get you started. In this exercise, you are expected to use *your own best judgment* in handling the items. You should not assume that just because something is done or not done in a certain manner in the ABC Police Department that this is the correct or incorrect way to handle a similar situation in this exercise.

You *must* handle every item in the exercise. In an actual situation, you might desire more information before deciding on a course of action. In this case, however, you are limited to the information at hand and must make a decision *based only on the available information*. Actually, this is not unlike real life, where you are often forced to take action under less than ideal circumstances or with less than optimum information.

So that we can determine how you handled the material, *write down everything that you decide to do*. You can handle items by either writing a separate memo or by writing on the item itself. You can either actually handle the item or you can simply describe what you would do. Or, you could do both. In either case, make sure that you tell everything or do everything that you would do in an actual situation.

Make memos to yourself about things you will want to do when you report to your new assignment. If you are going to do something, do it. If you would write a letter, *write it exactly as you would write it in an actual situation*. If you would hold something until a later date, indicate that fact on the item or by attaching a memo to it, and tell what you would do on that date. If you would not do anything with an item, indicate that on the item.

Make sure that every item you handle has some indication that you handled it, and what you did. Assessors will assume any item without a disposition on has not been handled.

You have exactly ninety minutes to respond to the four scenarios. You will only be given a five-minute warning that your time is about to expire. Therefore, budget your time and keep track of it carefully.

One of the test administrators will collect all of your materials at the end of the exercise.

If during the exercise you need clarification, ask the administrator the next time he/she comes into the room. We will check in periodically to see if there are any problems or questions.

SCENARIO 1

You are a newly promoted sergeant. You have just been called and told that one of your officers has just been involved in a shooting with a death. As a new supervisor, describe how you will handle this situation.

SCENARIO 2

It is now the late afternoon of the same day. You are on your way to a bank robbery in progress. The bank is an FDIC-insured bank. While on route, radio communication tells you that the suspect has left the bank on foot. The first officer on the scene gives dispatch a description and then the officer gets back on the radio and says he has caught the fleeing man and holding him at gun point. He has recovered the stolen money in a bag.

It is a very hot and humid day.

When you arrive at the bank, one of the bank clerks tells you that the robber said as he was leaving and that he had planted a bomb in the bank. You now expect to be at this scene for a long time. You also learn that there is a large church nursery about two blocks away that is in session with about thirty children.

Describe how you will handle the entire situation.

SCENARIO 3

One of your responsibilities is to oversee all off-duty details. One officer was supposed to report to a local hospital to work today. The hospital calls you at 9:00 am and says the officer did not show up. What do you do?

SCENARIO 4

The Chief of Police has mandated that all officers engage in at least two park-and-walks during their tour of duty. Your shift is failing miserably in that area, and the officers are not doing park-and-walks, but just filling out a form stating they'd done them. Describe how you will correct the problem and ensure compliance by your officers.

See **Exhibit 13** in the Exhibits Appendix for the Assessor Guide for this exercise.

INSTRUCTIONAL SUMMARY

Analysis and Discussion about Different Formats for In-Basket Exercises

The following are my summary instructions to you about IB exercises so read the contents as if you were listening to me giving you advice.

By now, you have probably finished a few strenuous practice sessions, but may still have more questions about IB exercises. This is to be expected because, in general, these are the most difficult exercises for all candidates I have coached and usually earn the lowest scores. I know that one of the reasons for this is that many people are not strong at processing paperwork, particularly when they are under pressure. Moreover, many of us do not enjoy handling paperwork because doing so is often tedious, sometimes boring, stressful and one of the least favorite parts of the work we do. This practice should bring those scores up.

Below are more important points to remember about how to tackle any IB exercise:

- You should always prepare a short outline or a bullet point list of the issues you feel are the most important.
- You can use your outline when making your oral presentation.
- An IB exercise is one of the best types of tests, if not the best, to measure a person's general management skills.
- Completing office paperwork includes knowing which items can or should be delegated, which are the most important to complete immediately, and which ones can be put off or filed.
- Each item should be reviewed very carefully and then read again before you determine what actions to take to deal with the item.
- Effective management does not mean that you delegate every item.

Chapter 8

DIFFERENT TYPES OF WRITTEN EXERCISES

INSTRUCTIONAL OVERVIEW

The following are my instructions to you about different types of written exercises so read the contents as if you were listening to me giving you advice.

In reality, almost all AC exercises are written exercises. As you know by now, when you participate in an AC process, there are many written components. Let's review those components.

CANDIDATE INSTRUCTIONS

The instructions are provided to each candidate and then a test administrator reads the instructions aloud to the candidate while they follow along on the written copy while listening to the administrator. Not all processes are done the same way by consulting firms. For example, the number of candidates may be too large to have enough administrators to read to each candidate. In that case the instructions are usually read by one person on a television monitor. You may be wondering why is it necessary for the instructions to be read aloud to candidates. The reason is: people learn differently. Some people hear better or would rather listen; others learn better by reading along with the presenter; and some people have a better recollection of what they read if it is also presented to them orally.

It is very important that the instructions are clear and concise, but specific enough such that the candidates do not have questions. The instructions should not be ambiguous or confusing, either. In other words, the contents should include all of the important things they must know to complete the exercise.

THE EXERCISE MATERIAL

Written test material can come in a variety of forms. The format is determined by the type of exercise. The degree of difficulty and time allotted for the actual exercise will vary. Blank sheets of lined paper are also usually part of the material candidates can use to write notes. However, those notes are rarely used to evaluate their skills. If they are, the instructions will be very clear on that point.

For some processes, candidates are provided with a test booklet in which they are instructed to write their responses. For some AC processes, all answers are typed on-line. Do not worry about the method used to record your responses, because what is important is that data is being collected.

At the end of the preparation time a test administrator escorts them to the presentation room where the assessors are seated. The candidate is allowed to refer to their material during this time and when time is called, the test administrator collects all of the materials. However, as stated previously, their written notes are generally not used in the evaluation process. The notes are shredded to ensure that the papers are not intermingled with the other materials.

THE ASSESSOR GUIDE

All AC exercises include an Assessor Guide. Its format and the level of detail included varies with the type of exercise involved, and with the consulting firm that is designing and administering the process.

There are two different written exercises in this chapter. The exercises appear as **Exercises 8-1** and **8-2** with titles and the instructions which you must read to yourself before you start work on the exercise. Remember to adhere to the time requirements.

EXERCISE 8-1
ABC POLICE DEPARTMENT
COMMUNITY POLICING PROBLEM ANALYSIS EXERCISE
LIEUTENANT

Candidate Instructions

Carefully review the following community policing problems and draft written responses to each one. Utilize your knowledge of community policing, problem-oriented policing, problem-solving strategies, report-writing, etc., in preparing your responses. Be clear and specific and do not assume that the evaluators know what experience you have.

You will have one hour and fifteen minutes to respond in writing to two problems. In this exercise, you will be evaluated on the following skill dimensions previously provided to you: **Judgment and Decision-Making; Planning and Organizing, Problem Analysis, and Written Communication**.

Write your candidate number on the upper right corner of each page. Write as legibly and neatly as you can. You may use as many pieces of paper as you need. Please number each page. No questions will be answered by the administrators after the start of the exercise. Your exercise will be collected by one of the test administrators at the end of the exercise. At the one-hour mark you will be informed of the time remaining. No materials are to leave the room.

Problem 1

A high school outside the city limits, but across the street from a city park, held a football game. During and after the game a lot of kids congregated at the park and left a big mess for park employees to clean up. A fight also broke out in the park during the game. One teenager was taken to the hospital emergency room with minor injuries. Additionally, when the game was over, the cars leaving the park caused a major traffic jam. Despite the fact that the school is not in the city, residents called the ABC City Police Department to complain about the traffic jam. Even though your officers ended the fight, the parents of the youths who got into the fight called the mayor to complain. They said that if the police had been patrolling the park at the time, the fights would not have broken out and nobody would have been injured.

How would you respond to these complaints?

Problem 2

Since there is a spillover into the city park and city streets, what would you do for future football games at this location to prevent a repeat of these problems, and what will you do if your plan does not work?

See **Exhibit 14** in the Exhibits Appendix for the Assessor Guide for this exercise.

EXERCISE 8-2
ABC POLICE DEPARTMENT ESSAY(S) EXERCISE CAPTAIN

Candidate Instructions

Carefully review the following four questions. The purpose of this essay exam is to place you the candidate, in four job-related situations. You will be required to respond to various questions in writing. Also, assume always that you are a police captain.

This exercise will be evaluated on the following skill dimensions; **Plan- ning and Organizing, Leadership, Interpersonal, Perception and Analysis, Judgment/Decision Making, and Written Communication**. However, not all questions measure each skill dimension. The skill dimensions are universally required for people promoted to the rank of police captain rank. Your final overall written communication score will be based on your performance in all four essays.

You will have two hours to hand write your answers when responding to the four problems.

Hand write as legibly and neatly as you can as this will be part of the assess- ment of your written communication skills. The assessors must be able to read your handwriting. There are plenty of pencils or pens and if you run out of ink or need a pencil sharpener let the administrator know.

You may use as many sheets of paper as you need. Please make sure you write your confidential candidate ID number in the upper right-hand corner of each page. Also, please number each page. You are allowed to use your dictio- nary.

No questions will be answered by the test administrator after the start of the exercise. Your essays will be collected by one of the administrators at the end of the exercise. Time will be noted at the one-hour mark. No materials may be taken from the room.

Question 1: New Technologies:
Promoting/Implementing/Maintaining

Outline your experience with promoting and implementing new technologies for the police department(s) you have worked for. Specifically, address the following:

1. When and where you were involved?
2. What were some of problems and challenges, and why were they so chal- lenging?

3. What was the extent of your involvement? Did you just delegate the work to subordinates or were you involved in a hands-on manner?
4. What are the names and telephone number of two people who can verify and validate your work?

Question 2: Mission Statement and Goals

The mission statement for the police department begins as follows:

"The mission of the ABC Police Department is to build a stronger community by working together."

You have recently been hired as a new captain for the ABC Police Department. The chief has asked you to identify and briefly discuss, in order of priority, what goals you would address in achieving this mission.

Question 3: Broken Windows

The policing theory of "broken windows" has been employed successfully in some communities and yet it has not been successful in others. Discuss why you believe this has occurred. That is, indicate under what, circumstances it has succeeded and under what circumstances it may have failed. Also, if applicable, include any work-related experiences you may have had dealing with this theory.

Question 4: Dealing with the Mentally Ill

Our state and community, as with other states and cities across the nation has its share of mentally ill individuals. Their behaviors, unfortunately, are sometimes quite bizarre, ranging from mass murder to having sex with animals. At times, new officers are not fully prepared to deal with these individuals. Your chief has asked you to prepare an in-service lesson plan for new and existing officers on how to deal with individuals who may be mentally ill. Discuss the steps you will take in developing this module as well as what topics you would include.

See **Exhibit 15** in the Exhibits Appendix for the Assessor Guide for this exercise.

INSTRUCTIONAL SUMMARY

Analysis and Discussion About Written Exercises

The following are my summary instructions to you about written exercises so read the contents as if you were listening to me giving you advice.

If you took the time to complete the exercise which included a review of the Assessor Guide after completion, you were probably surprised how many actions/behaviors you did not include in your written responses. Do not be surprised or dismayed that your evaluation of the situations fell short of perfection. Also, do not forget, because you completed the exercise for practice only, two or three trained assessors did not evaluate or score this exercise. Therefore, based on having gone through it here, you learned a lot and are one step ahead of your competitors.

To recap what you should have learned, the following points are important to remember when completing written exercises:

- You need to think as "macro" as possible in order to make decisions and plan and organize your responses.
- You must have the technical knowledge of your department's SOPs and current issues in your profession.
- Do not forget to consider what interpersonal behaviors and actions are required.
- After reading the items, the first thing you should do is prepare an outline. But when doing so, do not take too much time, or lose track of how much time you have left to write.
- Make sure to thoroughly proofread your writing.
- Make sure also that you leave enough time to practice a quick "dry run" of your oral presentation, if one is required as part of the exercise.
- Written exercises are designed to primarily measure your written communication skills, but the Assessor Guides can be useful to bolster your judgment and decision-making abilities.
- If you know that your written communication skill is one of your weaknesses, you should purchase a book on how to improve writing skills.

Chapter 9

ROLE-PLAYING EXERCISES

INSTRUCTIONAL OVERVIEW

The following are my instructions to you about different role play exercises so read the contents as if you were listening to me giving you advice. A role-play exercise is sometimes included in an AC process. However, a role-play exercise should not be used just because the test developers think that including one is a good idea or that other agencies they are familiar with have used role-play exercises. A role-play exercise (like all assessment exercises used in an AC process) should also not be used just because the agency, union, or HR Department staff thinks it is a good idea. The use of this type of exercise should be based on the job task analysis. The person who plays a role opposite a candidate must be specially trained to assume that role, and know how to play that role consistently to be fair to all candidates. That can be a tall order. Requiring a candidate to interact with a role-player is a way to measure their abilities. The abilities that are typically measured in this type of exercise are **Interpersonal, Coaching, Judgment, Decision-Making and Oral Communication**.

SOME RESEARCH ABOUT ROLE PLAY EXERCISES

A role-play exercise is based on a job-related situation which is designed to include a trained role-player. The important requirements of the job are in setting up as a simulation wherein the instructions for the role player are standardized. According to Eurich et al. (2009) approximately 76 percent of organizations that use the AC method conduct role-play exercises.

Later in this chapter the pros and cons of using role players are covered which is not based on any research articles but on my experience with using role players.

According to Goldstein and Ford (2002) no systematic studies examining the role of the role player in role-play exercises existed. What we do know and you will learn in this chapter, role players interact with the participants and should be consistent and objective (Thornton & Mueller-Hanson, 2004; International Task Force on AC Guidelines, 2009). When I was trained as an assessor and in turn when I trained assessors and role players, I made sure the role players played their roles as consistently and as humanely as possible, so to speak.

My first experience with AC methodology involved hiring local actors to play the roles. The local actors were paid to play the roles. In subsequent years, some of the assessors played roles, as did some of the AC's staff. We also used unpaid citizens to play the roles. A discussion of the pros and cons of using a live role player follows.

SOME PROS OF USING ROLE PLAYERS

There are several positive reasons for using one or more trained role players (each role player is assigned to a different exercise). Based on my knowledge and experience the pros include the following:

(1) **Face Validity**. The candidate is able to demonstrate their skills while speaking to a real person (versus an avatar or versus indicating what they would do with the problem employee or irate citizen, for example). On the "face of it", meeting with a real person is more related to the job for which the candidate is being tested.

(2) **Excellent Opportunity to Document Body Language**. When a candidate is interacting with a real person, they will demonstrate their true behavior. Given that it is difficult to "fake your way" through an AC, it is more difficult if not impossible, to fake your use of eye contact, gestures and body language (e.g., leaning forward, tapping on the table, not looking directly at the role player).

(3) **Same Role Player Used for Each Candidate**. The same role player should be used for each candidate. This provides for more safety in terms of standardization. However, if there are very large numbers of candidates, for example, over thirty-six (i.e., the role player plays the role six times a day for five days), then the role player may

get burned out. A paid role player will be less likely to burn-out because of the financial reward of the job.

SOME CONS OF USING ROLE PLAYERS

Overall, I think using role players is not a good idea. This is because based on my experience, there are more cons than pros which include the following examples.

(1) **Role Player Deviates from the Script**. A role player may ad lib because they forgot the script and did not want to open the folder where the script is kept. A role player may be forced to deviate from the script because of an aggressive candidate (e.g., a candidate may probe the role player, come too close to the role player, try to look at the role player's folder, etc.).

(2) **Not Enough Time to Memorize the Script**. Unless the agency has the luxury in terms of a large budget, hiring a trained actor or actress is out of the question. Therefore, non-actors or actresses more often do not memorize the entire script. They may not have enough time, during the training, to practice the role or to memorize the script word for word.

(3) **Cost to the Agency**. Using a role player in an AC process is much costlier than a standard oral assessment process. In fact, the cost per candidate for a comprehensive AC process can range anywhere from $500 to more than $1,000 per candidate and is contingent upon many variables. If a selection method results in selecting better employees who are retained on the job, then the process has utilitarian value. A multitude of utility studies of ACs with a specific discussion of role players, have been conducted in the United States and the findings as cited by Lievens (2002) are that ACs have more utility than unstructured assessment process. The utility of ACs resulted in higher utility because the process reduced adverse impact and because recent research on the utility of ACs has indicated that the process is superior to traditional selection methods in terms of selecting the best performing management personnel. In short, the benefits outweigh the costs (Lievens, 2002).

When police departments decide to use an AC process for promotional or whatever reasons (e.g., union contract requirement, consent decree, new management philosophy), it is inherent that top management staff are aware of the costs involved. Therefore, if they have budgeted for the process and using role players is part of the contract deliverables then finding, training and using role players adds to the overall cost.

The cost to hire trained actors or actresses will be based on the going-rate for the region of the country. Moreover, based on my knowledge and experience, the majority of agencies do not hire paid actors or actresses. Even so, the cost for a process goes up when role players are used because the agency should pay for their meals during the training and the actual AC process. Additionally, if they have to travel a long distance, then the agency should assume the cost of their housing for the duration of the testing process.

(4) **Potential Candidate Complaints About Being Treated Differently by the Role Player**. There is a possibility that a candidate will file a grievance because they felt that their role player did not stick to the script or something similar. However, in all the years I have been involved with the AC process I never have heard or read about a candidate doing this and being successful, but the possibility does exist.

(5) **Management and Monitoring of Each Role Player**. It is extremely important that the test administrators monitor the role players. This includes having someone watch/listen outside the door and listen to the role player, etc. I remember doing this during my training and the purpose was to make sure the role player was in the room, interaction was occurring, etc. The test administrators should meet with the role players after each assessment center session to review and discuss any issues or problems they encountered and make any necessary corrections.

There is one role-play exercise in this chapter. The exercise appears as **Exercise 9-1** with a title and the instructions which you must read to yourself before you start work on the exercise. Remember to adhere to the time requirements.

EXERCISE 9-1
ABC POLICE DEPARTMENT SUBORDINATE COUNSELING EXERCISE SERGEANT

Candidate Instructions

Today is May 30th, 20XX. You are to assume the role of newly promoted police sergeant, Kevin Spacey. You have just returned from a weeklong vacation and are anxious to begin work in your new position. You feel good because you completed some of your paperwork before you left town last week. The first item on your agenda today is to meet with one of your officers, Alec Baldwin.

While you were on vacation a female officer, Meg Ryan, filed a complaint with the human resources director. She claims that Baldwin used vulgar language when speaking with her in front of other male officers, looked her up and down and made sexual advances toward her which included putting his arm around her, kissing her neck, and asking her to come to his apartment. She also claims that he has done this in the past and she had previously asked him to "cut out the crap."

Captain Gandolfino has asked you to speak with officer Baldwin about this. The following information has been compiled about Baldwin from his personnel file for your review.

- He has worked for the department for five years.
- His performance evaluations have been above average for all five years.
- He has used up all of his family medical leave to care for his ailing son.
- He has received six commendations over the past five years for high arrest activity, officer of the month, etc.
- He had one accident and totaled a police car, but the accident was not his fault.
- You have seen his divorce paperwork.
- Two complaints have been filed about him. One was an allegation of harassing her at work filed by a woman within the past month; the other stated he had been rude to a man during his first year on the job. The older complaint was determined to have been unfounded.

You have twenty minutes to prepare for your meeting with Baldwin about this complaint and ten minutes for the meeting with him. Be sure to follow all General Orders and departmental procedures. Paper, paper clips, and marker pens are available for your use. Make sure you put your candidate number on all papers. The test administrator will collect your material at the end of the meeting.

See **Exhibit 16** in the Exhibits Appendix for the Assessor Guide for this exercise and **Exhibit 17** in the Exhibits Appendix for the role-player script for this exercise.

INSTRUCTIONAL SUMMARY

Analysis and Discussion About the Subordinate Counseling Exercise

The following are my summary instructions to you about role-play exercises so read the contents as if you were listening to me giving you advice.

To recap what you should have learned, the following are important things to remember when completing a coaching and counseling exercise:

- Many of the items in the exercise were related even though this is an exercise about an employee and not an IB exercise.
- You should be able to identify what the critical issues are with the employee.
- It should be fairly obvious to you that using your dealing with people skills is very important when meeting with a problem employee.
- Many items in the employee's personnel file for you to review during your preparation time are there to elicit your judgment and decision-making, planning and organizing skills, etc.
- No one is going to receive a perfect score.
- Remember the actions and statements of the role-player are not designed to trick or fool you. The role player's script is designed to elicit the most appropriate behaviors and actions from you.
- Handle any personnel coaching session with a role-player as you would if you were actually meeting with an employee who has had some recent performance problems, etc.
- If you have already read an entry level police supervisory textbook you should have already learned about how to conduct an employee counseling session.
- If you try to memorize how you should conduct an employee coaching/counseling meeting, you may miss many of the items contained in the personnel file.
- Pay close attention to the problems and issues about this employee and then jot down how you are going to run the meeting with the employee.

ANALYSIS AND DISCUSSION ABOUT
DIFFERENT ROLE-PLAYING EXERCISES

At this point in your studying and/or practice you have probably had enough of role-playing exercises and now know there is a great deal more involved in this type of exercise than you thought. However, given all of the sample exercises provided, you are one step ahead of your competitors.

I know you have learned a lot and have added to your knowledge bank of the AC process. Your toolbox keeps filling but there is still more to learn and remember. For example, do not forget this advice:

- Follow the policies and procedures of your department for responding to and dealing with face-to-face citizen complaints.
- *Do not* handle the situation the way your colleagues told you to handle similar situations based on their past experience with an AC process.
- Remember, we all have our individual differences, and, therefore, how your colleague interacts with people is going to be different than how you would proceed.
- Listen carefully to what the role player is saying and observe their body language.
- *Do not* try to size up the role-player or think that you can throw them off balance. Just be yourself and pretend the role player is a real person.
- Most, of my coaching clients are not strong in interpersonal skills. Therefore, when you receive your candidate orientation materials from the consulting firm or the HR department, and one of the exercises is a role-playing exercise with a live role-player, you must immediately know that one of the skill dimensions you will be expected to demonstrate is how to effectively deal with people.
- Regarding interpersonal skills, it is difficult to *fake* your behavior. In other words, *do not* make statements to the role player that you think demonstrate your interpersonal skills when the statements have nothing to do with the content of the exercise.
- Some of what the role player tells you is also designed to elicit your judgment and decision-making, and your planning and organizing skills, too.

- *Do not ever* think about how one of your colleagues told you to handle a role play exercise. For example, if one or more of them told you to just play a role yourself, this is bad advice.
- Being yourself is not acting. So be yourself.

Chapter 10

PROBLEM ANALYSIS (PA)
ORAL PRESENTATION EXERCISES

INSTRUCTIONAL OVERVIEW

The following are my instructions to you about problem analysis oral presentation exercises so read the contents as if you were listening to me giving you advice.

Problem Analysis exercises are also used in AC processes. This type of exercise can entail presenting a candidate with several written problems which they must respond to in a formal presentation. The problems can involve any number of relatively uncomplicated topics such as how to deal with:

- an employee who is found drunk or sleeping on the job and their personnel file reflects current family problems;
- a scheduling issue;
- an irate citizen who has plans to file a lawsuit after experiencing what was perceived as harassment during a traffic stop;
- two co-workers having a conflict which has begun to escalate;
- report-writing deficiencies;
- planning and coordinating a large-scale event.

A well-developed and difficult exercise should include several interrelated problems for which the candidate must devise a plan leading to a resolution. The problems can be very complex, detailed, and then escalate. If this type of exercise is designed properly, a candidate's innate abilities can be easily measured.

The PA exercise in this chapter was used for a former client. Please note that a map is not included because in the actual exercise the maps provided to the candidates were enlarged and a map for this book would be too small to read easily. Therefore, just read the departmental and geographic issues and the employee issues sections very carefully. Then read the candidate instructions. To practice this exercise, you can obtain a copy of the map of one zone in your department's coverage area. Then mark similar buildings noted on the map so you will experience using a map. If you do not want to do this, just carefully read the information and instructions and prepare your presentation.

There is one problem analysis oral presentation exercise in this chapter. The exercise appears as **Exercise 10-1** with a title and the instructions which you must read to yourself before you start work on the exercise. Remember to adhere to the time requirements.

EXERCISE 10-1
ABC POLICE DEPARTMENT
PROBLEM ANALYSIS ORAL PRESENTATION EXERCISE LIEUTENANT

Candidate Instructions

You are to assume the position of a police lieutenant with ABC Police Department located on the east coast of X state in X city is one of the fastest growing cities with 108,000 residents and an average of 100 new people moving into the city every day.

You are responsible for District 3 and Zone 34 (see map in your packet of materials). Zone 34 is a square, seven miles on each side. Assume your current staffing is one sergeant assigned to District I in Zone 34. The current staffing of the entire city per shift is sixteen officers with four in your district. Throughout the city, the day shift has one sergeant on duty per district, and on the midnight shift, there are two are on duty. A canine unit is also available twenty-four hours a day.

The entire department is currently understaffed but is in the process of hiring about fifteen new officers. However, on the day shift you are able to draw from other districts or divisions in the department to provide coverage.

The Police Chief has asked you to come up with specific goals, objectives, and strategies, to solve the problems addressed below. Assume it is the end of April 20XX. An action plan needs to be in place by the summer. What you prepare in this exercise will become part of a grand strategy based on input from other lieutenants in the department, subject to approval by the command staff. Each lieutenant will be presenting their ideas individually to the chief and command staff. So you should consider your contribution of critical importance.

ZONE 34 GEOGRAPHIC INFORMATION, ISSUES AND PROBLEMS

A large planned 2,700-acre residential community, Y, is becoming one of the larger commercial hubs in the city, too. It comprises a number of gated communities but maintains a down-home atmosphere. One exit of an interstate highway, I-5, provides citizens with easy ingress and egress. However, with its growth and popularity has come traffic congestion. Residents are complaining to the mayor's office and are afraid that crime may increase. Their concerns have also resulted in attention from the local news media.

Zone 34 has many warehouses, office buildings and light industry. The zone has some crime but it is not a hotbed of crime for the city.

A branch of a state university is located in the city. Like another, identical dormitory nearby, two new five hundred-student dormitories constructed in late 20XX also houses two students per room. Those 1,000 students have been good for the local economy, but already citizens are complaining about noise, late-night traffic and other problems. D state university has its own police department but has only staffed the dorm area with one officer. He has not been able to handle the problems sufficiently and they're getting prominent play in the local newspapers.

Many parishioners of a big Catholic church down the road from the university have written to the university and the police department about lewd sexual acts and behavior, underage drinking, and loud music playing late into the night in the dorms. They want it stopped. They also fear for their young daughters' safety and are outraged that there is an active LGBT student group on campus. Elderly residents in the local communities have also complained about the noise, increased traffic, and rude students at local restaurants.

Other complaints allege students are buying gas and then driving from the stations without paying, a spike in petty thefts, increased traffic on residential roads and an increased demand for public services. Some of the elderly residents have even been interviewed by the media and have stated that their tax dollars paid to the state and city are being misspent. Others have stated that they moved to the upscale community from a southern part of the state for a better quality of life and they fear that it is already starting to become like the densely urban southern part of the state.

A Walmart Supercenter is also located in the zone. The store has experienced an increase in crime, more shoplifting and even strong-arm robberies in the parking lot right after the store has closed. A city council member who lives in the area is putting pressure on City Hall to solve this problem. Additionally, some elderly residents who observed a strong-arm robbery said they are scared. One of them, a woman in her seventies, ended up in the hospital with a mild heart attack. These problems have been blamed on insufficient police presence at this store.

A Major League Baseball spring training facility is also located in Zone 34. Inappropriate behavior by some famous athletes has also occurred in the area. Residents have demanded that such problems should never reoccur. They also continually complain about the traffic problems before and after spring training games which they feel have not been sufficiently addressed. A new lower income housing area is also in the planning stages and residents are opposed; "Not in My Back Yard." This new development is located near I West, which is a prosperous enclave.

A skating rink is across the street from the stadium and so is a multiplex movie theater. A bowling alley is being built in that area, too. Five hotels are in the same vicinity which are at full occupancy during the winter-spring tourist season. An RV park and Gold's Gym are also located all within a three (3) mile radius. A few crimes have occurred at the RV Park and some vocal residents of the area are concerned that it may turn into a refuge for the homeless and criminal elements that might live in their cars or campers.

EMPLOYEE ISSUE

You had tasked your sergeant with conducting some research and compiling the data on the above problems. He has not met the deadline you gave him. When you queried him about the status of his research he said, "I have not started the work and do not have the time, due to insufficient staffing, and walked off." He is a long-term employee. His past performance has been above average. But this data is critical to your plan.

As noted previously, the Police Chief has asked you to come up with specific goals, objectives, and strategies to deal with the issues mentioned. What you prepare and present in this exercise will become part of a grand strategy based on input from other Lieutenants in the department. Each Lieutenant will be presenting his/her ideas individually to the Chief and Command staff. Subsequently, you should consider your contribution of critical importance.

You will have ninety minutes to prepare your presentation and fifteen minutes to present it to the assessor panel. When you make your presentation, you will be observed and evaluated by a team of trained assessors who will listen and document what they hear and observe. Assume that the assessors are the chief, the assistant chief and the district commanders.

The test proctor will be using a stopwatch to keep time, but you should also monitor your time with your own watch. You will be given a ten-minute warning at the eighty-minute mark.

You will also be given a five-minute warning and time will be called at the end of ninety minutes by the test administrator. Therefore, you should plan your time accordingly.

In this exercise, you will be evaluated on the following skills: **Planning and Organizing, Analytical Thinking/Problem Solving, Strategic Thinking/Innovation, Written Communication and Oral Communication.**

Paper, pencils, colored markers, paper clips, a stapler, an easel and paper, and a personal computer has been provided if you choose to use them. If you want to prepare slides or visuals for your presentation using the computer, you must use PowerPoint. This is to ensure that if candidates use a software program that they all use the same one in order to ensure the presentation material is uniform among the candidates.

During the ninety-minute preparation time, the test proctor will not answer any questions.

Your only reference material is what has been provided in the instructions. Therefore, it is expected that you will utilize your technical knowledge, job experience, planning and organizing, analytical thinking, problem solving and other skills to prepare your presentation. At the end of the exercise, the test proctor will collect all of your written material and notes and will escort you to the room where you will deliver your fifteen-minute presentation.

See **Exhibit 18** in the Exhibits Appendix for the Assessor Guide for this exercise.

Chapter 11

CRITICAL INCIDENT WRITTEN AND ORAL PRESENTATION EXERCISES

INSTRUCTIONAL OVERVIEW

The following are my instructions to you about critical incident/ issues written and oral presentation exercises so read the contents as if you were listening to me giving you advice.

A critical incident is another type of exercise used in AC processes and may also be called a problem-solving exercise. In this type of exercise the candidate has to solve several problems related to a critical incident. The most realistic exercises I have designed and administered have been for the firefighting profession in which the simulation is structured as if the candidate is in a fire engine and is called to assume command of a fire which is shown on a screen. The fire can start small and increase to the point it is out of control or can be contained. The candidate uses a hand-held radio and is receiving information from a person playing the role of the dispatcher.

For law enforcement management positions, the most realistic evaluation is a compstat exercise. At the time Henry's (2003) book, *The Compstat Paradigm* was written it was considered to be a paradigm. Law enforcement managers and executives meet in a room to discuss emerging crime trends and review statistical data. Each precinct commander presents their activities at the command and control center's podium to present their activities and accomplishments (Henry, 2003). However, to design and administer a compstat exercise is very expensive because of the number of people, video screens, computer equipment, and other materials needed. Some large city departments do regularly conduct compstat exercises, but it can be cost prohibitive for a significant majority of smaller police departments.

But a standard critical incident exercise can effectively evaluate candidates for police promotions and provide a very good measure of a candidate's skills. The ones I have used include written and oral components in which the candidate is to assume the incident is taking place, based on the information provided. The candidate is given time to review the material, prepare a written response (to obtain a measure of written communication skills) and then deliver an oral presentation to a panel of assessors who play the roles of top management police personnel. The candidate should save time at the end of the presentation for questions. The incident descriptions can be very short, just one or two paragraphs, or much longer, perhaps as many as four pages.

For the exercise that follows, the candidates were instructed to look at the screen and orally present their reports to a panel of assessors sitting in a room. It worked very well. Comments made by past clients include some of the following:

- **"It was very difficult, but very realistic"**
- **"I did not have enough time to edit my written report"**
- **"I spent too much time on the minute details"**
- **"Based on the Assessor Guide, there are many actions I should have taken and statements I should have made to my subordinates, etc."**

There are two critical incident/issues written and oral presentation exercises in this chapter. The exercise appears as **Exercises 11-1** and **11-2** with titles and the instructions which you must read to yourself before you start work on the exercises. Remember to adhere to the time requirements.

EXERCISE 11-1
ABC POLICE DEPARTMENT CRITICAL INCIDENT EXERCISE LIEUTENANT

Candidate Instructions

You will have fifteen minutes to review the incident, and at the end of the preparation period you will be escorted into a room where you will provide an assessment of the incident and an indication of your thinking process as you respond to the incident. Three assessors will be in the room, but you may not ask them any questions.

You should discuss your options for responding and anything else that you feel is important to address.

You will be given a maximum of seven minutes to provide your response to the initial incident description. Once you have completed your response, or seven minutes has passed—whichever comes first—you will be presented with an update that may affect your assessment of the incident. You will then have the remaining time to read, think about, and respond to the update. Your response to the initial incident description and update must be completed within the fifteen minutes allotted for this exercise.

You will be evaluated on the following skill dimensions: **Planning and Organizing, Judgment and Decision-making, and Oral Communication**.

Part 1: Initial Incident

You are to assume that you are a newly appointed lieutenant working for X City, in X state. You have just arrived at the scene of a multi-person argument where people are screaming at one another and a few fist fights have broken out. The location is a middle class to lower middle class multi-ethnic neighborhood. As you stop your vehicle, you also see people pushing one another. Some people are brandishing pots and pans. Others have baseball bats. In all, you see a crowd of about seventy-five women, men and young children in groups of about ten to twenty. As a result of a number of frantic 911 calls you observe seven police vehicles and at least eight to ten officers.

Your sergeant, whom you just met last week, tells you that from what she can gather since arriving five minutes earlier, was that two families began arguing because one refused to clean up after their dogs as they walked them past their yard. Within a very brief period of time, the situation mushroomed into at least, ten families loudly expressing their long-held concerns about one another, to include some racial and ethnic slurs. Your sergeant advises you she has not yet decided what to do, and notes that there is an elementary school in session four blocks away.

What you see now is basically a free-for-all, with pots banging, and possible shots fired. It is 1100 hours and you know that you will be in command for at least the next fifteen minutes.

Please explain to the assessor panel how you will prioritize your actions and take command of this situation.

Remember, you have just seven minutes to provide your initial incident description because you will be interrupted and provided with an update to the incident. It is up to you to keep track of your time.

Part 2: Seven Minutes Into the Incident

Another sergeant who has been in communication with dispatch tells you that there is an armed robbery in a strip mall two blocks away and that the suspects escaped in two vehicles, one of which may be headed your way.

You now have seven minutes to indicate how you will handle the scene now. You may utilize your seven minutes any way you choose.

After you have completed your responses, see **Exhibit 19** in the Exhibits Appendix for the Assessor Guide for this exercise.

EXERCISE 11-2
ABC POLICE DEPARTMENT PROGRAM DEVELOPMENT
WRITTEN AND ORAL PRESENTATION EXERCISE CAPTAIN

Candidate Instructions

You are to assume the role of newly promoted captain, Jean/Gene Hackman for X City Police Department which is in a northeastern state.

The chief calls a meeting with the captains and to review the portion of the department's strategic plan for designing, developing, implementing, and tracking gang problems. You should know that the city's program is based on the High Point Model. The intent of the High Point Model is to bring the best practices from around the country to address gang violence, open-air drug markets, and other negative elements that degrade the community and damage its residents' sense of safety in their neighborhood.

He briefly recapped the history of the High Point model by stating, "It began in Boston in 1996, when an intervention called Operation Ceasefire largely stopped gang violence in that city. Operation Ceasefire combined problem-oriented policing with collaboration between law enforcement organizations and community stakeholders."

He has directed each captain to prepare a report outlining their strategies for combatting the problem. After receipt and review of their reports, he will call another meeting with the captains. During that meeting, each captain will present key aspects of their program to the entire group. The meeting will be conducted similar to what happens in a compstat meeting. Later, the best ideas from all of the captains will be used in the strategic plan.

Part 1: Written Portion

You will have four hours to develop and write a program for dealing with the gang problem in the city. You may use the knowledge you have about gangs in the city you work for to design and write your report.

You are expected to use the Internet to conduct research on young gang programs around the country and may use this material in your program. You must also cite your references at the end of your report.

The program, which may include some bullet points, is to be no longer than seven pages, double-spaced with one-inch margins on all four sides. You are to use the Times New Roman font, with 12-point type.

You have been provided with a computer, printer, paper, pens and other office supplies. There are also back-up computers available in case your computer malfunctions at which point you are to notify the proctor in the room who will move you to a different work station. Any lost time will be added to your allotted time.

You will be evaluated on the following skills: **Planning and Organizing, Problem Analysis and Decision-Making, Dealing with People and Written Communication**. You were previously provided with the skill dimension list. These skills will be evaluated through the use of an assessor checklist.

Part 2: Oral Portion

You will have ten minutes to present the key components of your plan. During your presentation, you may refer to your written material. An easel and colored marker pens will be available to you to use. If you were actually getting ready to present your program to the assessors you would more than likely be given between fifteen and twenty minutes to prepare your presentation by writing on the easel board, making notes on note cards, or highlighting your report and using it for the presentation. However, for this exercise you would just present to Dr. Willis over Zoom. You should prepare for this part of the exercise on your own and use any format you desire.

During your ten-minute presentation, you will be evaluated only on your **oral communication skills**. Dr. Willis will take notes while you are presenting, use a stopwatch, and then complete the Assessor Guide. Her notes and Assessor Guide will be scanned and sent to you prior to the feedback session.

See **Exhibit 20** in the Exhibits Appendix for the Assessor Guide for this exercise.

INSTRUCTIONAL SUMMARY

Analysis and Discussion About Critical Incident Written and Oral Presentation Exercises

The following text are my summary instructions to you about critical incident/issues oral presentation exercises so read the contents as if you were listening to me giving you advice.

Based on your experience in handling various critical incidents, you know that some are very complex, rich in detail and substance, whereas others were less complex. A way to learn more about how to handle critical incidents in an AC process is just brainstorming with colleagues.

The following points are important to remember when completing this type of exercise:

- Read the incident very carefully and then read it again.
- Determine what the most important elements of the incident are.
- Prepare an outline which includes the steps you would follow.
- Pull from your memory the steps outlined in your department's policies and procedures manual as well as other reports and documents.
- Carefully consider how you would handle it if you were on the scene and in charge.
- Make sure you fully utilize your subordinate staff, as you cannot do everything yourself.
- Assume and continue to assume that you are in the rank being tested for, *not* the rank you now hold.
- Focus on the *big picture* first, then drill down to the smaller details.
- *Do not* get hung up on the small details, because if you were really on the scene, you would not handle every detail yourself.
- *Do not* forget to consider that several things are happening simultaneously, and therefore you must consider everything.

Chapter 12

THE LEADERLESS GROUP DISCUSSION (LGD) EXERCISE

OVERVIEW

The following are my instructions to you about leaderless group discussion exercises so read the contents as if you were listening to me giving you advice.

A leaderless group discussion (LGD) exercise is employed in an AC process if the job analysis data reflects that the incumbent spends a significant percentage of their time meeting with peers in an attempt to solve organizational problems. The candidates are told to conduct the meeting as if they were actually at work but no one in top management is available for feedback or input. The purpose of this exercise is to observe how candidates who are told they hold the same rank and title work together to solve a problem. They are given the same instructions, problem and amount of time to read the exercise instructions and when the time is called by the test administrator the exercise starts. There are assessors in the room who are assigned to observe and take notes on no more than two candidates during a typical forty-five to sixty minute exercise.

HISTORICAL OVERVIEW

The LGD was first developed for use in the military prior to WWII. It was first used by the German Army and also by its Navy. It was later used by the United States Army and British Navy (Bass, 1954; Ansbacher, 1951).

Eurich, Krause, Cigularov and Thornton (2009) identified 43% of organizations in the United States as using LGDs. This type of exercise provides unique and different perspectives on how candidates get along with others and get ahead. One of the positive aspects of an LGD exercise is that, based on research, assessors are consistent in their ratings of the candidates and the exercise does predict future behavior on the job. But it is more difficult to coach someone on how to behave in an LGD exercise, based on research by Kurecka, Austion, Johnson and Mendoza (1982). My experience supports the research.

EXERCISE MECHANICS

A former client of mine asked me to evaluate the materials, including videos, for some AC exercises he had previously completed including an LGD exercise. He was not selected for the position and did not feel that the HR department had provided him with enough information so he could understand why he did not do well enough to be promoted. I reviewed the videotape and gave him feedback on what he could have done better. For example, he made very few comments during the exercise, looked down much of the time instead of looking at the other candidates, and did not look at the candidate who was speaking.

Based on my experience designing and administering numerous LGD exercises over the years, there are a few downsides to using an LGD. One is cost. Another involves logistical issues, especially with a large number of candidates, say twenty or more competing for the same position. In an actual exercise, the candidates are sitting at a round table or in a circle and the assessors are assigned to observe no more than two candidates situated in a place in the room where they can easily observe each of their assigned candidates. The candidates' identifying numbers are affixed to their clothing so the assessors know which ones to observe. They focus on their two candidates and take notes on what each one says or does, including body language, raised voices, hand gestures, tapping a pencil on the table, etc.

A round table is the best setting, because it enables the candidates to better see each other, compared to a square or rectangular table. The assessors' job is somewhat easier in this type of exercise when there are no more than six to eight candidates in the room, with three to four assessors in the room. No one candidate should be allowed to dominate the discussion. Therefore, the Assessors will not be taking as many notes as they would in an Oral Presentation exercise.

It is common for many candidates to perceive that the exercise is only measuring a person's ability to lead others and does not include listening and other skills. As you pursue additional professional knowledge, you will find that the word *leadership* means different things to different people. It has many definitions and actually comprises a multitude of sub-skill dimensions.

Below are some examples of the erroneous perceptions many candidates have regarding how they should behave and actions they think they should take in an LGD exercise. You are the leader if:

- You are the first person to speak after the preparation period.
- Take immediate control of the marker pen.
- You take charge of the group and start to assign roles to the others.
- You essentially control the meeting.
- You are the candidate who is the strongest in problem analysis and wears the "black hat"—finding fault with some of the other candidates' ideas.
- You, essentially, do the most talking.
- You interrupt other participants in order to stay on time.

As you will learn after reading the Assessor Guide, the most effective candidate demonstrates a variety of behaviors.

This exercise is difficult to practice because it is unlikely that you will have six or seven other colleagues to practice with. The best way to get some hands-on experience with the exercise materials is to read the instructions, write down your ideas according to the instructions and then read the Assessor Guide. It is also a good idea to find examples of LGD exercises on the Internet. Many consulting firms have actually recorded actual exercises (of course with the candidates' permission) and have used those videos for training because a real exercise is much better to learn from versus one where actors play the candidates. Since law enforcement agencies are moving away from the military model and the pyramid-shaped hierarchy, it is also advantageous for you to watch LGD exercises—and not just law enforcement examples—on the Internet to see how other organizations use this model.

The candidate instructions, which include the full exercise and Assessor Guides, follows over the next few pages.

There is one leaderless group discussion exercise in this chapter. The exercise appears as **Exercise 12-1** with a title and the instructions which you must read to yourself before you start work on the exercise. Remember to adhere to the time requirements.

EXERCISE 12-1
ABC POLICE DEPARTMENT
LEADERLESS GROUP DISCUSSION EXERCISE
LIEUTENANT

Candidate Instructions

In 20XX, the city annexed approximately seventy-five percent of the property located east of the Keller Canal, south of Tenth Avenue North and north of Lake Roam Road. See the attached map. As a result of the annexation, the department created another zone, Zone 13, but it is for analysis purposes only. Officers working in Zones 2 and 5 currently handle calls in the annexed area. However, Zone 2 officers handle most of the calls in Zone 13.

Note: A map is not included because the original maps used for this exercise were very large and if reduced in size for this book would be very difficult to read.

The following partially describes the annexed property:

It is primarily industrial with two trailer parks and some scattered housing. Both trailer parks are in very poor condition, and the one off Lake Roam Road is known as a haven for drug dealing. Houses in the area are substandard. The remainder of the area is industrial with some large businesses and also some smaller warehouses and auto repair businesses. The 2200 block of Tenth North did not get annexed. Boutwell road presents traffic issues as a result of its becoming a major connector from Tenth Avenue North to Lake Roam Road when the new extension was completed. The city found out later that Boutwell road was not included in the annexed area, either, meaning the city cannot enforce traffic laws or any crimes on that road.

Much of the area is not up to code, including many of the residential properties. There is a trailer park south of Tenth on the west side of Boutwell road which is considered an eyesore. The same applies to some of the residential properties on the Lake Roam side.

The annexation also includes an apartment complex called the Varsity Club Apartments formerly known as Cypress Park which consists of some student housing for X Community College and some family rentals. Property crime and vehicle burglaries, mostly associated with commercial and industrial property, occur in this area. Also, fights, disturbances and thefts occur.

There is a very large vagrant problem, mostly from the wooded areas. Vagrants camp there and come into the commercial properties and commit auto burglaries and thefts. The department has seen evidence of this when they cross into the trailer park on Boutwell road. Stolen autos are also frequently dumped in the industrial area.

A call for service printout for the annexed area from X Sheriff's office and X City for December 1, 20XX through December 31, 20XX revealed the following data:

X Sheriff's Office and X City Logged Calls and Dates
12/01/XX–12/31/XX

X Sheriff's Office Logged Calls and Dates	X City Logged Calls and Dates
1,315 calls for service in the proposed annex area 12/1/XX thru 12/31/XX. City 12/1/XX thru 12/31/XX.	56,343 calls for service for the whole
Approximately 448 Part One Crimes in the annex area 12/1/XX thru 12/31/XX.	3,388 Part One Crimes for the whole City 12/1/XX thru 12/31/XX.
The annexation has (11) Sexual Batteries (19) Robberies (97) Assaults or Batteries (2) Arsons (155) Burglaries (164) Thefts (47) Criminal Mischief (50) Hit & Run Accidents (144) Other Accidents (47) Drug- or Alcohol-Related Calls (85) Domestic Disturbances	increased X City's calls for service by approximately 2.3%. The annexation increased X City's Part One Crime rate by 13.2%. Out of the 1,315 total calls for service in the annex area, approximately 448 were Part One crimes. That leaves 867 calls for service that include Part Two crimes.

Note: Part One crimes are the most serious and include murder, robbery, rape, aggravated assault, burglary, theft and auto theft, and arson. Part Two crimes include, assault (simple), criminal mischief, embezzlement, drug dealing, gambling violations, domestic disturbances, driving under the influence and other alcohol related incidents, prostitution, weapons violations, trespass, hit and run accidents, etc.

It should also be noted that only about half of the 867 remaining calls for service were criminal in nature. The other half was non-criminal calls, but still required law enforcement responses.

You are to assume the role of police lieutenant, working in the patrol division. Each of you has many years of experience in the various functional areas of the Police Department and is familiar with the recent annexation. The chief has asked you to work together and come up with a plan that covers staffing, patrol, equipment and other relevant components of a plan, to include some preliminary, estimated cost figures for dealing with the problems in the annexed area.

You each have two sergeants under your command and a zone team complement of six police officers each working on either the A, B or C shift. All of them are familiar with the current situation.

You will have forty-five minutes to come up with a plan. Prepare it assuming you will all make a formal presentation to the deputy chief and chief at a later date. When working with other group members, you will be observed and evaluated by a team of trained assessors who will document what they observe.

Papers, pencils, colored markers and easel paper have been provided.

You will be evaluated on the following skill dimensions in this exercise: **Planning and Organizing,Relationships with Others, Perception and Analysis, Leadership and Oral Communication**.

During the forty-five-minute meeting, the assessors and test administrators will not answer any questions. You are to conduct the meeting as if you were actually at work but no one in top management is available for feedback or input.

Your only reference material is what has been provided in the instructions. Therefore, is it expected that you will each utilize your management and leadership skills, and technical knowledge in order to participate and make contributions to preparing the plan. At the end of the exercise, the test administrator will collect all of your written material and notes. However, only your oral statements and responses will be evaluated by the assessor panel. See **Exhibit 21** in the Exhibits Appendix for the Assessor Guide for this exercise.

INSTRUCTIONAL SUMMARY

Analysis and Discussion About
Leaderless Group Discussion Exercises

The following are my summary instructions to you about leaderless group discussion exercises so read the contents as if you were listening to me giving you advice.

After having read the exercise and Assessor Guide, you may have had some difficulty visualizing participating in the exercise. As stated previously, a way to learn more about how an LGD exercise works is to conduct a search on Google or YouTube and typing: leaderless group discussion exercise. There you should find more information about this type of AC exercise.

Important points you should consider when participating in an LGD exercise include:

- Read the instructions thoroughly and while doing so do not worry about how long or little time it takes the other participants to read them.
- Do not worry about what you think the other participants are going to do or say.
- *Be yourself* and for some candidates this means talk early, long and forcefully; take control; assign tasks others, etc.
- *Do not* forget to consider what interpersonal behaviors are necessary.
- *Do not* just echo what others have already said just because you think this is the right thing to do. Orally present your case, to showcase your judgment and decision-making abilities.
- *Do not* assume that the most talkative person has the strongest skills and therefore, is the strongest leader.

Chapter 13

VIDEO-BASED TESTING (VBT) AS PART OF AN ASSESSMENT CENTER PROCESS

INSTRUCTIONAL OVERVIEW

The following are my instructions to you about video-based testing so read the contents as if you were listening to me giving you advice. However, this chapter does not include any practice exercises.

VBT is a method of testing wherein applicants view job-related scenarios, respond orally, and are later scored on at least five dimensions by trained assessors. A VBT can be used as part of an AC process particularly if the entire process is video taped. With this method, candidates are presented with video-recorded scenarios and then must provide oral and behavioral responses to each one. Based on my knowledge of several different types of VBTs, they differ from AC exercises because vivid depictions of job-related situations using recorded video with live actors or avatars are presented to the candidates. Even though VBTs differ, they can be included in an AC process. In VBTs, there are no live role players or assessors in the room. The assessors score the candidates' video responses at a later date.

SOME SPECIFICS

VBT scenarios can be used to depict close details of working environments, mannerisms, nonverbal cues, tone of voice, and the placement of physical objects. Also, video scenarios may more closely model actual work behaviors than scenarios that are presented in writing. Moreover, video scenarios can enhance face validity (e.g., the extent to which a test subjectively measures what it intends to measure), which has been shown to be related to applicant test performance (see Chan & Schmitt, 1997; Edwards & Arthur, 2007; Smither, Reilly, Millsap, Pearlman & Stoffey, 1993).

One of the positive aspects of VBTs is that facial expressions, hand gestures, voice tone and other components of body language can be picked up. However, the latter does not make the process less threatening for a candidate, especially one who has never been tested this way.

VBTs measure what a candidate actually says or does in response to a scenario and thus provide a more detailed measure of demonstrated performance. When presented with a situation depicting an upset citizen for example, it is one thing for candidates to simply indicate that they would calm the citizen; it is quite another thing for them to demonstrate how to do this.

SOME ADMINISTRATIVE ISSUES

I recently read a book about simulations in personnel testing (Editors Tuzinski & Fetzer, 2014). The authors summarized and critiqued different aspects of using simulation technologies. Given that some of you probably work for very large police departments or a federal agency, you might have to participate in an AC process that is administered entirely online. This is why the following points should be of interest to you.

- You will more than likely have to interact with a character that looks almost like a real person (an avatar) who is able to speak to you via computer-generated speech.
- Make sure you carefully and thoroughly read the candidate orientation materials.
- Take the online practice exercises more than once or as many times as allowed.
- If you have to watch and listen to an avatar, pretend the avatar is a real person.
- Do not *allow the fact that the avatar is not a live role-player to* confuse, upset or cause you to think that the exercise is not real, job-related, or fair. It is.
- Given that you will probably be provided with at least four options for how to respond to the avatar, pick the best option.

- Regarding test security, the system will be set up to prevent cheating, or sharing of information among candidates taking the assessment at the same testing center.
- More than likely, once you submit your answer, you will not be allowed to backtrack. Therefore, be careful not to hit the submit button until you are absolutely sure of your answer.

Chapter 14

SITUATIONAL JUDGMENT TESTS (SJTs)

INSTRUCTIONAL OVERVIEW

The following are my instructions to you about situational judgment tests so read the contents as if you were listening to me giving you advice. However, this chapter does not include any practice tests but does include a few samples.

Situational judgment tests (SJTs) have been frequently used as one of the exercises in an AC. These tests can be in either written or video form. SJTs are personnel selection instruments that present job applicants with job-related situations and possible responses to the situations. These tests are developed based upon an extensive job analysis and are composed of job-related issues or scenarios that describe a dilemma or problem requiring the application of relevant knowledge, skills, abilities, or other characteristics to solve SJT problems. They may be presented in written, oral, video, or computer-based formats (Pereira, Wiechmann, Schmitt, & Harvey, 2001; Motowidlo et al., 1990) and usually contain options representing alternative courses of action from which the test taker must choose the most appropriate response (see Christian, Edwards & Bradley, 2010).

Before I cover the theory and some research about SJTs, I will tell you about coaching a candidate who was testing for a management position in a very large law enforcement agency. After about a two-year process, he was selected as Agent in Charge for a state. He partially credited our coaching sessions for his success.

Typically, several thousand candidates compete to be placed in rank order on a state or federal test registry. Once they pass the national exam and are on the register, they can then apply for openings around the state or country. Then they would go through a structured assessment process with officials from the chosen agency.

Overall, the testing process is very rigorous. The particular process in which my client participated was designed by a nationally known company. The entire process was online and had many components. One part of the testing involves the candidate watching and listening to an avatar before being presented with options as to they would handle the situation. The options are similar to those found on a typical multiple-choice written exam.

Each choice is weighted. The candidates receive points for their selection on each question, with the most points awarded for the most appropriate choice. The questions the candidates are presented with tap into their innate abilities and their knowledge of agency standard operating procedures.

HANDLING STRESS

It can be very stressful for candidates to take an online test and have to pretend they are interacting with a person played by an avatar. In this situation, the skills you learned in the role-playing experience will be invaluable in understanding how to respond to the avatar, including which is the best answer to select. Based on having spoken with some of my clients about speaking into a camera or interacting with an avatar, they said they experienced heightened stress which may have adversely affected their scores. I do not know because I have no information on the extent to which candidates demonstrate stress and whether or not any of the thousands of candidates tested complained to the HR staffers about this. Nonetheless, here are my suggestions for minimizing your stress:

- Focus your attention on the scenario that is being presented to you by the avatar.
- Do not think about that the fact that the avatar is not a real person. Just listen and watch.
- Do not think about how the testing methodology was designed, or whether it is valid. It is.
- Take a deep breath before selecting the answer on the screen.

- Take your time and if backtracking is allowed before you hit the final submission button, then go back and make sure you are absolutely sure of the answer you selected.
- Pause a few seconds before moving on to the next vignette.

SOME RESEARCH ABOUT SJTs

Using online testing is the most efficient, effective method for testing large candidate pools spread all over the United States. Taking an SJT is not much different than a candidate presenting answers to person while looking at a screen or just speaking while an audiotape is playing. Regardless of the type of equipment used, the candidate needs to pretend that they are a sergeant, lieutenant, captain, agent in charge or other rank depending on the promotion being sought.

Motowidlo, Dunnette, and Carter (1990) first introduced SJTs as low-fidelity simulations, and since then a large body of research and practical experience has been presented which substantiates the validity and practical usefulness of SJTs (McDaniel, Morgeson, Finnegan, Campion, & Braverman, 2001).

There are typically two types of instructions which are behavioral tendency and knowledge-based. Behavioral tendency instructions ask respondents to identify how they would likely behave in a given situation and they choose the option they think is the best. Knowledge-based instructions ask respondents to evaluate the effectiveness of possible responses to a particular incident (McDaniel & Nguyen, 2001). Furthermore, because researchers have contended that SJTs predict performance because they measure job knowledge (Motowidlo, Borman, & Schmitt, 1997), practical intelligence (Sternberg, Wagner, & Okagaki, 1993), or general cognitive ability (McDaniel et al., 2001) it makes sense that some law enforcement agencies have started to use various forms of SJTs.

I found an SJT item designed by (Ployhart, Weekley, Holtz, & Kemp, 2003) and rewrote the scenario for law enforcement with some sample response standards. The exercise appears as **Exercise 13-1** with a title and the instructions which you must read to yourself before you start work on the exercise. There are no time requirements because it has been provided as an example.

EXERCISE 14-1 SITUATIONAL JUDGMENT SCENARIO WITH RESPONSE STANDARDS

Scenario: Assignment from Lieutenant

It is now 11:00. Your lieutenant has given you an assignment to be completed by noon. You are working on the assignment and are not finished yet. A citizen calls you and starts asking you questions about a police report she is waiting for from one of your subordinates.

Select the best action below you would take:

1. Answer her questions, but be quick about it.
2. Take your time to answer her questions.
3. Ask if she minds waiting while you contact your subordinate who is out on the road.
4. Tell her to please call back because you need to obtain the report from your Sergeant.
5. Tell her you will have someone call her back in a few minutes.

What would you most likely do?

What would you least likely do?

INSTRUCTIONAL SUMMARY

According to research (Bledow & Frese, 2009) candidate responses express a variety of different thoughts when answering SJT questions. I have included some of their thoughts here because when I coach my clients, I continue to remind them to pretend they are actually the rank they are being tested for and handle the situation as if they were on the job. Bledow and Frese noted that candidates indicated, "I tried to visualize the situation and thought how I would act." And for some questions that were excluded from further consideration, test-takers said things like, "This does not make sense"; "I don't think that is the right thing to do"; and "That is not enough, I need more control" (Bledow & Frese, 2009). Also, test takers "frequently based their decision on the consequences they thought an action would have, and selected the response option they thought would bring about the outcomes they valued" (Bledow & Frese, p. 243, 2009).

In summary, if your candidate orientation materials indicate that you will be taking an SJT, you should mentally prepare yourself to select the most appropriate option on the list.

As previously mentioned, a SJT can also measure a person's understanding of how to work with a team and team processes. Marks et al. (2001) developed ten:

✓ Mission analysis
✓ Goal specification
✓ Strategy formulation
✓ Monitoring progress toward goals
✓ Systems monitoring
✓ Team monitoring and backup behavior
✓ Coordination
✓ Conflict management
✓ Motivation and confidence building
✓ Affect management

As outlined by Adams et al. (2012), a scenario was created for each of the ten individual processes. Each scenario is accompanied by six behavioral responses, measured on a Likert scale, ranging from 1 (Very Unlikely) to 7 (Very Likely). Respondents were asked to review each scenario and then rate how likely they would be to take the proposed actions.

I adapted the following scenario and accompanying behavioral responses adapted from the aforementioned article. It pertains to a team process of strategy formulation and planning. The scenario appears as **Exercise 14-2** with a title and the instructions which you must read to yourself before you start work on the exercise. There are no time requirements because it has been provided as an example.

EXERCISE 14-2 SITUATIONAL JUDGMENT SCENARIO WITH RESPONSE STANDARDS

Scenario: Sergeant Task Team

You are part of a sergeant task team that has been working on a project for six months. It has become apparent to the team that the original strategy set for completing the project is not working out. The team is unsure of how to proceed.

Please rate each response choice on how likely you would be to take the listed action:

1. Suggest that a new strategy be created and implemented to better complete the team's task.
2. Continue with the current strategy but try to revise sections of the plan that need improvement.
3. Just use this experience to highlight the importance of having alternative strategies for when problems arise.
4. Verbally criticize the team's strategy as well as their lack of productivity in completing the task.
5. Develop an alternative strategy and present it at the next meeting for discussion.
6. In front of the lieutenants, place the responsibility of the failed strategy on the other team members.

INSTRUCTIONAL SUMMARY

Of the latter six actions presented, two reflected effective behavior (responses 1 and 5), two moderate behaviors (2 and 3), and two actions that represented ineffective behavior (4 and 6). According to Lievens, Peeters and Schollaert (2008), the strength of SJTs is that they effectively predict future job performance. SJTs have also been shown to have less adverse impact on minority candidates. In addition, based on research, applicant reactions towards this type of test are positive. Regarding weaknesses, SJTs might be susceptible to faking, practice, and coaching effects. If a SJT is poorly designed and subsequently some candidates are promoted even though they faked their way through the test, then they may not perform well in the position.

INSTRUCTIONAL OVERVIEW

Three Motivating/Confidence-Building Scenarios

On the next few pages are some other SJT items from Smith (1996). The scenarios are about motivating and building confidence in employees.

I adapted the following scenarios and accompanying behavioral responses adapted from the aforementioned article. It pertains to a team process of strategy formulation and planning. The scenarios appear in **Exercise 14-3** with a title and the instructions which you must read to yourself before you start work on the exercise. There are no time requirements because the scenarios have been included as examples.

EXERCISE 14-3 SITUATIONAL JUDGMENT SCENARIOS
WITH RESPONSE STANDARDS

Scenario 1: Motivation

Your work is shared with a co-worker. You work every afternoon and the co-worker works every morning. The co-worker is not doing a fair share of the work and as a result you have too much to do in the afternoon. Do you:

1. Give it to your boss to take care of?
2. Talk with the co-worker and that ask that he do more work?
3. Reduce your work effort and productivity to match?
4. Try to have a friendly, non-threatening meeting with the co-worker to more equitably divide the tasks?
5. Ask the boss if you can work with someone else?

On the next page are two more examples which could be modified and used for a law enforcement management position.

Scenario 2: Confidence Building

A district supervisor discovers from the dispatch log that one of the associates has regularly been stealing and shipping layaway merchandise to her home. Should the district supervisor:

1. Confront the associate with the information and try to obtain a confession.
2. Report the matter to the police department.
3. Set up surveillance on the associate's residence until a shipment is delivered.
4. Terminate the associate.
5. Alert the store manager.

Scenario 3: Motivation

A long-tenured associate is going to retire in less than a year. This associate is widely respected by the other associates. Recently, the associate's performance has slipped badly and his attendance has become irregular. Would you:

1. Let the associate work out the year until he retires.
2. Reduce the associate's hours and put him on the easiest assignments.
3. Coach the associate and, if necessary, take disciplinary action.
4. Suggest to the associate that he take early retirement.
5. Encourage the associate to transfer to another area (Weekley & Ployhart, 2005, p. 11).

INSTRUCTIONAL OVERVIEW

Analysis and Discussion About SJTs

My prediction is that more law enforcement agencies will use SJTs in the future for many of the reasons covered in this chapter. There are also several important points you should remember if you are advised that your AC process will include a SJT:

- The questions will be similar to those in a written exam.
- There will be between four and five options to choose from (e.g., a-e) and you will receive points for choosing one or more answers.
- You will be put under pressure.
- The questions will be tapping into your abilities, but with a different testing method.
- Some of the questions will tap into technical knowledge, therefore make sure you are totally familiar with your agency's SOPs, directives and general orders, etc.
- If you are required to write or type your answers (in an online test where there will be white box), the test is also tapping into your written communication skills.
- The SJT may also require you to answer questions posed to you by avatar.
- You will be given some credit for having selected the second most appropriate response, etc.
- SJTs are not designed to trick or fool you.
- SJTs are very difficult to develop and the companies that design these tests should know what they are doing. They must be able to defend the testing process if it is legally challenged.

Chapter 15

THE FUTURE OF POLICING EXERCISES

OVERVIEW

In January 2020, with the arrival of a life killing virus COVID 19, the world as we knew it, experienced dramatic changes in the way we live, and business and industry had to adjust. Public service professionals were swept up in the changes and this included police professionals. Considering the extensive, continual and sometimes inflammatory media coverage individual police officers and departments have received since George Floyd's death on May 25, 2020, police departments had to respond. Many have already made significant modifications in philosophy, policy, procedures and attitude. My reaction to the events is evidenced in this update to the 2017 edition of this book.

The most recent shooting and deaths of several civilians (see Table 1 on next page) have resulted in a great deal of pressure on police departments throughout the U.S. to change their methodology of response to resistance and arrest, especially in respect to the use of deadly force. The issues that I have written about in this chapter are ones that are continually being addressed by today's police leadership personnel.

Serious national issues such as domestic terrorism and mob violence are frightening. The insurrection of January 6, 2021 in the nation's capital present new and dangerous challenges for law enforcement professionals who are responsible for protecting our lives and maintaining the peace. At all levels police officers must be prepared to deal with these horrors. Therefore, there is an exigent need to solve internal police problems, some of which are presented in this chapter so that efforts can be directed toward dealing with external and internal situations that police departments face.

Table 1: Police Officer Shootings 2014–2020

Date	Who	Circumstances	Police Dept	Outcome/Other
7/17/14	Eric Garner	Under suspicion for illegally selling cigarettes. Chokehold, Uttered, eleven times, "I can't breathe."	NYPD, NY	Officer fired. No prosecution. National protests.
8/9/14	Michael Brown	Shot 6 times. Department of Justice report determined that racial bias was involved and excessive force use.	Ferguson, MO	Officer resigned. No prosecution.
11/22/14	Tamir Rice	Juvenile reported to have a gun pointed at passers-by. The weapon was probably a fake.	Cleveland, OH	No prosecutions after this case. Officer fired 3 years later for lying on employment application.
4/5/15	Walter Scott	Mr. Scott was pulled over for having a defective light on his car and ran away from the police officer after a brief scuffle.	North Charleston, SC	White male was fired and later sentenced to 20 years in prison. Protests in N. Charleston and chants of "No justice, no peace."
7/5/16	Alton Sterling	Police shot Mr. Sterling when they responded to reports of a disturbance outside a shop.	Baton Rouge, LA	The two officers were not charged. One was dismissed and the other suspended.
7/6/16	Philando Castile	When Mr. Castile and his girlfriend were pulled over for a routine check He advised the officer that he had a license to carry the gun in his possession. When he reached for license he was shot.	St. Paul, MN	No prosecution; cleared of charges.

Table 1—*Continued*

Date	Who	Circumstances	Police Dept	Outcome/Other
3/18/18	Stephan Clark	Police were investigating a break-in.	Sacramento, CA	No prosecution; officers feared for their lives.
3/13/20	Breonna Taylor	During execution of a search warrant no drugs were found but Ms. Taylor's partner thought they were being burglarized and fired in self-defense and police shot 8 times and killed her.	Louisville, KY	Family filed a lawsuit for wrongful death and use of excessive force. The family was awarded $12 million.
5/25/20	George Floyd	Police were called to the Cup Foods establishment because Floyd had been accused of trying to pay for an item with a counterfeit $20 bill. Interaction ended with Floyd on ground with knee on his neck for over 8 minutes	Minneapolis, MN	One officer was charged with second-degree murder and manslaughter, and three others face charges of aiding and abetting murder. Mr. Floyd continually pleaded that he couldn't breathe. Protests broke out in cities across the US, and there were demonstrations in other parts of the world.

continued

Table 1—Continued

Date	Who	Circumstances	Police Dept	Outcome/Other
6/12/20	Rayshard Brooks	Devin Brosnan responded to a complaint that Brooks was asleep in a car blocking a restaurant drive-through lane. Officers conversed with Brooks for 40 minutes in friendly interaction. He failed a breathalyzer test, a physical interaction ensued, he grabbed a Taser from the officer, ran and was shot while running because he appeared to point (e.g., a flash occurred) Taser in Rolfe's direction.	Atlanta, GA	Rolfe was fired and Brosnan placed on administrative duty. Garrett Rolfe was charged with Felony murder, Aggravated assault (5 counts), Violation of oath (4 counts), Damage to property. Devin Brosnan was charged with Aggravated assault, Violation of oath (2 counts).

Adapted from https://www.cnn.com/2020/08/05/us/rayshard-brooks-garrett-rolfe-bond-revoke-request/index.htmlapted; https://www.bbc.com/news/world-us-canada-52905408

Despite much negative commentary on police departments; e.g., systemic racism, implicit bias, calls for defunding, protecting officers through qualified immunity, etc., many positive changes can occur in police departments.

Chief Medina Arradondo of Minneapolis started the rebuilding process by immediately firing the officers involved in the death of George Floyd. Before George Floyd's death Mayor Jacob Frey and Chief Arradondo were already taking steps to demilitarize the police department (Coy, 2020).

An example of what could be accomplished had already occurred in the city of Camden, N.J which, with many sweeping reforms had remade its police department. The transformation of that department commenced in 2012 because of an increase in homicide. The police department was dissolved by the mayor and city council and now operates under a signed agreement for Camden county to provide shared services. The union still exists, citizen and police non-contact interaction has increased, de-escalation and body camera training has been provided, and more cameras were installed throughout the city. The healing of the department continues. For example, the white Chief Wysocki "brandished a "Standing in Solidarity" poster alongside residents holding "Black Lives Matter" signs (Holder, p. 37, 2020). The police department made a strategic shift toward community policing and the results were positive (Vallas, 2020). Per Vallas, despite the changes the union was not dismantled, and stated that, "Violent crime fell 23% and nonviolent crime plunged 48% from 2010 through 2018. While homicides increased slightly from 2019 from the year before, they've fallen 63% since 2010. The absentee rate among police officers on the new force plummeted" (Vallas, p. A11, 2020).

Many media outlets have reported different recommendations for changing/re-organizing/modifying/monitoring police departments and the examples include:

- Strengthen rules around misconduct.
    - Establish an independent agency to investigate misconduct (Li & Lodhi, 2020).
- Facilitate more accountability and accountability.
- Make it easier to prosecute and sue law enforcement officers.

- Establish a national misconduct registry.
  - o Require state and local law enforcement agencies to report disaggregated use-of-force data.
  - o Tighten the definition of criminal misconduct.
  - o Ban chokeholds.
  - o Build public databases of traffic stops (Li & Lodhi, 2020).
  - o Invest $300 million in community policing.
  - o Repeal a state statute that blocks police records from public view.
  - o Divert some of police department budgets to youth and social service programs (Albright, Wasson, Varghese & Mosendz, 2020).
  - o Develop an entirely new training regime which would include first responders providing meditation, social work, EMT skills and other kinds of training (Friedman, 2020).
  - o Conduct Critical Incident Training and follow the Memphis model where officers who completed specialized training to respond to mental health crises (Friedman, 2020).
  - o Update the 911 system with a program like that created by the city of Houston created where crisis counselors rather than patrol officers are dispatched to mental health calls (Friedman, 2020).

The death of George Floyd has also transported the issue of police abuse of use-of-force, general misconduct, bias and other behavior, to the national stage (Carter, 2020) and although they do not make the laws, they must enforce them appropriately that I am quite sure most Americans are saddened by the horrific event as well as those other civilians who died in 2020. And across the U.S. a great deal of pressure has been put on police departments to reform, change their cultures and some cities (e.g., New York, Los Angeles) have already reduced their police department budgets and moved the money to social services and other line items. The Los Angeles City Council voted 12–2 to cut the police department's budget by $150 million and reduced the number of officers by 2.5 percent (i.e., 9,988 to 9,757) (AP, Friday, July 3, 2020).

The pressure on police departments that have lost the confidence of citizens and elected officials will continue for the foreseeable future until significant changes are instituted in the departments. Moreover, even when some police positions are converted to civilian positions, promotions will have to occur because supervisors are critical in any organization and necessary to the implementation of changes. Considering this, the assessment center exercises in this chapter focus on the aforementioned issues.

INSTRUCTIONAL OVERVIEW

Five new exercises for the Sergeant, Lieutenant, Captain and Assistant Chief and Chief ranks were written in response to all that has transpired in 2020. Assessor guides for each exercise may be found in the Exhibits Appendix.

EXERCISE 15-1
ABC POLICE DEPARTMENT
BIAS IN POLICING
PROBLEM ANALYSIS ORAL PRESENTATION EXERCISE
SERGEANT

Candidate Instructions

You are to assume the role of newly promoted Sergeant, Jerry/Jerrie Jones for ABC Police Department which is in a northeastern state.

Your Lieutenant has asked you to:

1. Provide an analysis of the research findings presented in the about implicit bias and stereotyping.
2. Elaborate on how you will reinforce the importance of not engaging in bias with your officers.
3. Describe how you handle a racial bias complaint made against one of your officers.

You will have two hours to prepare an oral presentation which you will deliver to your officers. You will have ten minutes to make your presentation. During your presentation you may make reference to your agency's policies and procedures (the actual one you work for) as well as your own knowledge and experience. Also, you may be asked questions by the panel members.

You have been provided with a computer, printer, easel paper, pens, sharpie highlighters, and other office supplies. There are also back-up computers available in case your computer malfunctions at which point you are to notify the test proctor in the room who will move you to a different computer. PowerPoint is set up on the computer if you choose to use it. If your computer malfunctions you will be given additional time. The lost time will be added to your time.

Three Assessors holding the rank of Sergeant or while also performing the Lieutenant will assume the roles of the officers their Assessor duties, i.e., observation, documentation and evaluation.

You will be evaluated on the following skills: **Planning and Organizing, Perception and Analysis, Judgment/Decision Making, Adaptability, and Oral Communication**. You were previously provided with the skill dimension list. These skills will be evaluated through the use of an Assessor checklist.

Problem

The Captain calls a meeting with the Lieutenants and Sergeants to discuss how the department will inhibit and reduce racial bias against African Americans, Hispanics and other people of color with particular focus on patrol officers. His comments include:

"You should all know that biases can influence a person's experience of the world, and that experience can also affect our implicit biases."

Then the Captain read a quote from Spencer et al, "We encounter more criminals (or at least know when they do) in the course of doing our jobs than the average person does. If any of our officers, like most people, associate negative concepts, such as crime, with African American people, these biases cause them to more likely perceive an African American civilian as a criminal which is reinforced whenever they encounter African American individuals committing crimes" (Spencer, Charbonneau & Glaser, 2016).

He references a copy of a summary report the Chief obtained from the IACP about implicit bias (known as biased-based policing for police) in policing. The Captain hands out excerpts from the report and directs everyone to read it carefully:

- Discrimination is prevalent across many professions and areas in society, but particularly in police departments (Council of Economic Advisors, 1998; Glaser, 2014).
- Bias and what is referred to as implicit bias have been found to have the strongest influence on judgment and behavior when a situation is ambiguous (i.e., when it is not instantly clear what another person is doing or is going to do).
- Regardless of whether it is conscious or unconscious, prejudice and stereotypes occur when attempting to resolve uncertain situations (Spencer, Charbonneau, & Glaser, 2016). Examples are:
- A study by Eberhardt, Goff, Purdie, and Davies (2004) found that college students and police officers were faster to identify images of weapons as they became de-pixilated (i.e., causing an image to not break up into pixels, as by over-enlarging the image) when they were preceded by subliminal images of Black, rather than White, faces.
- This study is highly relevant to policing because it illustrates the role of disambiguation when applying racial stereotypes.

- Correll, Park, Judd and Wittenbrink (2002) and Correll, Hudson, Guillermo and Ma (2014) conducted research about "The Shooter Task". Their research findings provided further evidence of how racial/ethnic bias can be used to disambiguate policing-relevant situations.
- Participants were presented with images of Black and White men who were holding guns or non-gun objects and were directed to "shoot" armed targets.
- Some of the findings were that participants tended to respond faster and/or more accurately when the target was consistent with prevailing racial stereotypes (i.e., unarmed White and armed Black targets).
- Numerous studies have now indicated that police officers, when tested, exhibit shooter bias (e.g., Correll et al., 2007; Peruche & Plant, 2006; Plant & Peruche, 2005).
- Glaser and Knowles (2008) found that implicit stereotypic associations between Blacks and weapons predicted the strength of the shooter bias.
- Eberhardt, Goff, Purdie, and Davies' (2004) research reinforced implicit bias in police officers and college students. Both groups identified crime-related objects in an easier manner after being presented with (subliminally) African American faces. Some of the findings were:
- They paid more attention to the African American faces after a crime concept was initiated and when crime-related objects were presented to them.
- Both biases tended to be larger particularly when the faces were judged to have been more representative of African Americans as a social group.
- Walsh et al. (1995); and Park & Banaji, (2000) found that when participants were provided a list of names and asked to select the ones they thought were criminals they were far more likely to select the African American sounding name.
- Stereotypes link African Americans with aggressive behavior which caused the individuals to view the African American person as more aggressive compared to a White person (Duncan, 1976; Sagar & Schofield, 1980).
- Other studies have revealed prevalent implicit and explicit stereotypes that African Americans are dangerous, violent, and hostile (Bargh, Chen, & Burrows, 1996; Devine; Devine & Baker, 1991; Devine & Elliot, 1995; Dovidio, Evans & Tyler, 1986; Schaller, Park, & Mueller, 2003). Some of the findings were:
- Considering that the aforementioned characteristics are related to criminal behavior they are also important reasons when deciding whether the per-

son poses a threat to public safety. Subsequently, there are also important factors when deciding whether someone poses a threat to personal safety, which is a serious element of a police officers' decision to use force.

Finally, the Chief noted that the inquiry into 72 of the 330 Philadelphia officers included in the Plain View Project database prioritizes posts "clearly advocating violence or death against any protected class such as ethnicity, national origin, sex, religion and race."

Remember, you have ten minutes to make your presentation.

EXERCISE 15-2
ABC POLICE DEPARTMENT
USE OF NON-LETHAL FORCE TRAINING EXERCISE
SERGEANT

Candidate Instructions

You are to assume the role of newly promoted Sergeant, Jason/Jenny Statham for ABC Police Department which is in a Midwestern state.

Your Lieutenant has asked you to:

1. Make sure all of your officers receive training on the use of non-lethal force amended rule 500.
2. Prepare an outline of what you will cover in the training session.
3. Include how you reinforce the importance of the rule during the training.
4. Include what instructional methods will you use to deliver the training.
5. Include any other information that you feel is important.

The rule starts on the next page.

You will have two hours to prepare an oral presentation which you will deliver to the Lieutenant and some of the officers as a pilot session. He wants to make sure that you have covered what he thinks are the most important sections of the rule. You will have ten minutes to make your presentation and may be asked questions by the Assessors.

You have been provided with a computer, printer, easel paper, pens, sharpie highlighters, and other office supplies. There are also back-up computers available in case your computer malfunctions at which point you are to notify the test proctor in the room who will move you to a different computer. PowerPoint is set up on the computer if you choose to use it. If your computer malfunctions you will be given additional time. The lost time will be added to your time.

Three Assessors holding the rank of Sergeant or while also performing Lieutenant will assume the roles of the officers, i.e., observation, documentation and evaluation.

You will be evaluated on the following skills: **Planning and Organizing, Perception and Analysis, Judgment/Decision Making, and Oral Communication**. You were previously provided with the skill dimension list. These skills will be evaluated through the use of an Assessor checklist.

Remember you have ten minutes to make your presentation.

Rule 500—Use of Non-Lethal Force

June 11, 20XX

Statement on Use of Force:

The ABC Police Department is committed to de-escalating incidents to negate the need for the use of force. When force is necessary the ABC Police Department is committed to using only the amount of force that is reasonably necessary to overcome the resistance offered.

ABC Police Department is equally committed to preventing unnecessary force, ensuring accountability and transparency, and building trust with our community. The ABC Police Department respects the inherent life, liberty, dignity, and worth of all individuals by preserving human life, and minimizing physical harm and the reliance on use of force.

De-escalation: Prior to using physical, non-deadly and/or deadly force, all ABC police officers, when possible and feasible, will use proper de-escalation techniques to decrease the likelihood that officers will need to utilize use of force, and to minimize the level of force required. This includes using effective communication techniques to engage with individuals who are not compliant with orders by establishing rapport, asking questions and providing advice to defuse conflict and achieve voluntary compliance before resorting to force options.

Where feasible, police officers will try to determine whether an individual's failure to comply with an order is the result of one of the following factors:

- Medical conditions
- Mental impairment
- Developmental disability
- Physical limitation
- Language barrier
- Drug interaction
- Behavioral crisis, or
- Other factors beyond the individual's control

When feasible, after evaluating whether the individual's failure to comply with an order is based on one of the factors listed above, the police officer may determine whether physical force, and what level of physical force, is necessary and appropriate to resolve the situation in a safe manner.

When feasible and safe, officers should give verbal warnings when use of force is going to be used. In some cases, there may not be an opportunity to give verbal commands or warnings.

If the situation is not an arrestable offense, the manner cannot be resolved safely, the officer may disengage.

See Special Order 20-2 Street Outreach Unit and Referral Procedures. The Street Outreach Unit is a resource available to support all officers when dealing with individuals suffering from substance use disorder, mental health and/or homelessness.

Due to Intervene. Police officers are reminded of Rule 113 Public Integrity Policy, Sec. 5 Cannon of Ethics, Number Nine.

Two or more officers may effect an arrest, without the use of force which one officer cannot complete without resorting to the use of force.

Neck Restraints: ABC Police Department officers are not permitted to perform chokeholds, strangleholds, carotid artery neck restraints, or any other similar tactic on any individual that restricts oxygen or blood flow to the neck or head, except in the very limited situations when deadly force is necessary to address an imminent threat of serious bodily injury or death.

As a result of the increased potential for injury, officers should refrain from utilizing restraint techniques that include squeezing of trachea, windpipe or throat area to stop a subject from ingesting any controlled substance. This does not preclude an officer from using other reasonable methods to secure evidence that may be destroyed or lost during an encounter. As with all use of force it must be reasonable and suitable to the confrontation.

When the officer believes that an individual has swallowed a controlled substance, the officer shall take the following actions: if the officer has probable cause to arrest the individual, the officer shall make the arrest and detain the individual. If the officer does not have probable cause to arrest the individual, the officer shall ask the individual to remain at the scene. The officer shall notify dispatch of his belief that the individual swallowed a controlled substance and so requests EMS to come to the aid of the individual. The officer shall protect the scene and the individual while awaiting EMS.

All officers are to use the use of force model developed in 1991 by Dr. Franklin Groves, Federal Law Enforcement Training Center and Professor Gregory J. Connor, University of Illinois Police Training Institute. The model is available on-line.

Sec. 3 TRAINING AND QUALIFICATION: Police officers in the Department will be held accountable for proficiency, as well as compliance with Department policy in the use of non-lethal force. Specifically, sworn members shall qualify by successfully completing the course of instruction on non-lethal force approved by the Training and Education Division.

This course will be conducted as part of in-service training and will include a practical application segment and the written test component. Whenever the Department adopts new non-lethal force implements, officers will qualify in their use prior to carrying or using them on duty.

In the event officer fails to complete the required certification, the officer will be temporarily reassigned to the Academy. The Academy will then provide a remedial training program in order to ensure such certification. Officers who still fail to qualify will be subject to evaluation as to their fitness to continue to perform the duties of a police officer.

Sec. 4 INCAPACITATING AGENT: Officers will carry only the type of incapacitating agent issued by the Department.

In electing to use an incapacitating agent against an armed subject, officers should understand that its effects are not uniformly predictable and certain individuals may remain undeterred by its application. Any such use should be accompanied by a realization that officers may need to take further action to ensure their safety. Conversely, all officers should be aware of the potential, however limited, for serious injury arising from the use of an incapacitating agent.

For this reason, officers should generally confine the use of incapacitating agents against armed or unarmed persons to the following situations:

1. In self-defense or to defend another person.
2. When an officer, during an encounter is met with active resistance.
3. Officers should be aware of the increased potential for serious injury to the suspect when incapacitating agents are used under the following circumstances:
   a. When the subject is less than two feet away.

    b. When the subject is an enclosed area without ventilation.

    c. When the subject lacks normal reflexes, such as the ability to blink, or is otherwise incapacitated.

When an incapacitating agent has been applied to a subject; officers should upon securing the suspect, provide for the thorough dousing of the exposed areas with water as soon as is practicable. This should be done as soon as possible since the seriousness of any injury or burn is directly related to the length of time the exposed area remains untreated.

Sec. 5 SERVICE BATON: The Department currently authorizes several baton-type implements for use as non-lethal weapons against assailants. Upon issuance to and qualification by an officer, the only baton type implements authorized for that officer's use shall be their Department issued baton.

The primary purpose of these weapons is to provide officers with an advantage when fending off and subduing an UNARMED assailant. Officers should not rely on these weapons to overcome an ARMED attack, since they are not intended for such use.

All officers should bear in mind the essentially defensive nature of the use of non-lethal force, as outlined above General Consideration, Section 2, when using these weapons. Except in extreme situations, where the officer is in imminent danger of serious injury, no blows should be struck above the thigh, other than to the arms.

Additionally, officers should be aware of the potential for permanent disability arising from a blow to the groin and should limit such blows to extreme situations.

Sec. 6 EVALUATION OF SUSPECT BY EMERGENCY MEDICAL TECHNI-CIANS: The process of booking and jailing a suspect is often time consuming and confusing, allowing for the possibility of overlooking an injury that might have been brought about by police use of force. Indeed, many injuries may not be obvious even to the injured party. Such injuries, if left untreated, could result in serious problems for both the victim and the Department.

Therefore, this Department will have Emergency Medical Technicians examine all suspects who fall under either of these categories:

1. The suspect has an obvious injury, which in the opinion of the Duty Supervisor, requires treatment.
2. The suspect requests medical treatment for any injury, whether obvious or not.
3. The suspect ingests or swallows any controlled substance.

Sec. 7 INVESTIGATION OF USE OF FORCE: This Department will thoroughly investigate every incident in which an officer strikes someone with any object when an incapacitating agent is used on a subject, or when a visible injury occurs with officer(s) on scene.

All such applications of force or visible injury as described above shall be immediately reported verbally to the involved member's patrol supervisor. By the end of the tour of duty, an officer who has used non-lethal force shall make out a written report describing the incident including the names of the officer and other persons concerned, the circumstances under which such force was used, the nature of any injury inflicted and the care given afterwards to the injured party.

Upon receipt of verbal notification, the Patrol Supervisor shall respond to the scene and make an initial assessment of the incident. During this assessment if the officer(s) involved are assigned to and working in a capacity for a Division/Unit out of the chain of command of the Patrol Supervisor, the Patrol Supervisor shall make contact with a supervisor from that Division/Unit if available and request he/she respond to the scene. The investigation of the incident shall then be the responsibility of that Division/Unit supervisor.

Prior to the end of the tour of duty the Patrol/Unit Supervisor shall conduct a complete investigation of the use of such non-lethal force and submit a report to the Commanding Officer of the District or Unit where the officer(s) is assigned. Such report shall include the Supervisor's findings and recommendations based upon the assessment of facts known, as to the justification for the use of force. A complete Supervisor's investigation shall consist of the following, where applicable:

Supervisor's investigative report:

1. A copy of the incident report ABC Police Department form 1.1;
2. Reports from the officer(s) alleged to have utilized non-lethal force;
3. Reports from all Department personnel that were present;
4. Reports on all interviews of civilian witnesses to the incident;

5. Use of Force Tracking Form (0027-ABCPD-1106), with above information attached.

At the discretion of the involved member's Commanding Officer, further investigation of the incident may be undertaken. Once all the facts have been compiled and substantiated, the Commanding Officer shall submit a report of the incident through the channels to the Police Commissioner within seven (7) days.

Once the Police Chief indicates that the report and associated investigation is satisfactory, copies of every such report shall be forward to the Bureau or Professional Standards, the Human Resources Division and the Training and Education Division.

The Bureau of Professional Standards shall maintain a comprehensive file of all use of force reports. Further, the Bureau of Professional Standards, acting on its own authority may, or at the request of the Police Commissioner shall, investigate all incidents involving the use of non-lethal force that, based on the information at hand, indicate non-compliance with Department policy.

The Bureau of Professional Standards shall forward the results of all investigations undertaken to the Police Chief, who may accept it and act upon its recommendations, in total or in part, or return the report with a request for further information or clarification. In every case, the authority and responsibility for final departmental disposition of a Use of Non-Lethal force incident rests solely with the Police Commissioner.

Note: Rule 304, issued by Special Order 94-37 on October 11, 20XX, was amended by the issuance of Special Order 95-16, which made clear what constitutes a proper Patrol Supervisor's report (see section 7, para 3).

EXERCISE 15-3
ABC POLICE DEPARTMENT BODY CAMERAS PROBLEM ANALYSIS
ORAL PRESENTATION AND WRITTEN EXERCISE LIEUTENANT

Candidate Instructions

Your Captain has asked you to come up with a plan for dealing with the use of body cameras. Assume that you will be making your presentation to your boss, the Police Chief, all command staff, elected officials, members of the media, and concerned citizens.

You are also to prepare an outline for your presentation which will be evaluated (i.e. written communication) separate from your presentation. You must include and properly cite all of your references.

You will be evaluated on your **Planning and Organizing, Perception and Analysis, Interpersonal, Oral Communication and Written Communication Skills**.

Easel paper, colored marker pens, sticky notes and other materials are available to use in preparing your presentation. You will have fifteen (15) minutes to make your presentation.

The parameters for your outline are:

1. Use Word or WordPerfect.
2. Put your name and candidate number in the upper right had corner of the first page.
3. Include a cover page (which cannot be one of the 6 pages).
4. Use roman numerals.
5. Use Times New Roman 12 pitch font.
6. Use 1 inch top and bottom margins; 5 inch left and right margins.
7. Include page numbering.
8. Write no more than 4 double spaced pages.
9. Grammar and spelling with be checked.
10. All reference sources must be cited using the APA standard.
11. You **must** sign the last page of the report in acknowledgement that you wrote using your own words and did not plagiarize any part of the document.

Problem

You are the newly promoted police Lieutenant for ABC Police department, which has recently been awarded a grant for the purchase of body cameras. The police department has one-hundred and forty-three (143) employees which includes eighteen (18) civilians. Ninety-five (95) officers work in traffic patrol. Every officer will be equipped with the cameras.

There are numerous pros and cons regarding body cameras, many which have already been reported via many media sources. How your police department is going to measure the successfulness of using cameras has yet to be determined and will be an aspect of your presentation.

You will have 2.5 hours to conduct internet and/or library research on body cameras and prepare a fifteen minute presentation. Based on your research it is expected that at minimum, the following issues will be addressed:

- Pros and cons
- Storage and retrieval
- State of usage in U.S.A.
- Measurement criteria
- Evaluation criteria
- Training

EXERCISE 15-4
ABC POLICE DEPARTMENT PRESIDENT'S TASK FORCE
ON 21ST CENTURY POLICING PROBLEM SOLVING WRITTEN
AND ORAL PRESENTATION CAPTAIN OR DEPUTY CHIEF

Candidate Instructions

You are to assume the role of promoted Deputy Chief, Tommy/Tammie Jones for ABC Police Department which is in a southeastern state. Assume that you were promoted from inside the agency after a rigorous assessment center process and have only been at work for two weeks. Therefore, you have not had sufficient time to get to know everyone under your command. However, as an internal candidate you, in the past, have some contact with most of your staff.

You will have 2.5 hours to prepare a written and oral presentation which you will deliver to the Chief, Mayor, City Manager and council members. You will have fifteen minutes to make your presentation. Use your own knowledge and experience to prepare your presentation. Also, you may be asked questions by the panel members.

You have been provided with a computer, printer, easel paper, pens, sharpie highlighters and other office supplies. There are also back-up computers available in case your computer malfunctions at which point you are to notify the test proctor in the room who will move you to a different computer. PowerPoint is set up on the computer if you choose to use it. If your computer malfunctions you will be given additional time. The lost time will be added to your time.

Three Assessors holding the rank of Chief or Assistant/Deputy Chief will assume the roles of the aforementioned personnel while also performing their Assessor duties: i.e., observation, documentation and evaluation.

You will be evaluated on the following skills: **Planning and Organizing; Judgment/Decision Making; Adaptability; Oral Communication and Written Communication**. You were previously provided with the skill dimension list. These skills will be evaluated through the use of an Assessor checklist.

To reiterate, you will have fifteen minutes to make your presentation. During your presentation, you may refer to your written material, but the assessors will not use your notes to evaluate your performance.

The parameters for your written plan are:

1. Use Word or WordPerfect.
2. Put your name and candidate number in the upper right had corner of the first page.

3. Include a cover page (which cannot be one of the 6 pages).
4. Adhere to standard report writing protocols (e.g., introduction, body, conclusion).
5. Use Times New Roman 12 pitch font.
6. Use 1 inch top and bottom margins; 5-inch left and right margins.
7. Include page numbering.
8. Use headings where applicable.
9. Tables may be used but must be properly labeled.
10. An outline and some bullet points are allowed.
11. Write no more than 6 double spaced pages.
12. Grammar and spelling with be checked.
13. All reference sources must be cited using the APA standard.
14. You **must** sign the last page of the report in acknowledgement that you wrote using your own words and did not plagiarize any part of the document.

Problem

Since the Final Report on the President's Task Force on 21st Century Policing was published in 2015, agencies have considered where they should begin to implement the recommendations as well as determine the prioritization of the recommendations and if more research is needed in order to apply the recommendations to their agencies (theiacp.org).

As a result of the killing of George Floyd and the Black Lives Matter movement, it is anticipated that the recommendations will take front and center stage in many police departments.

The Police Chief has assigned you the task of preparing and action plan for implementing a few of the pillars, as soon as possible.

Pillar 1: Building Trust and Legitimacy
Key themes of the pillar's recommendations include:

- o Agencies should do the following to build trust and legitimacy:
  - track the community's level of trust by administering annual community surveys
  - strive to have as diverse a workforce with respect to race, gender, religion and sexual orientation as possible
  - work to build trust in immigrant communities and separate immigration enforcement from local policing (theiacp.org)
  - focus on several ways to build trust to include the emphasis on non-enforcement community activities

Pillar 2: Community Policing & Crime Reduction
Key themes of the pillar's recommendations include:

- o Agencies should do the following engage in community policing and crime reduction which includes:
  - cascade community policing throughout the culture and organizational structure
  - evaluate officers on their efforts to engage members of the community
  - encourage communities to evaluate the efficacy of team-oriented crisis intervention
  - work and collaborate with community residents to identify problems and meaningful results for the community

EXERCISE 15-5
ABC POLICE DEPARTMENT
CULTURE CHANGE
WRITTEN AND ORAL PRESENTATION EXERCISE
DEPUTY CHIEF OR CHIEF

Candidate Instructions

You are to assume the role of newly hired Police Chief, Shawn/Sean Bean for ABC Police Department which is in a southeastern state. Assume that you were hired from outside the agency and have only been at work for thirty days. Therefore, you have not had sufficient time to get to know everyone under your command.

You will have 2.5 hours to prepare a written and oral presentation which you will deliver to the Mayor, City Manager and council members. You will have fifteen minutes to make your presentation. Use your own knowledge and experience to prepare your presentation. Also, you may be asked questions by the panel members.

You have been provided with a computer, printer, easel paper, pens, sharpie highlighters, and other office supplies. There are also back-up computers available in case your computer malfunctions at which point you are to notify the test proctor in the room who will move you to a different computer. Power point is set up on the computer if you choose to use it. If your computer malfunctions you will be given additional time. The lost time will be added to your time.

Three Assessors holding the rank of Chief or Assistant/Deputy Chief will assume the roles of the aforementioned personnel while they will also be performing their Assessor duties; i.e., observation, documentation and evaluation.

You will be evaluated on the following skills: **Planning and Organizing, Judgment/Decision Making, Adaptability, Oral Communication and Written Communication**. You were previously provided with the skill dimension list. These skills will be evaluated through the use of an Assessor checklist.

To reiterate, you will have fifteen minutes to make your presentation. During your presentation, you may refer to your written material but the assessors will not use your notes to evaluate your performance.

The parameters for your written plan are:

1. Use Word or WordPerfect.
2. Put your name and candidate number in the upper right had corner of the first page.
3. Include a cover page (which cannot be one of the 6 pages).

4. Adhere to standard report writing protocols (e.g., introduction, body, conclusion).
5. Use Times New Roman 12 pitch font.
6. Use 1 inch top and bottom margins; 5-inch left and right margins.
7. Include page numbering.
8. Use headings where applicable.
9. Tables may be used but must be properly labeled.
10. An outline and some bullet points are allowed.
11. Write no more than 6 double spaced pages.
12. Grammar and spelling will be checked.
13. All reference sources must be cited using the APA standard.
14. You **must** sign the last page of the report in acknowledgement that you wrote using your own words and did not plagiarize any part of the document.

Problem

The culture within the police department is very strong and despite turnover in the position every 3-5 years, none of the previous chiefs were successful in changing the culture. Given the recent death of George Floyd and other use of force deaths caused by police officers, the Mayor, city council members, community watch groups, leaders of the clergy and citizens living in the lower economic sections of the city, are demanding that radical change takes place ASAP.

All personnel were recently made aware of some facts published and/or stated by members of the national media to include: 72 police officers were removed from working the streets of Philadelphia because the city found their racist and offensive social media posts; the Plain View project uncovered social media posts from police departments in eight jurisdictions across the U.S. and thousands of racist and offensive social media posts were found.

An article by Armacost (2016), entitled, "The Organizational Reasons Police Departments Don't Change," was disseminated to everyone immediately prior to your arrival. After reading it you were left with little confidence that the culture of your department could easily change. It was disconcerting.

A paragraph, which started with one of the reasons culture is hard to change, "Departments blame 'rogue cops'", reinforced what you already know. Armacost's other statements, "Often, you will hear police chiefs or other spokespeople referring to a small number of 'rogue cops' in cases of brutality. In reality, these claims are nearly always false. While claims of police abuse do tend to cluster around a relatively small group of police officers, those officers *tend to repeat their abusive behavior with impunity*. Repeated brutality that is not addressed by higher-ups is a systemic problem, not a problem of rogue individuals. It means that the organizational message being conveyed, whether or not explicit, is that some level of abusive behavior is okay" (Armacost, 2016, p. 1).

However, Armacost (2016) did provide some hopeful information about departments that have made progress: Dallas and Baltimore. You only know this much about the culture of your department as follows:

- Top management staff are currently dealing with lawsuits regarding officer misconduct, misuse of force and bias against people of color.
- Two sergeants and two recently hired officers resigned stating they could not deal with the conflict and pressure coming from all directions.
- One officer who served more than fifteen (15) years was recently terminated for posting derogatory racial comments on his Facebook page (i.e., It is a good day for a chokehold; I should have pulled the trigger on the n....r).

The staffing complement in your department is:

a. Chief
b. Deputy Chief (vacant)
c. Three (3) Captains (one vacancy)
d. Eight (8) Lieutenants
e. Twelve (10) Sergeants
f. Eighty-one (81) officers including Patrol Officers and Detectives. There are six (6) vacancies and the department has had difficulty filing the positions.
g. Two (2) Animal Control Officers
h. Nine (9) Dispatchers
i. Five (5) records staff
j. Executive Secretary

The city population is approaching 100,000—55% of the residents are Caucasian, 20% are Hispanic, 17% are African American and 8% are Asian and other. A majority of the Caucasian communities are upper middle class and above. A significant part of the Hispanic and African American communities is middle to lower middle class. Unemployment is the highest in the Hispanic and African American communities and 20% of the citizens receive some governmental support.

The Mayor, City Manager and council members have directed you to:

1. Prepare a plan for changing the culture of the police department.
2. Elaborate on how you will ensure that the changes cascade throughout the organization.
3. Include how you plan to resolve the turnover and recruitment problems.
4. Indicate how you will deal with the concerned and angry citizens.

Chapter 16

SO, DO YOU THINK YOU STILL NEED ONE-ON-ONE COACHING?

OVERVIEW

The following text is my summary of advice to you about one-on-one coaching, so read the contents as if you were listening to me giving you advice. However, this chapter does not include any practice tests but does include a few samples.

When some people open a new book to read, they read the first few and the last few pages, to see if they want to read the entire book. I hope you are not one of these people. If you aren't, by now you may have practiced some or all of the exercises. You may have some of the thoughts or feelings below. Are you:

- Overwhelmed because of the detailed Assessor Guides?
- Exhausted?
- Surprised?
- Worried?
- Anxious?
- Wishing someone had been there to take notes when you made a presentation?
- Wondering what it would have been like had a real role-player been used?
- Wishing you had a video of your presentation?
- More than ready for your AC process?
- Not quite ready?
- Not at all ready, but have an idea of what to expect?
- In need of skill improvement?

- Aware of your strengths but also aware of many weaknesses?
- Unable to score your in-basket items despite the Assessor Guide?
- Impressed with the exercises?
- Hoping for more practice and more exercises?
- Thinking about face-to-face coaching?

Despite these feelings, you may not feel you need to purchase a coaching package, attend a seminar where you learn more about the AC method or receive coaching from your supervisor, friend or mentor. Your reasons may include:

- Oh, the cost is prohibitive.
- I feel I know enough about what to expect now.
- My spouse will not approve the expenditure.
- I have already paid for group coaching.
- My boss who just retired is coaching a bunch of us and he has extensive experience as an assessor and a wealth of knowledge.

Overall, you will decide how important your long-term career development is. Let's now discuss your long-term career goals.

YOUR CAREER GOALS

Every police officer may have a somewhat different career, and we may be at a different stage in our life cycle. Some officers know they want to move up the hierarchy. You should ask yourself some of these questions: How badly do I want to be promoted? What does the investment of more of my valuable time and money mean to me and my family over the long run? Do I want to take the next step? Will my spouse support the expense for this process?

If this book aided you in developing the innate abilities you already have, then I have made a positive contribution to your life. On the other hand, if you feel the book is not enough, then you might consider purchasing one of my firm's coaching packages or attending a workshop on the AC method, etc. Finally, you should consider some of the characteristics covered in the next section.

PAST CLIENT CHARACTERISTICS

Based on my experience coaching men and women all over the United States, there are several characteristics that set them apart from the many people I have spoken with over the phone who decided not to be coached. Those officers who chose to purchase an individualized coaching package were:

- Not cost conscious
- Proactive
- People who have a career plan
- Time conscious
- Genuinely interested in learning
- Serious about the process
- Serious about being promoted
- Not worried about their friends' opinions
- Willing to commit the time
- Willing to be coached in the evening or on a weekend
- Insightful
- Able to take criticism

Many of my clients have documented that even after undertaking many different practice exercises and reading extensively, the extra dimension that contributed to their being promoted was the individualized coaching they received directly from me and my associates. Their letters of thanks often attributed their success, in a large part to our coaching style and personalities. We do not water down our feedback because we know that feedback is essential to the learning experience. We have never guaranteed any client will be promoted as a result of our coaching because in the end, the evaluation performance is ultimately up to the client. Also, each candidate must already possess many of the innate abilities that are covered during coaching, although we work together, to enhance these abilities.

The next section deals with some of the research on coaching.

WHAT SOME OF THE RESEARCH SAYS ABOUT COACHING

Lievens (2002) conducted research regarding the use of what he referred to as slogans in the assessment center process. One of the slogans in his review of the literature was that coaching did not have any effect on a person's performance in an assessment center. I included his research in this book for several reasons; (1) there are many people around the country who provide either group or individual coaching; (2) some of my past clients have participated in group coaching that fell short, such as learning nothing about their strengths and weaknesses; and (3) to provide you with some evidence that coaching can help you.

Lievens looked for studies about three commonly used exercises; the in-basket, role-playing, and group discussion. He reviewed Brannick et al. (1989), Brostoff and Meyer (1984) and Gill's (1982) research. Their research determined that students were able to improve their performance on particular aspects of the in-basket exercises. However, the improvement occurred after studying workbooks which were designed to help them (Brannick et al., 1989; Brostoff & Meyer, 1984; Gill, 1982). The workbooks also taught them about planning and organizing, how to make the best use of their time, and when they should delegate specific tasks or IB items. Even though the latter studies may be dated, the findings are extremely relevant to the coaching my firm provides. Based on the large number of police personnel who have completed an IB exercise, some of their scores increased when they completed another exercise which measured the same skill and they were promoted. A number of my past clients have also told me that had they not completed the exercises and received the face-to-face coaching and in-depth feedback, they might not have been promoted.

Moses and Ritchie (1976) published a study about the effects of what was called "supervisory relationship training" on performance in role-playing exercises. Lievens (2002) also reviewed their study. They found that first level supervisors who modeled the behaviors they learned in the training, which was about how to deal with problem subordinates, were much more effective in dealing with problem employees compared to untrained supervisors.

Overall, based on some of the research training does help elevate scores. I included the Moses and Ritchie study because of my hands-on knowledge, from having trained several hundred people to be assessors. In each training session role-playing exercises were used and in leadership development workshops I have conducted I found that participating in the role-playing exercises either as the supervisor or the subordinate developed the participant's skill levels.

Several studies have also been conducted on LGD exercises. The studies date back to 1974 starting with Petty's research that year. Based on my knowledge and experience, it is plausible that providing a briefing will help improve participant's performance, which his study substantiated. Even though his research sample included students, his findings are important (Lievens, 2002). Lievens was able to review an unpublished study by Bracken (1989) who found that participating in training on the LGD improved both knowledge and performance compared to just discussion participation or no training at all. One of the most interesting studies, completed by Kurecka et al. (1982), found that the group that not only participated in an LGD exercise and a second exercise, but received feedback on their behaviors and subsequent performance on a second group exercise, did better than a control group (the group that did not participate in a practice exercise), and a group that received bad advice on how to behave in a group exercise. Again, even though Kurecka's study is a bit dated, it is still relevant. A few years ago, during one AC process my firm had designed and was administering, a candidate was faking his behavior in the LGD exercise. He had apparently been told how to behave in a LGD exercise—he told the other participants what to do, etc.

I was sitting in the room as a monitor in the back corner and was not surprised by this behavior because of his inappropriate behavior when I was reading the instructions to him during another exercise. He eyed me up and down, and interrupted me a few times during my reading and started to ask questions. I continued to read to him and ignored this behavior and then told him that candidates should not interrupt the test administrator. In the end, he was not ranked among the top candidates.

Overall, there is limited research which substantiates the trainability of performance in an AC. Nonetheless, the research that has been published and my clients' experiences provide support for Lievens' (2002) paper on AC slogans. His statement about the research is eloquent,

> In sum, research on the trainability of AC performance does not lend support for the slogan that it is difficult to prepare oneself for an AC.
>
> Assessee coaching appears to significantly improve performance in in-baskets, role-plays, and group discussions. However, due to the limited number of studies, no definite conclusions can be drawn. Note also that only a snapshot of possible coaching tactics has been studied and the effects of assessee coaching on subsequent job performance are unknown. (p. 95).

Moreover, research has been conducted since 2002. A study by Lievens et al. (2012) of a high-stakes educational testing program that had been ongoing for ten years in Belgium. They noted that their study provided two key contributions to the literature on the effect of coaching on candidates before they take tests, and that even though the study was done in Belgium in an educational setting, it is relevant to a high-stakes, large-scale public sector selection process in the military and police fields. They determined that in a formal coaching program candidates had an augmentable effect over and above someone preparing on their own (Lievens, Buyse, Sackett & Connelly, 2012). Based on my experience I know that people can improve their skills with coaching. In fact, I designed an SJT assessment process for a candidate whose performance improved such that his overall score moved him up on a federal register. As a result, he was able to participate in the assessment process processes for vacancies throughout the U.S.

The coaching my firm provides is very experiential because the clients actually complete AC exercises and receive both written and verbal feedback via Zoom (or over the telephone, if for some reason the client is unable to install or use Zoom).

That is what this book is all about. It is very hands-on and experiential. You are provided with many different exercises that have been used to coach our clients, and the exercises have been used in past processes that my firm has either developed or customized. The customized exercises are prepared after we conduct our first telephone assessment process with clients and learn about their backgrounds and the law enforcement agency where they are competing for a promotion, and the type of tests which will be given in their AC—and the name of the company that is designing and administering it.

Our associates have extensive knowledge or do research into the philosophy of most of the companies who specialize in the AC process. We also do an Internet search about the community (size, demographics, etc.) so that our exercises are relevant to the position for which the candidate is testing. This knowledge is essential in creating the customized exercises utilizing items from our testing bank. However, there is an additional charge for customizing a new exercise for a client.

In conclusion, if you decide to purchase a coaching package, attend a group coaching session, receive mentoring and coaching from your current supervisor or read all of the books published on the assessment center process for law enforcement, you will be a few steps ahead of your competition. However, given what I know about my competition, your best choice for coaching is L.J. Craig & Associates, Inc. You can reach us at www.ljcraig.com. Our number is (561) 750-8669.

Chapter 17

SAMPLE CANDIDATE FEEDBACK REPORTS

OVERVIEW

When I was initially trained as an assessor, I learned how to write comprehensive candidate feedback reports, which is one of the most difficult assessor roles. There is no requirement that candidates be provided with a feedback report, but experts in the field believe they are essential. However, writing such a report requires a huge commitment of time and energy, especially when most assessors are not paid for their service. For all of the AC processes I have been involved with since 1984, the assessors did not write the reports, the staff of the consulting firm did. The reasons for that include:

- The cost for each report increases the cost of the contract.
- If large numbers of candidates are competing in the process, more assessors are needed which raises the overall cost of the contract.
- Agencies do not want to commit more than 1–2 days for the AC process.
- There is no need for a feedback report if the AC process particularly is not being used for developmental purposes.
- The staff working in the police department's HR section or the city's Human Resources department do not know enough about the AC process to write a comprehensive feedback report.

In general, the agencies who were willing to pay for feedback reports want the reports to be as complete as possible and for the least amount of money. One past client did not have the reports in the bid specifications and when my firm was selected, the HR director said they wanted these reports and expected my firm to write them—for free. Since we believed that, in this case, the reports were appropriate and necessary, we negotiated a modest fee for 2–3 single-spaced typed pages for each candidate. I have included a few sample reports for developmental purposes. I believe that if you read the reports, you will have a better understanding of how scores are determined.

THERE IS NO STANDARD REPORT FORMAT

There is no generally accepted standard for writing a candidate report. When I first learned how to write them, I remember that many assessors were exhausted after writing detailed reports. I was later hired by the same vendor that designed the large-scale AC processes for the Miami-Dade Police Department. I remember writing reports for one of their corporate clients until well after midnight. Each Assessor wrote six reports. We were trained to cross every *t* and dot every *i.* Because of the comprehensiveness of each report, the candidates received developmental feedback even if they were not promoted.

A few reports have been provided for your review from a past AC process my firm completed. The police department name, original candidate numbers or social security numbers have been omitted.

The following report numbers 5 and 18 are from a sergeant AC process.

CANDIDATE 5

This report summarizes the performance of Candidate No. 5, sergeant AC. Four exercises are discussed in this report. Candidate 5's strongest skill is relationships with others/human relations. His performance in each exercise is summarized separately. Brief summary comments are provided regarding his performance with respect to each skill dimension across exercises. Not every example listed in the Assessor Guide or every note taken is referenced due to the large volume of material collected.

CITIZEN COMPLAINT

Candidate 5's overall performance was more than adequate or acceptable. He received the following consensus ratings from three assessors in each skill dimension:

3,3,2 in **Judgment/Decision-Making**
5,4,4 in **Relationships with Others/Human Relations**
4,4,4 in **Planning and Organizing**
5,5,5 in **Interpersonal Communication (Verbal Aptitude)**

SUMMARY COMMENTS

Judgment/Decision-Making

Candidate 5 apologized to the role player that no one returned his call (i.e., "Sorry for the inconvenience."), listened attentively while he vented, tried to calm him down (i.e., "Let's talk about it. I'm sure your complaint will be addressed."), and told him that he would handle the situation. He did not ask the role player to see a copy of the ticket, explain the charges to him, explain the process of officers giving out tickets or assure him that the police department does not single out people due to race, sex, or ethnicity and does not discriminate against any group.

Relationships with Others/Human Relations

Candidate 5 asked the role player to have a seat, thanked him for coming to the department to discuss his concerns (i.e., "Thank you for coming in here; sorry it was for a complaint."), listened attentively to his complaint before responding, and apologized for the inconvenience of having to call and then come in. He also maintained a cooperative and courteous demeanor and tactfully handled the situation (i.e., "How can we help you?").

Planning and Organizing

Candidate 5 told the role player he would talk to the officer as soon as possible regarding the circumstance of giving the ticket (i.e., "Meet with officer, find out what happened."), indicated that he would get back in touch with him ASAP (i.e., "Contact you, tell you about meeting with officer."), did not fidget or shuffle papers during the meeting, and demonstrated an appropriate level of assertiveness without being aggressive. He did not take a few minutes to review the man's traffic ticket, indicate that he would like to handle the most important complaint first, or tell him that he had only a few minutes to meet (because of having to attend another meeting) and, therefore, wanted to address all of his concerns.

Interpersonal Communication (Verbal Aptitude)

Candidate 5 maintained eye contact with the role player; spoke in an audible tone with poise and confidence; listened attentively, and used voice inflection when appropriate. He did not explain the process of giving tickets to citizens in a confident, specific and clear manner, or convey to the role player, in an efficient and effective manner that the department does not single out or discriminate against minority groups.

SUBORDINATE COUNSELING

Overall, Candidate 5's performance was more than adequate or acceptable. He received the following consensus scores from three assessors in each skill dimension.

4,5,4 in **Judgment/Decision-Making**
4,4,4 in **Relationships with Others/Human Relations**
4,4,5 in **Planning and Organizing**
4,4,4 in **Leadership (Leading/Staffing)**
5,5,5 in **Interpersonal Communication (Verbal Aptitude)**

SUMMARY COMMENTS

Judgment/Decision-Making

Candidate 5 told the role player the purpose of the meeting (i.e. "We will get over this hump, action plan, resolution, we do not turn our backs, professional behavior."), reviewed his current problems and acknowledged concern for his recent problems (i.e., "Happy he's getting out of hospital"; "If I can't help, we'll find someone."); told him that the allegations would be investigated, and advised him of the seriousness of the offense if substantiated and why. He did not ask him for his side of the story, explain that retaliation against his accuser was illegal and in violation of current policy and federal law or redirect the conversation at hand when the role player acted like he had done nothing wrong and blamed the female officer.

Relationships with Others/Human Relations

Candidate 5 advised the role player of the importance of meeting with him to discuss a few issues, established rapport with him by explaining that he was new to the position and had reviewed his personnel file etc. (i.e., "How are you doing, new, commendations, incredible performance, we do not turn our back."). He also listened attentively to the role player's explanation of the alleged sexual harassment before responding. He also offered him financial assistance (i.e., "Financial help from the city."). He did not assure him that the department would investigate the complaint thoroughly or apologize that a meeting about a serious matter had to be their first encounter.

Planning and Organizing

Candidate 5 took a few seconds to explain to the role player about the complaint and why he was asked to come to the meeting, (i.e., "I will meet with citizen about complaint, game plan, objective, help you deal with it."), reviewed items in his personnel file (i.e., candidate instructions), did not fidget and shuffle papers during the meeting and did not allow the role player to dominate the meeting. He also set a date and time for a follow-up meeting (i.e., "thirty-day performance plan, action plan"). He did not explain to the role player the type of behavior that was expected of him based on internal G.O.s and other city policies and procedures or explain the procedures of investigating sexual harassment complaints.

Leadership (Leading/Staffing)

Candidate 5 asked the role player if he knew that a female officer had filed a sexual harassment complaint against him (i.e., the role player is playing the role of the employee), told him directly about the purpose of the meeting, and acknowledged to him that he was aware of his personal problems and would provide whatever support and assistance he could (i.e., Have you tried to get to EAP for assistance?" "Confidential, explain your issues to them; we will try to *nullify* the other citizen complaint."). He also told him the importance of all staff following policies and procedures (i.e., "Will adhere to policies.") and that he would be monitoring his behavior. He did not explain to him the reasons for possible disciplinary action, or direct him to read all GOs and Personnel Policies and Procedures pertinent to sexual harassment.

Interpersonal Communication (Verbal Aptitude)

Candidate 5 spoke in an audible tone and with poise and confidence. He listened attentively when the role player was speaking, smiled when appropriate and took notes during the meeting. He did not explain the process of investigating sexual harassment complaints in a non-threatening and assured manner and did maintain regular eye contact with the role player.

COMPETENCY-BASED STRUCTURED
SITUATIONAL INTERVIEW

Candidate 5's performance in this component of the AC was evaluated across all written scenarios and skill dimensions. Therefore, comments are provided only on some actions that he did not say he would take to handle each situation. Candidate 5's performance was consistent across all skill dimensions with the exception of Interpersonal Communications. The questions are included so you do not have to try to recall the question when reviewing the report. He received the following consensus scores from three assessors:

2,2,2 in **Judgment/Decision-Making**
3,3,3 in **Relationships with Others/Human Relations**
3,3,2 in **Planning and Organizing**
3,3,3 in **Leadership (Leading/Staffing)**
5,5,5 in **Interpersonal Communications (Verbal Aptitude)**

Trucker's Strike: Your officers have received information that as many 300 trucks are going to picket a rock pit. If the truckers strike, their actions could shut the whole city down. One of your officers is already assigned to the location. Your officer calls you and says that five people responded to the scene. He also tells you that five men are jumping on the trucks of the independent truckers. The situation is getting heated up; i.e, a lot of shouting and threats. There are more trucks coming up from the county and they may end up tying up traffic for hours. The majority of truckers are Spanish speaking. What do you do? Candidate 5 did not indicate that he would pool employees from different divisions in the city, deploy officers on motorcycles, hold personnel on overtime for as long as necessary, call in shifts early, prepare an After-Action Report or provide relief staff as necessary. He also did not make plans for vehicles exiting the interstate.

Community Policing: A recently built elementary school in town was not designed properly around housing elements for proper egress and ingress of vehicles. As a result of this, the department and your officers get constant complaints about traffic flow, speeders and others coming down the sides of the roadway and speeding. Recently, the situation has gotten out of hand in your zone. Describe the actions you would take to address this situation.

Candidate 5 did not indicate that he would change the way people pick up their children, set up ongoing running of radar, increase the number of crossing guards at active intersections or ensure that speeders are ticketed. He also did not note that he would keep his boss informed or provide moral support to officers in the zone.

Man with Gun in Apartment Having Psychotic Episodes: You are a sergeant working the midnight shift. You are in the office completing your paperwork. You hear on the radio that a man who lives at a five-story apartment complex is threatening to kill anyone who comes near him. He says he is talking to the devil. He appears to have a gun in his hand. A neighbor called the police. He is breaking glass and throwing it out his apartment window. Your current staffing is 8 officers. How do you handle this situation?

Candidate 5 did not indicate that he would evacuate apartments on both sides and above and below the perpetrator's; set up officers with rifles in case the man tries to leave the apartment; or call in the next shift early to assist or call in additional personnel. He also did not note that he would have a debriefing with the officers after the scene is cleared or inner and outer perimeters are set up.

Disruptive Employee: You have an officer who is allegedly spreading rumors about another employee. When you previously spoke to him about this he denied it and said everyone was out to get them. Now a few officers come to your office and tell you that he is bringing down the morale of the unit and nothing is being done about it. They leave your office angry. How will you handle this situation?

Candidate 5 did not indicate that he would explain the situation to the employee, tell him that there is to be no retaliation against officers who brought this to his attention, attempt to get him to admit to spreading rumors or tell him that his behavior it is bringing morale down and how this affects the entire unit.

Officer-Involved Shooting: You hear over the radio that one of your officers has been involved in a shooting. You arrive on the scene and crowds are forming at the shopping center. Meanwhile a robbery is taking place nearby at a check cashing store. Describe how you will handle these situations.

Candidate 5 did not indicate that he would make sure other officers are handling the rest of the scene, call for additional backup, monitor other emergency situations in the city, obtain a briefing from the shooter as to what occurred or call in additional personnel as needed. He also did not note that he would get medical assistance for all persons if they needed it, or make assignments as to who is going to write a report.

IN-BASKET

Overall, Candidate 5's performance was adequate or acceptable in all dimensions except Leadership. In Written Communication, his performance was strong. He received the following consensus scores from three Assessors:

   3,3,3 in **Judgment/Decision-Making**
   3,3,2 in **Relationships with Others/Human Relations**
   3,3,3 in **Planning and Organizing**
   2,3,2 in **Leadership (Leading/Staffing)**
   5,5,4 in **Written Communication (Language Ability)**

SUMMARY COMMENTS

Due to the number of items and issues addressed in the In-Basket exercise, it is not feasible in this report to note each action Candidate

5 did or did not do. Therefore, brief summary comments are made regarding each skill dimension across the entire In-Basket.

Judgment/Decision-Making

Candidate 5 only exercised judgment and made decisions in less than half of the seventy-three judgment/decision-making items in the In-Basket. He did not note to counsel the officer who received the citizen complaint for rudeness or make plans to meet with the citizen. He did not make a note to call Mr. Olson regarding his overgrown grass. or call Eileen Medeiros to find out what kind of statistics she wanted.

Relationships with Others/Human Relations

Candidate 5 did not note to offer assistance to officers Bender and Douglas regarding their recent problems, or prepare a letter for the chief's signature from the citizen who wrote a commendation letter about an employee. But he thoroughly handled all of the issues pertinent to the three telephone calls.

Planning and Organizing

Candidate 5 completed less than half of the sixty planning and organizing items. Although he addressed some of the items, he did not complete all of the expected planning and organizing actions for each item. He did not make plans to meet with his boss regarding the officer who received a citizen complaint of rudeness, note to offer assistance, thoroughly handle the Injury Accident Report for the officer, or mark the calendar to meet with the employee who had a death in his family.

Leadership

Candidate 5 did not take all the expected leadership actions in the In-Basket. He did not note that Bender and Douglas needed assistance or that Douglas should be referred to EAP due to potential psychological problems. He also did not deal with the employee's vacation request which would cause a staff shortage. He also did not demonstrate any leadership with respect to required performance evaluations or obtain information from their personnel files.

Written Communication

Candidate 5 utilized notes or memos to convey information to people, with appropriate grammar, punctuation and word usage.

CANDIDATE 18

This report summarizes the performance of Candidate No. 18, sergeant AC. Four exercises are discussed in this report. Candidate 18's strongest skill was Written Communication. His performance in each exercise is summarized separately. Brief summary comments are provided regarding his performance with respect to each skill across exercises. Not every example listed in the Assessor Guide or every note taken is referenced due to the large volume of material collected.

CITIZEN COMPLAINT

Overall, Candidate 18's performance was adequate or acceptable. He received the following consensus ratings from three assessors in each skill:

3,3,3 in **Judgment/Decision-Making**
3,3,3 in **Relationships with Others/Human Relations**
3,3,3 in **Planning and Organizing**
4,4,4 in **Interpersonal Communication**

SUMMARY COMMENTS

Judgment/Decision-Making

Candidate 18 asked the role player to see a copy of the traffic ticket ("Have citizen meet with for running a red light."), apologized that no one returned his call, explained the process of going to traffic court, and listened attentively while he vented ("If you feel that it's a racial issue get with a command staff."). He also maintained his composure and self-control throughout the exercise when the role player was raising his voice, acting hostile and agitated. He did not tell him calls are always returned, and he would find out why the call was not returned, explain the process of officers giving out tickets, and assure him that the police department does not single out people due to race, sex or ethnicity, or discriminate against any group.

Relationships with Others

Candidate 18 asked the role player to have a seat, thanked him for coming into the department to discuss his concerns, and listened attentively to his complaints before responding. He also continued to calm him down whenever he continued to be hostile, and emphasized the importance of the department's role in the community, ("We only do what we think is right; that's why we need community input."). He did not politely interrupt him when necessary, assure him that the department does not single out minorities for tickets, etc., or inform him politely about the responsibility of the department with respect to issuing tickets.

Planning and Organizing

Candidate 18 took a few minutes to review the role player's traffic ticket, did not fidget and shuffle papers during the meeting, demonstrated an appropriate level of assertiveness without being aggressive ("Is there anything else I can help you with?") and accomplished most of the goals of the meeting: the test administrator did not have to call time. He did not indicate he would like to handle the most important complaint first; the issue of the ticket, then the issue of discrimination, or indicate that he would get back in touch with the role player ASAP.

Interpersonal Communication

Candidate 18 maintained eye contact with the role player and spoke with poise and confidence. He listened attentively, clearly and concisely expressed his ideas to the role player, and took notes during the meeting. He did not smile when appropriate, explain the process of giving tickets to citizens in a confident, specific, and clear manner, or convey to the role player in an effective manner that the department does not single out or discriminate against members of minority groups.

SUBORDINATE COUNSELING

The performance of candidate 18 was inconsistent across all skills His performance overall ranged from adequate and acceptable to weak. He received the following consensus scores from three assessors in each skill:

2,2,1 in **Judgment/Decision-Making**
3,3,2 in **Relationships with Others**
2,1,1 in **Planning and Organizing 1,1,1 in Leadership**
2,2,2 in **Interpersonal Communication**

SUMMARY COMMENTS

Judgment/Decision-Making

Candidate 18 told the role player the purpose of the meeting, blamed his financial problems for his high stress level, as well as his son's recent accident. He stated, "Are there any problem besides that?" "EAP, I would suggest you do it." "It's voluntary and confidential. You can meet with a pastor." He also offered him assistance with his problems, and solicited his input on the issues ("PBA (Time Pool)? "Perhaps a leave of absence?"). Candidate 18 did not tell the role player the purpose of the meeting, ask for his side of the story, advise him of the seriousness of the offense if substantiated, or that possible disciplinary action could be taken against him. He did not explain that retaliation against his accuser was illegal and in violation of current policy and federal law.

Relationships with Others

Candidate 18 asked the role player to have a seat, established rapport with him by telling him that he is new to the position and that he had reviewed his personnel file and noted a commendation in it. He listened patiently to him when he was venting about his personal problems. He also empathized with him about his recent divorce, his child's accident and emotional trauma that results from such events. He also offered to help him find a source of financial assistance. ("Is there anything I could do?"). He did not advise him of the importance of the meeting, try to calm him down when he was venting about his personal problems, assure him that the department would investigate the complaint thoroughly and that he would not be retaliated against.

Planning and Organizing

Candidate 18 did not fidget or shuffle papers during the meeting, reviewed the items in his personnel file, and did not allow the role player to dominate the meeting. Candidate 18 did not explain the procedures of investigating sexual harassment complaints, explain what type of behavior was expected of him, demonstrate an appropriate level of assertiveness without being aggressive, set a date and time for a follow-up meeting or accomplish all the goals of the meeting.

Leadership

Candidate 18 did not demonstrate any leadership in this exercise. He only acknowledged that he was aware of the role player's personal problems and would provide whatever support is necessary ("Is there anything I could do?" "Light duty position." "EAP suggest, can't force you, confidential, pastor."). He did not ask the role player if he knew that a female officer had filed a sexual harassment complaint against him, tell him directly the purpose of the meeting, ask for his side of the story, or tell him that disciplinary action may be taken against him, or the reasons for the possible action. He also did not tell him the importance of following policies and procedures and direct him to read all the department G.O.s and Personnel Policies and Procedures pertinent to sexual harassment.

Interpersonal Communication

Candidate 18 maintained eye contact with the role player, spoke audibly and listened attentively when the role player was speaking. He also nodded when necessary. He did not smile when appropriate, explain the process of investigating sexual harassment complaints in a non-threatening and assured manner, and did not take notes during the meeting. He also did not address all issues and questions in an organized manner or speak in a manner that was understandable.

COMPETENCY-BASED STRUCTURED SITUATIONAL INTERVIEW

The performance of candidate 18 in this component of the AC was evaluated across all written questions and skills. Therefore, comments are provided only on some actions he failed to suggest he would take to handle each situation. The questions are included so you do not have to try to recall the question when reviewing the report. The performance of candidate 18 overall was adequate and acceptable. He received the following consensus scores from three assessors:

3,3,3 in **Judgment/Decision-Making**
3,3,3 in **Relationships with Others**
3,3,3 in **Planning and Organizing**
2,2,2 in **Leadership**
3,3,3 in **Interpersonal Communication**

Trucker's Strike: Your officers have received information that as many 300 trucks are going to picket a rock pit. If the truckers strike, their actions could shut the whole city down. One of your officers is already assigned to the location. Your officer calls you and says that five people responded to the scene. He also tells you that five men are jumping on the trucks of the independent truckers. The situation is getting heated up; i.e., a lot of shouting and threats. There are more trucks coming up from the county and they may end up tying up traffic for hours. The majority of truckers are Spanish speaking. What do you do? Candidate 18 did not indicate that he would deploy officers on motorcycles, set up a command post, hold personnel on overtime as long as necessary, prepare an After-Action Report, nor mention any plans for vehicles exiting the interstate. He also did not note whether he would maintain communications with various other agencies involved, seek intelligence from departmental detectives, or provide staff with relief as necessary.

Community Policing: A recently built elementary school in town was not designed properly around housing elements for proper egress and ingress of vehicles. As a result of this, the department and your officers get constant complaints about traffic flow, speeders and others coming down the sides of the roadway and speeding. Recently, the situation has gotten out of hand in your zone. Describe the actions you would take to address this situation.

Candidate 18 did not indicate that he would have officers on bicycles each day, set up ongoing radar to ensure speeders are ticketed, act on ideas that are logical and doable, solicit feedback from homeowners to see if the plans are working, or work with the school board to educate teachers, parents, and students regarding traffic flow and speeding.

Man with Gun in Apartment Having Psychotic Episodes: You are a sergeant working the midnight shift. You are in the office completing your paperwork. You hear on the radio that a man who lives at a five-story apartment complex is threatening to kill anyone who comes near him. He says he is talking to the devil. He appears to have a gun in his hand. A neighbor called the police. He is breaking glass and throwing it out his apartment window. Your current staffing is 8 officers. How do you handle this situation?

Candidate 18 did not indicate that he would deploy officers at each stairwell, in the parking lot and near the elevators to prevent people from coming into the building, He also did not mention stationing officers with rifles in case the man tried to leave the apartment, or call in the next shift early to assist or call in additional personnel. He also did not note that he would set up a media staging area or provide staff with emotional support as necessary

Disruptive Employee: You have an officer who is allegedly spreading rumors about another employee. When you previously spoke to him about this he denied it and said everyone was out to get them. Now a few officers come to your office and tell you that he is bringing down the morale of the unit and nothing is being done about it. They leave your office angry. How will you handle this situation?

Candidate 18 did not indicate that he would review the employee's personnel file, ask him for his side of the story, attempt to convince him to admit to spreading rumors, or tell him such behavior would not be tolerated. He also did not note that he would inquire as to whether the officer is having personal problems, order him to cease his behavior, or continue to monitor and document the situation.

Officer-Involved Shooting: You hear over the radio that one of your officers has been involved in a shooting. You arrive on the scene and crowds are forming at the shopping center. Meanwhile a robbery is taking place nearby at a check cashing store. Describe how you will handle these situations.

Candidate 18 did not indicate that he would monitor other emergency situations in the city, maintain the integrity of the officer's firearm, call the victim advocate, or say he would separate everyone involved in the shooting, including witnesses. He also did not note that he would get a briefing from the shooters as to what occurred, set up a command post or ensure the officer has legal representation.

IN-BASKET

Candidate 18's performance varied by skill dimension and exercise. His performance ranged from less than adequate or acceptable to strong. In Written Communication, his performance was strong. He received the following consensus scores from three Assessors:

3,3,3 in **Judgment/Decision-Making**
2,2,3 in **Relationships with Others**
3,3,3 in **Planning and Organizing**
3,2,2 in **Leadership**
5,5,5 in **Written Communication**

SUMMARY COMMENTS

Due to the number of items and issues addressed in the in-basket exercise, it is not feasible in this report to note each action Candidate 18 did or did not do. Therefore, brief summary comments are made regarding each skill dimension and some actions.

Judgment/Decision-Making

Candidate 18 completed slightly less than half of the seventy-three judgment/decision-making items in the in-basket. He did not fully complete any item. He did not note that he would counsel officer Bender regarding the inappropriateness of his actions as outlined in the citizen complaint he received, or make plans to meet with his boss to obtain his input. He did not send an officer's leave slip back to him to sign, approve another officer's training request, or thoroughly handle the three phone calls. Regarding the phone calls, he did not send an e-mail to the field operations lieutenant or community standards about Mr. Olson's call, or make a note to call Eileen Medeiros to find out what kind of statistics she wanted, etc. He did not complete the timecards for officers Penn and Downey.

Relationships with Others

Candidate 18 did not note to offer assistance to officers Bender and Douglas regarding the citizen complaints they received, or make plans to meet with them. He did not write a commendation letter for the employee who received a thank-you letter from a citizen, or prepare a letter to the citizen for the chief's signature. He also did not mark his calendar to arrange to speak with the employee who had experienced a death in the family upon his return from vacation.

Planning and Organizing

Candidate 18 completed less than half of the sixty planning and organizing items in the In-Basket exercise. He did not complete all of the components of each item. Candidate 18 did not make a copy of the citizen complaint letter about Officer Douglas for the field operations major, write a memo to the lieutenant telling him that the complaint had been turned over to OA to handle, or forward the complaint to IA. He did not return the officer's leave request to him, or log the sick time on the timecard. He also did not sign off on all the forms for the worker's compensation and injury accident reports.

Leadership

Candidate 18 did not note that officers Bender and Douglas needed assistance, or that he may refer Officer Douglas to EAP due to potential emotional problems. He did not note that he will find out from the officer what steps will be taken to respond to the commissioner's e-mail message. He did not mark his calendar to speak to the employee who had experienced a death in his family in order to console him and provide support. He did not note to obtain information from the personnel files of officers Bender and Douglas in preparation for completion of their annual performance evaluations.

Written Communication

Candidate 18 utilized notes or memos to convey information to people, used appropriate grammar and spelling and sentence structure. He did not write legibly.

EXHIBITS APPENDIX

Exhibit 1

POLICE SERGEANT SKILL DIMENSIONS, DEFINITIONS AND IMPORTANCE PERCENTAGE (%) WEIGHTS OUT OF ONE-HUNDRED PERCENT (%)

Perception and Analysis: Ability to quickly identify a problem and to analyze it; to notice details or phenomena; to sort out pertinent information; to foresee the consequences of various alternative actions. To what extent can the individual obtain relevant information from available information and screen out less essential details? Does the individual misinterpret information? To what extent can the individual use data and related information in order to evaluate a problem? To what extent does the individual logically interpret information in order to solve problems?

12.86% out of 100%

Decision-Making: Ability to make sound decisions promptly on difficult problems; the exercise of judgment and consideration of available information; the willingness to make a decision when required. Does not overly delegate; does not delay action on important items; takes a firm position and makes position clear. Evaluates situation to determine action to be taken; assigns tasks to subordinates when nature of the incident requires coordinated efforts of several subordinates. Basically, to what extent does the individual use all information to take the most appropriate action and exhibit a willingness to make decisions when necessary?

19.64% out of 100%

Dealing with People: Ability to establish and maintain effective and harmonious working relationships with other employees, other agencies and citizens; work as a member of team; respect and encourage working cooperatively with subordinates and co-workers and others without regard to their gender, age, race, beliefs or cultural background. Ability to deal with people beyond giving and receiving instructions. Respects ideas of others; praises subordinates for good and outstanding performance; investigates disputes and complaints against subordinates.

18.40% out of 100%

Adaptability: Ability to remain flexible and patient in the face of constantly changing needs and to influence events and execute the required actions to complete cases. Ability to modify behavior to accommodate needs and feelings of others.

11.70% out of 100%

Planning and Organizing: Ability to plan and organize daily work routine; establish priorities for the completion of work in accordance with sound time-management methodology. Ability to avoid duplication of effort, estimate expected time of completion of work elements and establish a personal schedule accordingly. Ability to know and understand expectations regarding such activities to ensure such expectations are met, and in a timely manner. Develops and formulates ways, means and timing to achieve established goals and objectives. Ability to effectively and efficiently utilize resources to achieve such goals and objectives. Ability to break work down into smaller tasks and prioritize these subtasks so it can be done effectively; to anticipate problems before they come up; to prepare effective plans to control problems; to set objectives and priorities.

12.50% out of 100%

Oral Communication: Ability to speak and signal people to convey or exchange information; receive or provide assignments or directions;

Exhibit 1   209

speak with others with poise, voice control and confidence. Ability to record and deliver information, explain procedures; to follow and give verbal and written instructions; communicate effectively with persons of varying educational backgrounds and in a variety of technical or professional languages including law enforcement staff and other personnel. Speaks clearly and is easy to follow; uses good grammar; displays self-assurance; appears unflustered; is orally fluent; is well organized; is persuasive; is enthusiastic; uses gestures effectively; does not talk too fast; does not talk haltingly; does not have distracting verbal mannerisms (uh, um, you know).

14.20% out of 100%

Written Communication: Ability to express ideas concisely and effectively in writing; to organize information effectively; to communicate at an appropriate level for any audience; use proper grammar, spelling and punctuation. Basically, to what extent can the individual present material clearly in writing?

10.70% out of 100%

Total = 100%

Exhibit 2

POLICE DETECTIVE SKILL DIMENSIONS, DEFINITIONS AND IMPORTANCE PERCENTAGE (%) WEIGHTS FOR DAY AND NIGHT SHIFTS OUT OF ONE-HUNDRED PERCENT (%)

Problem Analysis: Identifies, assimilates, and comprehends the critical elements of a situation; to assess the implications of alternative courses of action; evaluates factors essential to a problem's solution; separates relevant from irrelevant information exercising judgment.

15% AM shift; 15% PM shift = 12.5% out of 100%

Judgment and Reasoning: Exercises analytical judgment in areas of responsibility. Identifies issues or situations as they occur and specifies objectives. Identifies or assists in identifying alternative solutions to issues or situations. Implements decisions in accordance with prescribed policies and procedures and with a minimum of errors. Seeks expert advice where appropriate and researches issues, situations and alternatives.

15% AM shift;10% PM shift = 12.5% out of 100%

Dealing with People: Ability to establish and maintain effective working relationships with other employees, other agencies and citizens; work as a member of team; respect and encourage working cooperatively with subordinates and co-workers and others without regard to their gender, age, race, beliefs or ethnic background. Dis-

Exhibit 2 211

plays sensitivity to the feelings of others; comforts families of victims. Ability to deal with people beyond giving and receiving instructions.

10% AM shift; 15% PM shift = 12.5% out of 100%

Planning and Organizing: Plans and organizes daily work routine. Establishes priorities for the completion of work in accordance with sound time-management methodology. Avoids duplication of effort. Estimates expected time of completion of work elements and establishes a personal schedule accordingly. Attends, on time, required meetings, planning sessions and discussions. Implements work activity in accordance with priorities and schedules. Plans, coordinates and uses information effectively to enhance activities and production. Knows and understands expectations regarding such activities and works to ensure such expectations are met and in a timely manner. Effectively uses resources to achieve goals and objectives.

20% AM shift; 15% PM shift = 17.5% out of 100%

Initiative: Ability to work independently without direct or regular supervision; to be proactive and able to commence and complete cases without prompting or follow-up by other authorities.

10% AM shift; 10% PM shift = 10% out of 100%

Adaptability: Ability to remain flexible and patient in the face of constantly changing needs and to influence events and to execute the actions required to complete cases.

10% AM shift; 10% PM shift = 10% out of 100%

Oral Communication: Ability to speak or signal people to convey or exchange information; receive or provide assignments or directions; speak with others with poise, voice control and confidence. Ability to record and deliver information, explain procedures, to follow and give instructions; communicate effectively and efficiently with persons of varying educational backgrounds using a variety of technical and professional vocabularies, including law enforcement, personnel management, etc.

10% AM shift; 10% PM shift = 10% out of 100%

Written Communication: Ability to prepare and write reports using proper grammar, sentence structure, word usage, spelling, and punctuation, and to carefully analyze, clarify and document information in a well-organized and understandable matter.

10% AM shift; 15% PM shift = 12.5% out of 100%

Total = 100%

Exhibit 3

COACHING SKILLS ASSESSOR GUIDE

Below are some of the actions a candidate should indicate if asked to describe how they would coach a subordinate.

_____ 1. Periodically review all personnel records of subordinates to determine their level of growth, competencies, etc. in order to assess future advancement opportunities.

_____ 2. Discuss employee's career goals, the skills needed to advance.

_____ 3. Provide career-building options available within the organization, such as additional training, career ladders, cross-training and temporary assignments.

_____ 4. Work out a plan of responsibility with employee that goes with their advancement opportunities; and coach them on their strengths and weaknesses.

_____ 5. Reassure employee of my confidence in his or her ability to take on a new challenge.

_____ 6. Make myself available for coaching sessions, by keeping an open door.

_____ 7. Provide employee with benchmarks to be met along the way.

_____ 8. Set mutually agreed upon goals and timelines needed to reach final objectives.

_____ 9. Point employee to possible resources to assist in carrying out new assignments.

_____ 10. Set regular follow-up meetings to discuss progress and provide encouragement.

_____ 11. Praise and acknowledge successes along the way.

_____ 12. At completion of special assignments, conduct post-review and progress on employee's process.

_____ 13. Listen to employee's concerns and frustrations, provide encouragement and support.

_____ 14. Document other behaviors or actions not listed above.

_____ **RATING**

Exhibit 4

LEADERSHIP SKILLS ASSESSOR GUIDE

Below are some of the actions a candidate should indicate if asked to describe how they would lead their staff.

_____ 1. Share mission of department with staff in staff meetings or one-on-one.

_____ 2. Hold regular staff meetings to update one another and maintain open lines of communication.

_____ 3. Review annual goals and objectives for your unit or division and update when needed.

_____ 4. Solicit input from staff when setting annual goals and objectives.

_____ 5. Follow up with each staff person when goals and objectives are not being met.

_____ 6. Provide guidance and assistance to staff to aid them in achieving their goals.

_____ 7. Facilitate teamwork and its importance.

_____ 8. Provide regular update reports (orally or in writing) to my Chief.

_____ 9. Ensure all staff receive the training they need.

_____ 10. Discourage "we versus they" thinking.

_____ 11. Engage in ongoing self-development activities: study how to better communicate; read books on leadership; learn how to better organize, plan, make decisions, analyze, and how to be a better coach.

_____ 12. Stay abreast of current trends in law enforcement by reading books and articles, attending conferences, and share what you learn with staff as appropriate.

_____ 13. Document other behaviors or actions not listed above.

_____ **RATING**

Exhibit 5

INTERPERSONAL SKILLS ASSESSOR GUIDE

Below are some of the actions a candidate should indicate if asked about using their interpersonal skills to build relaationships with others in their organization.

_____ 1. Learn to curb my competitive nature.

_____ 2. Get to know everyone on a personal level with attentiveness and interest.

_____ 3. Do not backbite or gossip.

_____ 4. Keep disagreements within group; maintain confidentiality.

_____ 5. Be open and honest to build trust, since I am the newcomer.

_____ 6. Be an active and willing candidate in fulfilling the team's objectives.

_____ 7. Keep everyone in the loop.

_____ 8. Share information and do my part to facilitate open communications.

_____ 9. Facilitate trusting relationships.

_____ 10. Be responsive to any feedback I receive from my staff, peers and superiors.

____ 11. Treat everyone with respect.

____ 12. Document other behaviors or actions not listed above.

____   **RATING**

Exhibit 6

BARS FOR ORGANIZATIONAL CHART REVIEW AND 60–90 DAYS QUESTION

5   Candidate indicated that they would:

_____   review each employee's personnel file.

_____   find out what the organization's culture is like.

_____   not repeat past mistakes.

_____   advise staff about their management style.

_____   be a team player and expect same from the entire staff.

_____   become familiar with all written material about the organization.

_____   meet with all key employees weekly or twice a month as a group.

_____   maintain an open-door policy.

4   A score of 4 reflects that the candidate covered between 4–5 of the above statements.

3   Candidate indicated that they would:

_____   get to know who was who in the organization.

____ outline their management style for employees.

____ become familiar with all written material about the organization.

____ meet with all key employees on a weekly or semimonthly basis as a group.

____ Focused more on the "big picture," rather than getting to know the staff.

2 A score of 2 reflects that the candidate covered between 2–3 of the above statements.

1 A score of 1 reflects that the response was very vague or tangential.

Exhibit 7

THE FIVE-POINT RATING SCALE

Strong (5)

A strong rating does not mean that a candidate is perfect or without weaknesses. Rather, a strong rating means that, based on the candidate's performance in the assessment process, the candidate is likely to be strong in that skill upon assuming the job. The candidate is expected to not only step into the job and perform in a competent manner but will be expected to perform in a superior manner almost immediately upon assuming the new position, with little additional training or experience required to achieve that level of performance.

More Than Adequate or Acceptable (4)

A more than adequate rating means that, based on performance in the assessment process, the candidate is likely to perform more than competently upon assuming the position. It is expected, however, that the candidate will still be capable of improving to a considerable degree, given additional time and training in the position, but require only minimal direct supervision.

Adequate or Acceptable (3)

An adequate or acceptable rating means that, based on performance in the assessment process, the candidate is likely to perform at a competent level after assuming the position. However, additional training and experience will be necessary for the candidate to perform at a more than competent basis, and the candidate will need closer supervision than someone in the first two categories.

Less Than Adequate or Acceptable (2)

A less than adequate or acceptable rating means that, based on performance in the assessment process, the candidate is likely to perform at a less than a competent level upon assuming the position. Extensive training, experience, and supervision will probably be necessary to bring the candidate up to a competent or higher level of performance.

Weak (1)

A weak rating means that the candidate is not prepared to perform at a higher level based on the candidate's performance in the assessment process. If promoted, the candidate's performance is likely to be consistently substandard, even with direct and frequent supervision. The candidate is simply not ready to assume the position at this time.

Exhibit 8

A DIFFERENT FIVE-POINT RATING SCALE

Highly Desirable (5)

A highly desirable rating does not mean that the candidate is perfect or without weaknesses. Rather, a highly desirable rating means that based on the candidate's performance during the assessment process, they are likely to be strong in that competency upon assuming the job. The candidate is expected to not only step into the job and perform in a competent manner, but is expected to perform in a superior manner almost immediately upon assuming the new position, with little training or experience required to achieve that level of performance.

Desirable (4)

A desirable rating means that, based on performance during the assessment process, the candidate is likely to perform more than competently upon assuming the position. It is expected, however, that the candidate will still be capable of improving to a considerable degree, given additional time and training in the position, but should require only minimal direct supervision.

Somewhat Desirable (3)

A somewhat desirable rating means that, based on performance during the assessment process, the candidate is likely to perform at a competent level after assuming the position. However, additional training and experience will be necessary for the candidate to perform at a more than competent level, and the candidate will need closer supervision than someone in the first two categories.

Would Consider (2)

A would consider rating means that, based on the candidate's performance during the assessment process, the candidate is likely to perform at a less than a competent level upon assuming the position. Extensive training, experience, and supervision will probably be necessary to bring the candidate up to a competent or higher level of performance.

Would Not Consider (1)

A would not consider rating means that the candidate is not prepared to perform at this level, based on the candidate's performance during the assessment process. If hired or promoted, the candidate's performance is likely to be consistently substandard, even with direct and frequent supervision. The candidate is simply not ready to assume the position at this time.

Exhibit 9

A TEN-POINT RATING SCALE

9–10   **Outstanding** means the need for improvement is minimal, although a composite score of 9-10 does not mean that the performance in the assessment process was perfect.

7–8   **Well above Satisfactory** means there is very little need for improvement, but the performance in the assessment process was much better than above average.

6–7   **Above Satisfactory** means that the performance in the assessment process was somewhat above average and needs some improvement.

5–6   **Satisfactory** means that the performance in the assessment process was average and substantial improvement is needed.

3–4   **Below Satisfactory** means that the performance in the assessment process was below satisfactory and in need of much improvement.

0–2   **Poor** means that the performance in the assessment process was well below satisfactory and in much need of improvement.

Exhibit 10

ABC POLICE DEPARTMENT
IN-BASKET EXERCISE
LIEUTENANT
ASSESSOR GUIDE

Candidate #:_____   Assessor Name #:_____

Date:_____

RATING TABULATION MATRIX

Skill Dimension	Tentative Score	Final Score
Problem Analysis/Decision-Making		
Planning and Organizing		
Interpersonal Relations		
Written Communication		
FINAL OVERALL RATING:		

Exhibit 10 227

PROBLEM ANALYSIS/DECISION-MAKING

- Keeps superiors informed of all **critical matters**, actions taken or past-due assignments (see item). Combines/coordinates items that are related e.g., (1/12, 2/15, 3/7, 15/16).
- List all items in order they were found when you opened the in-basket. Show items clipped together in brackets.
- List item numbers of items not handled:_____

  _____

- List item numbers of items *Held for future action:*_____

  _____

- List item numbers of items marked *No action taken:*_____

  _____

MOST APPROPRIATE PROBLEM ANALYSIS/DECISION-MAKING BEHAVIORS/ACTIONS

✓ Check All Behaviors That Apply

Item 1: **E-mail from Sergeant Ashley to Brite re: police misconduct in park (Shift III).**

_____ 1. Refers to AC and chief for investigation.

_____ 2. Advises AC and chief.

_____ 3. Checks on Shift III.

_____ 4. Advises Ashley to keep issue confidential.

_____ 5. Document other behaviors or actions not listed above.

Item 2: **E-mail from Killian to Brite Asking for more than a week off.**

_____ 1. Does not grant requested time off due to staffing levels in **Item 14.**

_____ 2. Document other behaviors or actions not listed above.

Item 3: E-mail from Snoke to Brite re: complaint about Slyck's alleged harassment and poor attitude.

_____ 1. Documents and refers to Professional Standards for assignment.

_____ 2. Notes Snoke's inappropriate reference to the complainant in official records and must address issue with Snoke.

_____ 3. Document other behaviors or actions not listed above.

Item 5: E-mail welcome from secretary Maxwell to Brite with organizational information attached.

_____ 1. Notes and responds to inappropriate comment ". . . who to trust." Make plans to speak to her about putting such a comment in writing.

_____ 2. Document other behaviors or actions not listed above.

Item 7: Letter from PTA commending Slyck.

_____ 1. Forwards to Arvilla and asks her to ensure that a commendation letter is written.

_____ 2. Document other behaviors or actions not listed above.

Item 8: Unofficial note from Bollen to Gage: sergeant's memo points to possible problems with officer.

_____ 1. Acts to obtain more specific information.

_____ 2. Does not overreact by assuming that innuendo is true.

_____ 3. Document other behaviors or actions not listed above.

Exhibit 10 229

Item 10: E-mail from Pesky to Gage: he requests input on proposed transfer of Slyck to Burglary Suppression.

_____ 1. Advises AC that pending investigation of complaints indicates need to place decision on hold pending outcome.

_____ 2. Or tells sergeant to put together an information packet and make a recommendation.

_____ 3. Document other behaviors or actions not listed above.

Item 11: E-mail from Bollen to Gage re: complaint from Meagher regarding his performance evaluation.

_____ 1. Obtains specific information as to basis for comment.

_____ 2. May note that employees cannot file a grievance over satisfactory evaluations

_____ 3. Notes also that the review should never have been issued without the employee first seeing it.

_____ 4. Document other behaviors or actions not listed above.

Item 12: E-mail from Grace to Pesky, passed to Gage about complaints from city officials re: criminal and nuisance activities in Meadows Park.

_____ 1. Ensures that AC and chief are aware that deadline will not be met.

_____ 2. Assures Pesky that action will be taken to promptly prepare plan in his absence.

_____ 3. Writes note to Sergeant to make sure that AC and DCs are notified.

_____ 4. Document other behaviors or actions not listed above.

Item 14: E-mail from Gage to Pesky regarding a staff shortage in Shift III, citing reasons for it, including budget issues.

____ 1. Decides that Killian's request for time off should be denied because of staff shortage.

____ 2. Notes importance of problem with staff shortages.

____ 3. Document other behaviors or actions not listed above.

Item 15: E-mail from Snoke to Gage regarding Slyck complaint.

____ 1. Refers to AC and chief for investigation.

____ 2. Snoke refers this to IA.

____ 3. Ensures that AC knows that Slyck has asked for a transfer.

____ 4. Document other behaviors or actions not listed above.

Item 16: Letter from citizen, Denis Menis, passed to Gage by Pesky. He complains about conduct, attitude, and language used by Slyck in issuing traffic summons.

____ 1. Refers to AC and chief for investigation.

____ 2. Document other behaviors or actions not listed above.

Item 17: E-mail from Chief to Brite regarding ideas on 3 districts due in office before Brite goes on military duty.

____ 1. This item cannot be delegated.

____ 2. It must be completed during the hour exercise.

____ 3. Document other behaviors or actions not listed above.

____ **RATING**

Exhibit 10 231

INTERPERSONAL RELATIONS

Summarize the *tone* of the candidate's overall communications. Was it polite, considerate, apologetic if not able to fulfill requests, appreciative when appropriate, and was "thanks" used when directing actions?

_____

_____

_____

MOST APPROPRIATE INTERPERSONAL BEHAVIORS/ACTIONS

✓ Check All Behaviors That Apply

Item 2:   E-mail from Killian to Brite asking for more than a week off.

_____   1. Must be sure that Killian is apprised of his decision and an explanation given based on the information in Item 15.

_____   2. Document other behaviors or actions not listed above.

Item 3:   E-mail from Snoke to Gage: report of complaint of Slyck's alleged harassment and poor attitude when issuing a summons.

_____   1. Must be sure some notification is made to citizen that the matter is being addressed.

_____   2. Document other behaviors or actions not listed above.

Item 4:   E-mail from AC Pesky to Brite with explanation of why AC won't be available and pass along his appreciation for Brite's efforts.

_____   1. A note of appreciation and understanding to new boss is appropriate.

_____   2. Document other behaviors or actions not listed above.

Item 5:   E-mail from Maxwell to Brite welcoming him with organizational information attached.

_____ 1. Should thank secretary for her efforts but should note in some fashion that they will have to discuss with her "whom to trust/not trust" comment as being inappropriate.

_____ 2. Document other behaviors or actions not listed above.

Item 6:   E-mail from Carter (911) to Brite about need for training in communications protocol, procedures, and supervision.

_____ 1. Indicates concern for Carter and Carter being absent.

_____ 2. Will follow-up with upon return.

_____ 3. Document other behaviors or actions not listed above.

Item 7:   Letter from PTA to Chief Grace commending Slyck for his fine job with the children.

_____ 1. Asks Arvilla to handle commendation and thank her for taking care of it.

_____ 2. Document other behaviors or actions not listed above.

Item 8:   Unofficial note from Bollen to Gage about officer Pace.

_____ 1. Should make plans to speak to Sergeant Bollen and Pace upon return from trip.

_____ 2. Makes a note of it and puts it on his calendar.

_____ 3. Document other behaviors or actions not listed above.

Exhibit 10 233

Item 9: **Letter from citizens to commanding officer commending Slyck for saving drowning child.**

____ 1. Should ensure that thank-you responses are provided to citizens.

____ 2. May include in commendation to Slyck despite his other problems.

____ 3. Document other behaviors or actions not listed above.

Item 11: **E-mail from Bollen to Gage regarding a complaint from Meagher regarding his performance evaluation.**

____ 1. Must make sure Meagher is aware that matter is being handled.

____ 2. Document other behaviors or actions not listed above.

Item 13: **Letter from to citizen Neal Jones to chief complaining about crime increase and invitation to community gathering.**

____ 1. Needs to notify citizen indicating a PD representative will attend.

____ 2. Document other behaviors or actions not listed above.

Item 15: **E-mail from Ashley to Gage regarding complaint about Slyck.**

____ 1. Complainant should be advised that an investigation is being conducted and he will be contacted.

____ 2. Document other behaviors or actions not listed above.

Item 16: Letter from citizen, Denis Menis, passed to Gage by Pesky complaining about conduct, attitude, and language used by Slyck in issuing traffic summons.

_____ 1. Must let citizen know matter is being investigated.

_____ 2. Document other behaviors or actions not listed above.

_____   **RATING**

PLANNING AND ORGANIZING

- How comprehensively was the exercise handled?
- What did the candidate do beyond the obvious—plan a shift staff meeting on return, send out a notice of absence to all concerned personnel—to complete the exercise?
- Which items were delegated or reassigned partially or completely to subordinate personnel?
- Was there an over-reliance on one or a few subordinate staffers while ignoring others?
- How extensively did the candidate make use of the calendar (if provided) to schedule due dates, assignments, meetings, and follow-up?
- To what extent did candidate delegate or reassign work have specific due dates when appropriate?
- To what extent did the delegated or reassigned work have specific objectives and tasks?
- To what extent did those delegated or reassigned tasks have knowledge of related activities and assignments? Was there appropriate coordination among them?

Exhibit 10 235

MOST APPROPRIATE PLANNING AND
ORGANIZING BEHAVIORS/ACTIONS

✓ Check All Behaviors That Apply

Item 2: **E-mail from Killian to Brite Asking for more than a week off.**

_____ 1. Must deny or pass on to AC Pesky because of shortage of personnel as noted in **Item 14**.

_____ 2. Document other behaviors or actions not listed above.

Item 5: **Pages 2 and 3; organizational chart and Shifts I-III staffing complement.**

_____ 1. Organizational chart is for informational purposes only.

_____ 2. Staffing complement can be used for delegation, filling gaps.

_____ 3. Document other behaviors or actions not listed above.

Item 6: **E-mail from Carter (911) to Brite about need for training in communications protocol, procedures, and supervision.**

_____ 1. Can start gathering info now from Carter and his sergeants to get a full perspective on the issue.

_____ 2. Document other behaviors or actions not listed above.

Item 9: **Letter to commanding officer commending Slyck for saving drowning child.**

_____ 1. Should also forward to the chief's office for preparation of a letter.

_____ 2. Document other behaviors or actions not listed above.

Item 12: E-mail from Grace to Pesky, passed to Gage from city officials regarding the complaint about criminal and nuisance activities in Meadows Park.

_____ 1. Needs to delegate development of a remedial plan to a sergeant.

_____ 2. Needs to inform Pesky and Grace of action taken.

_____ 3. Document other behaviors or actions not listed above.

Item 13: Letter to chief from citizen Neal Jones complaining about crime increase and inviting him to a community gathering.

Needs to:

_____ 1. assign a representative to attend.

_____ 2. gather specific complaints.

_____ 3. obtain crime data.

_____ 4. prepare a draft response to Jones.

_____ 5. make note to contact a staff person regarding who will be attending the meeting.

_____ 6. write a note to have a community policing officer attend.

_____ 7. Document other behaviors or actions not listed above.

Item 14: E-mail from Gage to Pesky regarding staff shortage for Shift III, citing reasons for the shortage, including budget issues.

_____ 1. Should make plans to deal with the issue upon return from military duty.

Exhibit 10 237

_____ 2. Document other behaviors or actions not listed above.

Item 17: E-mail from chief to Brite regarding ideas on three districts due in office before Brite goes on vacation.

_____ 1. This item must be completed in the time allotted.

_____ 2. Document other behaviors or actions not listed above.

_____ **RATING**

WRITTEN COMMUNICATION

- To which items did the candidate respond with written memoranda or letters?
- To which items did the candidate not respond with written memoranda, although the nature of the item required it?
- Summarize the quality of all the written materials in terms of grammar, spelling, punctuation, word usage, sentence and paragraph structure and legibility).
- Note and explain any exceptions, to the overall quality of the writing, by item number.

MOST APPROPRIATE WRITTEN COMMUNICATION

✓ Check All Behaviors That Apply

_____ 1. Used correct English grammar.

_____ 2. Used correct spelling.

_____ 3. Used appropriate sentence construction ? neither too long or too short—used paragraphs, and did not overuse bullet points or lists.

_____ 4. Used appropriate punctuation.

_____ 5. Writing was clear and succinct.

_____ 6. Writing was well organized.

_____ 7. Wrote for the appropriate audience – police officials, court personnel, etc.

_____ 8. Outlines or bulleted lists were prepared in appropriate format.

_____ 9. Document other behaviors or actions not listed above.

_____ **RATING**

Exhibit 11

ABC POLICE DEPARTMENT ORAL, WITH NOTES IN-BASKET EXERCISE SERGEANT ASSESSOR GUIDE

Candidate #:_____ Assessor Name #:_____

Date:_____

RATING TABULATION MATRIX

Skill Dimension	Tentative Score	Final Score
Problem Analysis		
Judgment and Reasoning		
Planning and Organizing		
Management/Supervision		
Oral Communication		
FINAL OVERALL RATING:		

MOST APPROPRIATE PROBLEM ANALYSIS BEHAVIORS/ACTIONS

✓ Check All Behaviors That Apply

_____ **Item 1:** Recognizes that someone else needs to attend due to drug sales.

_____ **Item 2:** Notes that employee can't be at work in this condition.

_____ **Item 2:** Will find out more about previous reported incident about drinking.

_____ **Item 2:** Employee needs to be observed on the job.

_____ **Item 3:** Notes importance of meeting with Ryan: he is a probationary employee; it was his first case, and a sexual assault, etc.

_____ **Item 4:** Vehicle can't be driven until it is repaired and needs repair ASAP.

_____ **Items 5–5a:** Department works closely with community associations.

_____ **Items 5–5a:** Recognizes need to address the problems ASAP; write letter as first action per lieutenant Smith's instructions.

_____ **Items 6–6a:** Recognizes importance of letter. Roundtree must be called and the candidate should schedule a time to meet with Reston to discuss the complaint of rudeness and abrasive behavior.

_____ **Items 7:** Recognizes that this is a problem as it prevents other officers from having Friday off and that there may be a pattern.

_____ **Items 8–8a:** Recognizes need to have a telephone complaint form completed.

Exhibit 11 241

_____ **Items 9:** Recognizes that someone needs to call her back, but it is not a top priority since the case is already a few months old.

_____ **Items 10:** Recognizes that task cannot be completed on time due to vacation; lieutenant needs to be reminded and needs an extension on initiative.

_____ Document other behaviors or actions not listed above.

_____ **RATING**

MOST APPROPRIATE JUDGMENT/REASONING BEHAVIORS/ACTIONS

✓ Check All Behaviors That Apply

_____ **Item 1:** Makes suggestion to have another sergeant or another person from a specialized unit attend due to the nature of the association's concerns regarding drug sales.

_____ **Item 2:** Recognizes serious nature of being drunk on the job.

_____ **Item 2:** Employee may need to be referred to EAP.

_____ **Item 2:** OIC lieutenant needs to be notified.

_____ **Item 3:** Ryan needs immediate intervention/assistance due to probationary status and nature of recent case (sexual assault), and lieutenant asked for an update.

_____ **Item 4:** Would make sure accident report is completed.

_____ **Item 4:** Accident needs to be investigated.

_____ **Item 5–5a:** Recognizes that in addition to a letter being written to Haines, a meeting should also be set up with the association.

____ **Item 7:** Needs to review sick leave for Bentley upon return from vacation but may consider referring to OIC lieutenant as the candidate is going on vacation, and situation needs to be dealt with ASAP.

____ **Item 10:** Due to nature of problem—prostitution—considers asking officers to brainstorm ideas on how to deal with the situation while the candidate is on vacation so the initiative will not be delayed.

____ Document other behaviors or actions not listed above.

1. How comprehensively did the candidate handle the exercise?
2. Did the candidate answer the questions listed in the instructions?

MOST APPROPRIATE PLANNING AND ORGANIZING BEHAVIORS/ACTIONS

✓ Check All Behaviors That Apply

____ **Item 1:** Makes plan to have someone else attend meeting; will schedule a meeting with the employee when the candidate returns from vacation; will refer to Lieutenant to meet with Stupor ASAP.

____ **Item 2:** Will get on telephone and talk to OIC about and ask him to send the person home; notify OIC Lieutenant to approve.

____ **Item 2:** Will schedule meeting with Stupor upon return from vacation.

____ **Item 2:** Will make plans to observe him on job upon return from vacation.

____ **Item 2:** Will call lieutenant regarding the Stupor situation and plans to deal with it upon return from vacation.

Exhibit 11 243

____ **Item 3:** Will schedule time to meet with recruit Ryan upon return from vacation; will call her before leaving to tell her of date change.

____ **Item 5–5a:** Will follow up with officers upon return from vacation to obtain update on response to Haines and homeowners' association.

____ **Item 6–6a:** Will make plans to meet with Reston upon return from vacation to discuss complaint letter.

____ **Item 7:** Will make plans to meet with Bentley upon return from vacation.

____ **Item 10:** Will review officer's suggestions regarding initiatives for combatting prostitution on King Street and meet with them upon return from vacation.

____ Document other behaviors or actions not listed above.

____ **RATING**

MOST APPROPRIATE MANAGEMENT
AND SUPERVISION BEHAVIORS/ACTIONS

✓ Check All Behaviors That Apply

____ **Item 2:** Will establish priorities for Stupor and specifically notes:

____ 1. He cannot be drinking on job etc.

____ 2. Will give him a specific time period during which he needs to improve his performance.

____ 3. He will be observed on the job.

____ 4. Will ask for his input.

____ 5. Will refer him to EAP if appropriate.

____ **Item 3:** Will provide one-on-one coaching and counseling with Ryan on an ongoing basis; will offer assistance when she needs it on anything else.

____ **Item 4:** Notes that the candidate may need to meet with Mayham regarding safe driving, especially if accident is his fault.

____ **Item 6–6a:** Will establish priorities for Reston and specifically notes:

____ 1. Will discuss incident with the reporter.

____ 2. Get his input.

____ 3. Coach him on better ways to deal with reporters.

____ **Item 7:** Will establish priorities for Bentley and specifically notes:

____ 1. Do not call in on other officers' Fridays off.

____ 2. This appears to be a pattern, if records reviewed are correct, based on Axelrod's e-mail complaint.

____ **Item 11:** Notes that the candidate would speak to the officer upon return from vacation, to find out about his assessment of the value of the training.

____ Document other behaviors or actions not listed above.

____ **RATING**

Exhibit 11   245

MOST APPROPRIATE ORAL COMMUNICATION

✓ Check All Behaviors That Apply

_____ 1. Had effective delivery (vivid, graphic, organized, concise, passionate, spirited, direct, and fluent (as opposed to awkward or halting).

_____ 2. Used gestures effectively (positive, supportive, varied).

_____ 3. Maintained eye contact while speaking and listening.

_____ 4. Used appropriate nonverbal communication and other body language that facilitated understanding rather than distracting—tapping a pencil, shuffling papers, looking around room—from the presentation.

_____ 5. Was clear in speaking at an appropriate speed, with good enunciation and diction.

_____ 6. Used an appropriate vocabulary and good grammar, avoiding jargon, slang and profanity.

_____ 7. Spoke appropriately to the point, rather than being excessively wordy and running on before getting to the point.

_____ 8. Used voice inflection to emphasize certain points and enhance clarity when appropriate.

The candidates are rated on the overall quality of their oral communication rather than looking at the extent to which each detail listed above was or was not effectively covered. That information is a guide, but it is not intended to be used to count the number of check marks to compute a score, or to measure one candidate against another to determine their overall rating for this category.

_____   **RATING**

Exhibit 12

ABC POLICE DEPARTMENT ORAL WITH WRITTEN SCENARIOS IN-BASKET EXERCISE SERGEANT ASSESSOR GUIDE

Candidate #:_____ Assessor Name #:_____

Date:_____

RATING TABULATION MATRIX

Skill Dimension	Tentative Score	Final Score
Judgment/Decision Making		
Relationships with Others		
Leading/Staffing		
Planning and Organizing		
Oral Communication		
Written Communication		
FINAL OVERALL RATING:		

Exhibit 12 247

MOST APPROPRIATE JUDGMENT/DECISION MAKING BEHAVIORS/ACTIONS

✓ Check All Behaviors That Apply

Item 1: **Complaint Letter from Major Re: Third Complaint of Officer Rudeness (Priority Item)**

_____ 1. Would document incident of rudeness of officer Bender in memo to IA (who reports to Sergeant).

_____ 2. Would set up meeting with officer as soon as possible after return from vacation and reach a conclusion about what punishment if any, Bender should receive.

_____ 3. Would obtain his side of the story.

_____ 4. Would counsel employee regarding inappropriateness of actions and that this is the third rudeness complaint if allegation is sustained.

_____ 5. Would make plans to meet with the major to get input as to whether the officer should be sent for counseling.

_____ 6. Would call citizen to let them know the situation will be handled upon return from vacation.

_____ 7. Noted during assessment process other actions that would be taken.

Item 2: **Complaint Letter Re: Officer Flirting/Making Sexual Comments to Citizen (Must Do)**

_____ 1. Makes copy of letter for Road Patrol major.

_____ 2. Copy to IA.

_____ 3. Writes memo to major and notes that is has been handled.

_____ 4. Noted during assessment process other actions that would be taken.

Item 3: Commissioner Nicholson's E-mail Message Complaint (Must Do)

_____ 1. Notes to speak with officer to find out circumstances of ticket.

_____ 2. Prepares notes about steps to be taken for commissioner

_____ 3. Notifies major that it is being handled.

_____ 4. Forwards to major a copy of the message from the commissioner.

_____ 5. Noted during assessment process other actions that would be taken.

Item 4: Leave Request Form (Must Do)

_____ 1. Sends back to officer to sign.

_____ 2. Noted during assessment process other actions that would be taken.

Item 5: Training Request—Field Training (Needs Some Action)

_____ 1. Approves request.

_____ 2. Routes to major for signature.

_____ 3. Call training division regarding training he has received during the year, or check employee file to review training received during year, or check with employee.

_____ 4. Notes that training request for a class is consistent with current duties.

Exhibit 12 249

_____ 5. Notes that training request is for career development and thus is appropriate.

_____ 6. Noted during assessment process other actions that would be taken.

Item 6: Workers Compensation On-the-Job Injury Paperwork (Must Do)

_____ 1. May refer to Risk Management, but not required.

_____ 2. Refers to major.

_____ 3. Notes that it is linked to item #11; both items are clipped together.

_____ 4. Noted during assessment process other actions that would be taken.

Item 7: Three Phone Calls to Return (Must Handle)

_____ 1. Sends e-mail to Field Operations major or Community Standards about the call from Mr. Olson about overgrown grass.

_____ 2. Calls Olson and tells him that it will be handled.

_____ 3. Makes call to get more information from Babson.

_____ 4. Notifies Field Operations major that Olson's complaint was sent to Community Standards.

_____ 5. Tells Babson who it has been referred to the CID to handle.

_____ 6. Sends e-mail to records supervisor with requester's telephone number.

_____ 7. Calls to get more information from person about statistics needed and how they want them broken out (Medeiros' call).

____ 8. Sends e-mail to Community Policing regarding information being requested as CPO may be at meeting (Medeiros' call).

____ 9. Notes to have appropriate personnel put together packet of information for person (Medeiros' call).

____ 10. Noted during assessment process other actions that would be taken.

Item 8:   Thank You Letter from Citizen to Employee (Name of Employee Not Given) (Should Do)

____ 1. Makes note to write commendation or cover letter to employee upon return.

____ 2. Notes that I did find out or will find out whom the employee was.

____ 3. Notes on calendar to write letter upon return from vacation.

____ 4. Noted during assessment process other actions that would be taken.

Item 9:   Vacation Request from Employee (Should Take Some Action)

____ 1. Notes potential problem; i.e., why is employee asking for time off; i.e. dates.

____ 2. Disapproves vacation (but does the latter).

____ 3. Routes back to employee.

____ 4. Noted during assessment process other actions that would be taken.

Exhibit 12 251

Item 10: Calendars for May and June (Should Use the Calendars)

____ 1. Marks calendars with appropriate dates for completion of tasks.

Item 11: Injury Accident Report for Officer (Must Do)

____ 1. Notes that this item is linked to Item 6. Both are clipped together (same officer).

____ 2. Completes Supervisor Accident Injury Report.

____ 3. Signs off on City of X form.

____ 4. Completes second page of form.

____ 5. Noted during assessment process other actions that would be taken.

Item 12: Police Vehicle Operation and Pursuit for Review and Comment—Due June 2nd (Should Take Some Action)

____ 1. Should start to review and comment on.

____ 2. Notes that because of due date, will handle upon return from vacation.

____ 3. Noted during assessment process other actions that would be taken.

Item 13: Employee Leave Request—Bereavement (Must Do)

____ 1. Signs off on leave request.

____ 2. Noted during assessment process other actions that would be taken.

Item 14: Completed Educational Request from Employee (Should Do)

_____ 1. Return to employee for proper completion of paperwork (Should not approve).

_____ 2. Noted during assessment process other actions that would be taken.

Item 15: Blank Performance Evaluation Forms for Two Employees (High Priority items: Officer with Citizen Complaint about Flirting, and Other Officer with Citizen Complaint)

_____ 1. Notes that a review will be due within 2 days upon return from vacation.

_____ 2. Marks calendar to complete reviews upon return.

_____ 3. Notes on review form or piece of paper to meet with both Douglas and Bender upon return from vacation to discuss complaints.

_____ 4. Links with item 2 regarding Douglas.

_____ 5. Links with item #1 regarding Bender.

_____ 6. Writes memo asking who should write reviews for Douglas and Bender given he has not been their supervisor for long.

_____ 7. May start to complete the review.

_____ 8. Noted during assessment process other actions that would be taken.

Item 16: Timecards for Penn & Downey (Must Sign)

_____ 1. Completes and signs cards for Penn (item 9) & Downey (item 13).

Exhibit 12 253

_____ 2. Notes during assessment process other actions that would be taken.

_____ **RATING**

MOST APPROPRIATE RELATIONSHIPS WITH OTHERS BEHAVIORS/ACTIONS

✓ Check All Behaviors That Apply

Item 1: Complaint Form from Major Re: Third Complaint of Officer Rudeness) (Priority Item)

_____ 1. Notes to make plans to meet with major to get his input regarding whether officer should officer be sent for counseling if complaint is founded.

_____ 2. Notes to offer assistance to officer.

_____ 3. Notes during assessment process other actions that would be taken.

Item 2: Complaint Letter Re: Flirting and Sexual Innuendoes

_____ 1. Notes to make plans to meet with major to get his input regarding whether officer should be sent for counseling, if complaint is founded.

_____ 2. Notes to offer assistance to officer if complaint is founded and if needed.

_____ 3. Notes to call person in and talk to him.

_____ 4. Notes during assessment process other actions that would be taken.

Item 3:   Commissioner Nicholson's E-Mail Message Complaint

____ 1. Notes to speak with officer to find out circumstances of ticket.

____ 2. Notes to talk to commissioner and explain steps to be taken if any, to resolve.

____ 3. Notes during assessment process other actions that would be taken.

Item 5:   Training Request–Field Training

____ 1. Notes that training request is for career development, and thus is appropriate.

____ 2. Notes during assessment process other actions that would be taken.

Item 7:   Three Phone Calls to Return

____ 1. Has appropriate personnel put together packet of information for the person.

____ 2. Notes that all personnel have been called.

____ 3. Notes during assessment process other actions that would be taken.

Item 8:   Thank-You Letter from Citizen to Employee (Name Not Given)

____ 1. Will write commendation or cover letter to employee upon return.

____ 2. Forward copy for file.

____ 3. Notes during assessment process other actions that would be taken.

Exhibit 12 255

Item 11: Injury Accident Report for Officer

____ 1. Noted during assessment process other actions that would be taken.

Item 13: Employee Leave Request—Bereavement

____ 1. Signs off on leave request.

____ 2. Marks calendar to speak to employee upon return.

____ 3. Notes during assessment process other actions that would be taken.

Item 15: Blank Performance Evaluation Forms for Two Employees (Priority one is for Officer with Citizen Complaint about Flirting)

____ 1. Notes may refer Douglas to EAP (per G.O. 123) due to potential psychological Problems (see item 2).

____ 2. Notes that Bender may need counseling (see item 1).

____ 3. Notes during assessment process other actions that would be taken.

____ **RATING**

MOST APPROPRIATE PLANNING AND ORGANIZING BEHAVIORS/ACTIONS

✓ Check All Behaviors That Apply

Item 1: Complaint Letter from IA Re: Third Complaint of Officer Rudeness (Priority Item)

____ 1. Notes to document incident of rudeness of officer Bender (who reports to Sergeant); review is forthcoming.

_____ 2. Sets up meeting with officer as soon as possible after return from vacation.

_____ 3. Makes plans to meet with major to get his input on whether officer should officer be sent for counseling.

_____ 4. Notes to offer assistance to officer if that officer needs help.

_____ 5. Makes call to citizen to let them know situation will be handled upon return from vacation.

_____ 6. Notes during assessment process other actions that would be taken.

Item 2: Complaint Letter Re: Officer Flirting/Making Sexual Comments to Citizen (Must Do)

_____ 1. Makes copy of letter for Road Patrol major.

_____ 2. Writes memo to major and says that it has been turned over to IA to handle.

_____ 3. Notes during assessment process other actions that would be taken.

Item 3: Commissioner Nicholson's E-mail Message Complaint (Must Do)

_____ 1. Notes to speak with officer to find out circumstances of ticket.

_____ 2. Notes to find out from officer what steps will be taken to resolve.

_____ 3. Sends memo to major that it is being handled.

_____ 4. Sends major a copy of commissioner's message.

_____ 5. Notes during assessment process other actions that would be taken.

Exhibit 12 257

Item 4: Leave Request Form (Must Handle)

_____ 1. Returns to officer to have him sign off on.

_____ 2. Notes to check form for correctness.

_____ 3. Logs sick time on timecard or notes it needs to be done.

_____ 4. Notes during assessment process other actions that would be taken.

Item 5: Training Request—Field Training (Needs Some Action)

_____ 1. Notes to check employee file to review training he has received during year.

_____ 2. Marks calendar to meet with employee about upon return from vacation to discuss.

_____ 3. Notes during assessment process other actions that would be taken.

Item 6: Workers Compensation On-the-Job Injury Paperwork (Must Do)

_____ 1. Returns to officer to sign.

_____ 2. May note to advise Risk Management via memo.

_____ 3. Refers to major for signature.

_____ 4. Notes that it is linked to item #11; both items are clipped together.

_____ 5. Notes during assessment process other actions that would be taken.

Item 7:   Three Phone Calls to Return (Must Handle)

_____ 1. Sends e-mail to Field Operations major or CID commander about the call and the drug dealing.

_____ 2. Makes call to get more information from Babson.

_____ 3. Notifies Field Operations major that it was sent to CID.

_____ 4. E-mails Babson it has been turned over to CID.

_____ 5. E-mails information to records supervisor with requester's phone number.

_____ 6. Calls to get more information from person about statistics and what kind and how they want them broken out.

_____ 7. Sends e-mail to Community Policing regarding information being requested as CPO may be at meeting.

_____ 8. Asks appropriate personnel to put together packet of information for person.

_____ 9. Calls Olson and tells him that it will be handled.

_____ 10. Notes during assessment process other actions that would be taken.

Item 9:   Vacation Request from Employee (Should Take Some Action)

_____ 1. Notes request is while on vacation.

_____ 2. Notes that person is asking for a month off.

_____ 3. Notes during assessment process other actions that would be taken.

Exhibit 12   259

Item 10: Calendars for May and June (Should Use Calendars)

_____ 1. Marks calendar with appropriate dates for completion of tasks.

_____ 2. Notes during assessment process other actions that would be taken.

Item 11: Injury Accident Report for Officer (Must Do)

_____ 1. Notes that this item is linked to item 6 and both are clipped together (same officer).

_____ 2. Completes Supervisor Injury Accident Report.

_____ 3. Signs off on all forms.

_____ 4. Completes Accident Injury Report (must be done during time).

_____ 5. Hand writes latter information on accident report.

_____ 6. Notes during assessment process other actions that would be taken.

Item 12: Police Vehicle Operation and Pursuit for Review and Comment—Due June 2nd (Should Take Some Action)

_____ 1. May start to review and comment if time allows.

_____ 2. Marks calendar to do and June 2nd due date upon return.

_____ 3. Notes during assessment process other actions that would be taken.

Item 13: Employee Leave Request—Bereavement (Must Do)

_____ 1. Notes to send e-mail to chief's office regarding death.

____ 2. Marks calendar to speak to employee upon return.

____ 3. Notes during assessment process other actions that would be taken.

Item 15: Blank Performance Evaluation Forms for Two Employees (Priority one is for officer with citizen complaint on flirting, but both need action)

____ 1. Notes that a review will be due within two days upon return from vacation May 30 (Per G.O., so reviews are due on June 3).

____ 2. Marks calendar to complete upon return.

____ 3. Notes on review form to meet with Douglas and Bender upon return from vacation to discuss complaints.

____ 4. Links with item 2 regarding Douglas; clips items 2 and 15 together.

____ 5. Notes may refer Douglas to EAP (per G.O. 123) due to potential psychological problems.

____ 6. Notes during assessment process other actions that would be taken.

Item 16: Timecards for Penn and Downey (Must Sign)

____ 1. Completes and signs cards for Penn (item 9), and Downey (item 13).

____ 2. Clips items 9 and 13 to completed timecards.

____ 3. Notes during assessment process other actions that would be taken.

____ **RATING**

Exhibit 12 261

MOST APPROPRIATE LEADERSHIP
(LEADING/STAFFING) BEHAVIORS/ACTIONS

✓ Check All Behaviors That Apply

Item 1: **Complaint Letter from IA, re: Third Complaint of Officer Rudeness (Priority Item)**

_____ 1. Notes to speak with officer to obtain his side of story.

_____ 2. Notes to meet with and counsel employee regarding inappropriateness of actions; note that this is the third complaint if allegation is sustained.

_____ 3. May note that officer needs professional assistance.

_____ 4. Notes during assessment process other actions that would be taken.

Item 2: **Complaint Letter Re: Flirting and Sexual Innuendoes**

_____ 1. Notes to speak with him to obtain his side of story.

_____ 2. Refers to IA to handle.

_____ 3. Notes to advise major upon return and cc's major.

_____ 4. Notes during assessment process other actions that would be taken.

Item 3: **Commissioner Nicholson's E-mail Message Complaint**

_____ 1. Notes I will find out from officer what steps will be taken to resolve.

_____ 2. Notes during assessment process other actions that would be taken.

Item 5:   Training Request—Field Training

_____ 1. Will check employee file to review training he has received during year.

_____ 2. Notes that training request is for career development, and thus is appropriate.

_____ 3. Notes to meet with employee after training to find out how it went.

_____ 4. Notes during assessment process other actions that would be taken.

Item 9:   Vacation Request from Employee

_____ 1. Notes potential problem with the dates requested and staffing shortage.

_____ 2. Notes during assessment process other actions that would be taken.

Item 13: Employee Leave Request - Bereavement

_____ 1. Notes to send e-mail to chief's office regarding death.

_____ 2. Marks calendar to speak to employee upon return to console, offer support.

_____ 3. Noted during assessment process other actions that would be taken.

Item 15: Blank Performance Evaluation Forms for Two Employees (Priority One is for Officer with Citizen Complaint on Flirting and Then Other Officer with Citizen Complaint)

_____ 1. Notes on review form to meet with Douglas and Bender upon return from vacation to discuss complaint.

Exhibit 12 263

_____ 2. Notes may refer Douglas to EAP (per G.O.) due to potential psychological problems (see item 2).

_____ 3. Notes during assessment process other actions that would be taken.

_____ **RATING**

MOST APPROPRIATE WRITTEN COMMUNICATION

✓ Check All Behaviors That Apply

_____ 1. Did the candidate utilize notes or memos to convey information to people?

_____ 2. Did the candidate utilize appropriate grammar?

_____ 3. Did the candidate utilize appropriate spelling?

_____ 4. Did the candidate utilize appropriate punctuation?

_____ 5. Did the candidate utilize appropriate word usage?

_____ 6. Did the candidate write legibly?

Note: Remember that written communication is evaluated across entire IB on a 1–5 scale for all items.

_____ **RATING**

Exhibit 13

ABC POLICE DEPARTMENT WRITTEN SCENARIOS IN-BASKET EXERCISE SERGEANT ASSESSOR GUIDE

Candidate #:_____   Assessor Name #:_____

Date:_____

RATING TABULATION MATRIX

Skill Dimension	Tentative Score	Final Score
Perception and Analysis		
Planning and Organizing		
Judgment/Decision-Making		
Interpersonal		
Written Communication		
FINAL OVERALL RATING:		

Exhibit 13 265

SCENARIO 1
MOST APPROPRIATE BEHAVIORS/ACTIONS

✓ Check All Behaviors That Apply

Perception and Analysis Behaviors

_____ 1. Maintain integrity of the crime scene.

_____ 2. Follow the Critical Incident Check List.

_____ 3. Separate officer from rest of people at scene.

_____ 4. Notify Professional Standards.

_____ 5. Notify CID.

_____ 6. Notify PIO.

_____ 7. Notify union representative for the officer.

_____ 8. Notes that some of these steps could be done by the lieutenant.

_____ 9. Document other behaviors or actions not listed above.

_____ **RATING**

Planning and Organizing Behaviors

_____ 1. Contact sheriff's office, if applicable, to handle calls.

_____ 2. Keep shift commander advised of situation.

_____ 3. Make sure officer's service weapon is taken away.

_____ 4. Document other behaviors or actions not listed above.

_____ **RATING**

Judgment/Decision-Making Behaviors

_____ 1. Go to scene immediately.

_____ 2. Notify Professional Standards.

_____ 3. Notify CID.

_____ 4. Notify PIO.

_____ 5. Notify union representative for the officer.

_____ 6. Make sure officer's service weapon is taken away.

_____ 7. Document other behaviors or actions not listed above.

_____ **RATING**

Interpersonal

_____ 1. Work as team with other peers and officers.

_____ 2. Be concerned with well-being of officer and other officers on scene.

_____ 3. Notify union representative for the officer.

_____ 4. Document other behaviors or actions not listed above.

_____ **RATING**

Written Communication

_____ 1. Utilized appropriate grammar.

_____ 2. Utilized appropriate spelling.

_____ 3. Utilized appropriate sentence and paragraph structure.

Exhibit 13   267

___ 4. Utilized appropriate punctuation.

___ 5. Utilized appropriate word usage.

___ 6. Wrote legibly.

___ **RATING**

SCENARIO 2
MOST APPROPRIATE BEHAVIORS/ACTIONS

✓ Check All Behaviors That Apply

Perception and Analysis Behaviors

___ 1. Obtain notification that officers have arrested the suspect.

___ 2. Make sure the cash recovered is secured.

___ 3. Act on additional information.

___ 4. Check with all officers at posts.

___ 5. Check on barricades and crime scene tape.

___ 6. Contact PIO.

___ 7. Evacuate bank and surrounding buildings.

___ 8. Notify captains and Detective Bureau.

___ 9. Take suspect to talk with FBI agent(s) as the bank was federally insured bank.

___ 10. Set up a perimeter around the area, and around the bank building.

___ 11. Send officers to block off all surrounding intersections.

_____12. Contact the city's Streets Division to bring barricades for intersections to assist in traffic control.

_____13. Call sheriff's office to have a bomb technician respond.

_____14. Document other behaviors or actions not listed above.

_____   **RATING**

Planning and Organizing Behaviors

_____ 1. Follow SOPs for shutting down communications.

_____ 2. Make contact with bank manager.

_____ 3. Call in fire rescue medics if necessary.

_____ 4. Act on any additional information.

_____ 5. Document other behaviors or actions not listed above.

_____   **RATING**

Judgment/Decision-Making Behaviors

_____ 1. Get notification that officers have arrested the suspect.

_____ 2. Make sure the money recovered is secured.

_____ 3. Follow SOPs for shutting down communications.

_____ 4. Act on additional information.

_____ 5. Check with all officers at posts.

_____ 6. Check on barricades and crime scene tape.

_____ 7. Contact PIO.

Exhibit 13   269

____ 8. Evacuate bank and surrounding buildings.

____ 9. Notify captains and Detective Bureau.

____10. Set up area perimeter and around building

____11. Take suspect to talk to FBI agents as it was a federally insured bank.

____12. Send officers to block off all surrounding intersections.

____13. Contact city's Streets Division to bring barricades for traffic control.

____14. Call Sheriff's Office to have bomb technician respond.

____15. Document other behaviors or actions not listed above.

____ **RATING**

Interpersonal

____ 1. Make sure patrons and employees are checked to ensure they are not injured.

____ 2. Check with all officers at posts.

____ 3. Arrange for water to be brought over due to heat of day.

____ 4. Made arrangements for officers to be relieved.

____ 5. Call other officers in early or approve overtime if scene lasts a long time and officers need to be relieved.

____ 6. Document other behaviors or actions not listed above.

____ **RATING**

Written Communication

_____ 1. Utilized correct grammar.

_____ 2. Utilized correct grammar.

_____ 3. Utilized correct spelling.

_____ 4. Utilized appropriate sentence and paragraph structure.

_____ 5. Utilized appropriate punctuation.

_____ 6. Utilized appropriate word usage.

_____ 7. Wrote legibly.

_____ **RATING**

SCENARIO 3
MOST APPROPRIATE BEHAVIORS/ACTIONS

✓ Check All Behaviors That Apply

Perception and Analysis Behaviors

_____ 1. Check with IA to check on his or her record.

_____ 2. If no other priors then decide how to deal with the issue.

_____ 3. If no priors, issue a written warning.

_____ 4. Prevent them from signing up for any other details for 30 days.

_____ 5. Document other behaviors or actions not listed above.

_____ **RATING**

Exhibit 13 271

Planning and Organizing Behaviors

____ 1. Prevent them from signing up for any other details for 30 days.

____ 2. Write them up according to SOP.

____ 3. Tell them what will happen according to SOPs.

____ 4. Document other behavior or actions not listed above.

____ **RATING**

Decision-Making/Judgment Behaviors

____ 1. Talk to officer and counsel them.

____ 2. Find out precisely what happened and why.

____ 3. Send officer over to stand by until another officer could go there, if available.

____ 4. Write officer up according to SOPs.

____ 5. Tell them will happen according to SOPs.

____ 6. Write up the disciplinary action.

____ 7. Have them sign it.

____ 8. Distribute copies.

____ 9. Document other behaviors or actions not listed above.

____ **RATING**

Interpersonal Behaviors

____ 1. Talk to officer and counsel them.

____ 2. Send officer over to stand by until another officer could go there, if available.

____ 3. Write officer up according to SOPs.

____ 4. Tell them what will happen according to SOPs.

____ 5. Write up the disciplinary action and explain why.

____ 6. Document other behaviors or actions not listed above.

____ **RATING**

Written Communication

____ 1. Utilized correct grammar.

____ 2. Utilized correct spelling.

____ 3. Utilized appropriate sentence and paragraph structure.

____ 4. Utilized appropriate punctuation.

____ 5. Utilized appropriate word usage.

____ 6. Wrote legibly.

____ **RATING**

SCENARIO 4
MOST APPROPRIATE BEHAVIORS/ACTIONS

✓ Check All Behaviors That Apply

Perception and Analysis Behaviors

____ 1. Carefully review all forms.

Exhibit 13 273

____ 2. Determine which officers are padding forms.

____ 3. Document the padding of forms for each officer's record.

____ 4. Review data and determine if there is a pattern.

____ 5. Determine which G.O. or SOP has been violated and document it.

____ 6. Document other behaviors or actions not listed above.

____ **RATING**

Planning and Organizing Behaviors

____ 1. Set up meetings with officers who have padded forms.

____ 2. Meet with captain to discuss situation.

____ 3. Set up meeting with entire shift to review situation.

____ 4. Meet with offenders, counsel and discipline.

____ 5. Document other behaviors or actions not listed above.

____ **RATING**

Judgment/Decision Behaviors

____ 1. Determine disciplinary action to take.

____ 2. Determine pattern if any.

____ 3. Meet with entire shift to discuss the padding of forms.

____ 4. Direct staff not to do this anymore.

____ 5. Start to go and monitor staff more.

____ 6. Tell them what actions will be taken if anyone continues to pad forms, especially what will happen to repeat offenders.

____ 7. Document other behaviors or actions not listed above.

____ **RATING**

Written Communication

____ 1. Utilized correct grammar.

____ 2. Utilized correct spelling.

____ 3. Utilized appropriate sentence and paragraph structure.

____ 4. Utilized appropriate punctuation.

____ 5. Utilized appropriate word usage.

____ 6. Wrote legibly.

____ **RATING**

Exhibit 14

ABC POLICE DEPARTMENT
COMMUNITY POLICING PROBLEM
ANALYSIS EXERCISE
LIEUTENANT
ASSESSOR GUIDE

Candidate #:_____ Assessor Name #:_____

Date:_____

RATING TABULATION MATRIX

Skill Dimension	Tentative Score	Final Score
Problem Analysis		
Judgment		
Planning and Organizing		
Written Communication		
FINAL OVERALL RATING:		

MOST APPROPRIATE PROBLEM ANALYSIS BEHAVIORS/ACTIONS

✓ Check All Behaviors That Apply

____ 1. Used the SARA model or some other problem-solving methodology with respect to problem analysis.

____ 2. Referenced *scan* and list ideas reference scanning.

____ 3. Would make plans to go out and see if there is a real problem. Will talk to people and find out if they really have a problem with the lack of police officers in the park during football games.

____ 4. Look at the history of problems in the park and with traffic.

____ 5. Determine if the juvenile problem still existed when no football games were being played.

____ 6. Listed other feasible ideas and likely solutions besides the above.

____ 7. Referenced *analyze* and listed ideas reference to analyze.

____ 8. Would determine who the players are: school officials, the parents, park staff, residents and students, and football fans who attend games.

____ 9. Noted to *analyze* what has been done in the past to manage large gatherings of teens in park, traffic jams during sporting events, fights in the park, etc.

____ 10. Considered outside resources—such as high school security officers, the sheriff's office, the local police department where high school is located.

Exhibit 14 277

____11. Would gather as much data as possible about the problems and find out what strategies have been successful and unsuccessful.

____12. Provided other feasible solutions with respect to analyze addition to the above.

____13. Referenced *response* and noted.

____14. The number of officers needed to cover park during ball games.

____15. That the department should coordinate with school staff and other police

____16. Departments to handle flow of traffic.

____17. The department should hold community meetings and meetings with school officials.

____18. Consider changes in park to discourage students from loitering in the park during ball games, such as having all the sprinkler systems come on at that time, or employing traffic devices to allow them to get out safely.

____19. Considered impact on all other patrol units in regard to increased staffing at these times.

____20. Referred to assess, in noting that the department should follow up to see if the above interventions have solved the problems.

____21. Would do periodic reassessments to determine if additional attention is needed.

____22. Document other behaviors or actions not listed above.

____ **RATING**

MOST APPROPRIATE JUDGMENT/DECISION-MAKING BEHAVIORS/ACTIONS

✓ Check All Behaviors That Apply

_____ 1. Utilized the SARA model or some other logical and workable problem-solving methodology to respond to these problems.

_____ 2. Re-identified the issues and problems when noting how she or he would work to solve them.

_____ 3. Would seek expert opinions and assistance when designing a plan, including the captain, school security officials, park employees, school administrators, and other police departments.

_____ 4. Noted in writing that if strategies did not work, they would develop and implement alternatives.

_____ 5. Utilized sound judgment when identifying courses of action, including stationing more police officers in park, making changes to the park, holding meetings with school officials and members of the community, and obtaining a football schedule so department can plan ahead for the games.

_____ 6. Noted that he or she would conduct research before implementing any plan as part of the analyze phase of the SARA process.

_____ 7. Document other behaviors or actions not listed above.

_____ **RATING**

Exhibit 14 279

MOST APPROPRIATE PLANNING AND ORGANIZING BEHAVIORS/ACTIONS

✓ Check All Behaviors That Apply

_____ 1. Report was well-organized and planned.

_____ 2. Report included what would be expected of staff in dealing with the problems addressed.

_____ 3. Report included a timeline and schedule.

_____ 4. Plan included who would attend meetings.

_____ 5. Plan included organization and allocation of manpower and other designated resources that would assist in achieving the goals of solving problems addressed in exercise.

_____ 6. Responded to each component of the problem(s).

_____ 7. Followed the instructions.

_____ 8. Finished plan in the allotted one hour and fifteen minutes.

_____ 9. Document other behaviors or actions not listed above.

_____ **RATING**

LIST OF EXPECTED RESPONSES IN WRITTEN DOCUMENT

✓ Check All Behaviors That Apply

Note: The actions below are many which the candidate should put in their written document. Also, the actions may fall under more than one skill dimension.

_____ 1. Meet with sergeants and staff to work out plans.

_____ 2. Emphasize to them it is not "Us against them."

_____ 3. Meet with school officials and obtain football schedule.

_____ 4. Strategize as to how could we better use our park rangers to help with managing congregating kids.

_____ 5. Have them call us before the crowd of teens gets too large.

_____ 6. Set up Neighborhood Watch groups; tell them that games will be occurring so we can be there before there are so many cars jammed up.

_____ 7. Have parents reinforce the importance of watch groups.

_____ 8. Work with community on regular basis.

_____ 9. Use all resources—not just the Police Department.

_____10. Provide more training to officers.

_____11. Reward and champion guys who are solving the problems.

_____12. Share success stories with shift.

_____13. Talk about training and make aware of community problems.

_____14. Schedule meetings at city hall with Parks and Recreation and Leisure Affairs.

_____15. Set up a training program with city hall personnel.

_____16. Note that it is a collaborative effort—call upon city staff.

_____17. Note that the community policing staff should make use of other city agencies (e.g., some things may be better handled by Engineering and Environmental Design Services).

_____18. Think outside the box.

Exhibit 14 281

_____19. Ensure open communication.

_____20. Have sector officers assigned to area.

_____21. Obtain ongoing reports on process.

_____22. Have officers identify quality of life issues with residents.

_____23. Address the root problems.

_____24. Ensure staff is looking at big picture and identifying ways to solve the problems.

_____25. Come up with solutions; route vehicles from area, get brighter lighting there.

_____26. Overall, teach citizens and employees what to do to solve problems in community.

_____27. Pull all divisions together to help with assistance.

_____28. Deal with people parking illegally or parking on homeowner's property.

_____29. Document other behaviors or actions not listed above.

Note: A rating is not assigned to the latter items because the written sections are scored using the checklist below.

MOST APPROPRIATE WRITTEN COMMUNICATION

✓ Check All Behaviors That Apply

_____ 1. Utilized correct grammar.

_____ 2. Utilized correct spelling.

_____ 3. Utilized appropriate sentence and paragraph structure.

____ 4. Utilized appropriate punctuation.

____ 5. Utilized appropriate word usage.

____ 6. Wrote legibly.

____ **RATING**

Exhibit 15

ABC POLICE DEPARTMENT
WRITTEN ESSAY(S) EXERCISE
CAPTAIN
ASSESSOR GUIDE

Candidate #:_____ Assessor Name #:_____

Date:_____

RATING TABULATION MATRIX

Question Topic	P&O	LD	IP	P&A	J/DM	WC
New Technologies: Promoting, Implementing, Maintaining						
Mission Statement and Goals						
Broken Windows						
Dealing with the Mentally Ill						
FINAL OVERALL RATING:						

1. NEW TECHNOLOGIES: PROMOTING/ IMPLEMENTING/MAINTAINING

Most Appropriate Planning and Organizing Behaviors/Actions

✓ Check All Behaviors That Apply

_____ 1. Read as much as I can about the department; read all of the most important files and reports; get to know the different sections; learn who is who in each division.

_____ 2. Set up meetings with key department personnel (individually or in groups as appropriate) in each bureau or section based upon my assignments.

_____ 3. Read policies and procedures (directives, general orders) related to each section.

_____ 4. Visit different sections' work sites.

_____ 5. Review all staff personnel files.

_____ 6. Manage my time accordingly.

_____ 7. Handle high priority work first and as it comes in.

_____ 8. Meet with my boss and get to know them.

_____ 9. Meet with all city officials and community representatives.

_____ 10. Plan to make a formal presentation to city officials regarding my overall vision and plans for change and improvement when and where appropriate.

_____ 11. Document other behaviors or actions not listed above.

_____ **RATING**

Exhibit 15 285

MOST APPROPRIATE LEADERSHIP BEHAVIORS/ACTIONS

✓ Check All Behaviors That Apply

_____ 1. Need to get to know who is who in the organization in order to be effective.

_____ 2. Collaborate with lieutenants and sergeants to solve cases.

_____ 3. Seek out help and information from my supervisor and other staff members to be the most effective.

_____ 4. Reading the department directives will help me with my job and to get up to speed the fastest.

_____ 5. Need to work as a team with everyone to obtain information from key people within the organization.

_____ 6. Meeting with and getting to know key personnel will help me solve cases.

_____ 7. Document other behaviors or actions not listed above.

_____ **RATING**

2. MISSION STATEMENT AND GOALS

Most Appropriate Planning and Organizing Behaviors/Actions

✓ Check All Behaviors That Apply

_____ 1. Would study and address response calls for assistance especially in urgent situations.

_____ 2. Placed suggested goals in priority order.

_____ 3. Somehow address individual and property rights and civil rights).

_____ 4. Mentioned or implies protection of Fourth Amendment rights.

_____ 5. Included a timeline for the implementation and dissemination of each goal.

_____ 6. Addressed school-based educational programs such as D.A.R.E. and gang membership avoidance programs.

_____ 7. Wrote about community involvement in crime prevention and other ways the police department and the community can work together to build a stronger bond.

_____ 8. Mentions community policing as an aspect of one goal.

_____ 9. Document other behaviors or actions not listed above.

_____ **RATING**

3. BROKEN WINDOWS

Most Appropriate Perception and Analysis Behaviors/Actions

✓ Check All Behaviors That Apply

_____ 1. Looks at models in other communities where crime prevention programs have succeeded.

_____ 2. Addresses both positive and negative aspects of the Broken Windows Theory.

_____ 3. Provides personal experiences with the theory.

_____ 4. Uses such terms as "proactive disorder enforcement," "hot-spot policing" or "zero-tolerance policing."

_____ 5. Discusses increase in misdemeanor arrests.

Exhibit 15   287

____ 6. In some way referred to the concept embodied in the statement, "If a window is broken and left unrepaired, all the rest of the windows will soon be broken."

____ 7. Document other behaviors or actions not listed above.

____ **RATING**

4. DEALING WITH THE MENTALLY ILL

Most Appropriate Planning and Organizing Behaviors/Actions

✓ Check All Behaviors That Apply

____ 1. Addressed need for caution in dealing with the mentally ill, many of whom are homeless.

____ 2. Discussed the use, and the dangers, of using non-lethal deterrents.

____ 3. Included module in *all* in-service training manuals.

____ 4. Provided the definitions of *mentally ill.*

____ 5. Would research model programs employed by other communities.

____ 6. Would consider community-based workshops.

____ 7. Would consults and coordinate with medical and EMR personnel in advising patrol officers.

____ 8. Outlined alternatives ranging from warnings, psychiatric hospital placement to outright arrests, and discussed the consequences of each.

____ 9. Would gather and circulate information concerning community mental health facilities.

_____ 10. Would establish a rapid response team to be called to a scene where officers believe the mentally ill individual is possibly a danger to them self or others.

_____ 11. Document other behaviors or actions not listed above.

_____   **RATING**

MOST APPROPRIATE WRITTEN COMMUNICATION

✓ Check All Behaviors That Apply

_____   1. Utilized correct grammar.

_____   2. Utilized correct spelling.

_____   3. Utilized appropriate sentence and paragraph structure.

_____   4. Utilized correct punctuation.

_____   5. Utilized appropriate word usage.

_____   6. Wrote legibly.

_____   **RATING**

Exhibit 16

ABC POLICE DEPARTMENT
SUBORDINATE COUNSELING EXERCISE
SERGEANT
ASSESSOR GUIDE

Candidate #:_____ Assessor Name #:_____

Date:_____

RATING TABULATION MATRIX

Skill Dimension	Tentative Score	Final Score
Judgment/Decision-Making		
Relationships with Others		
Leadership		
Oral Communication		
FINAL OVERALL RATING:		

MOST APPROPRIATE JUDGMENT/
DECISION-MAKING BEHAVIORS/ACTIONS

✓ Check All Behaviors That Apply

_____ 1. Told the role-player the purpose of the meeting was to discuss a sexual harassment complaint made against him and see if there were relevant personal problems.

_____ 2. Reviewed the role-player's current problems and acknowledged concern for his situation.

_____ 3. Asked role-player for his side of the story.

_____ 4. Told him that the allegations would be investigated by IA and/or the Human Resources Department.

_____ 5. Advised him of the seriousness of the offense if substantiated.

_____ 6. Directed him not to engage in this kind of behavior in the future, especially when the role-player admits to doing what he was accused of doing.

_____ 7. Told role-player that disciplinary action may be taken against him and why.

_____ 8. Explained the reasons for such disciplinary action.

_____ 9. Explained that any retaliation against his accuser would be illegal and in violation of current policy and federal law.

_____10. Redirected the conversation to the information at hand when the role-player acted as though he had done nothing wrong or blamed the complainant.

_____11. Asked about his recent divorce and if it may have any correlation to the behavior leading to the harassment allegation, suggesting that stress or anger might have been motivating factors.

Exhibit 16 291

____12. Asked if role-player's financial problems might have contributed his stress or anger level.

____13. Asked if his son's recent accident might have contributed to his stress level, especially in combination with the other stressors in his life.

____14. Offered him assistance with problems: a referral to the EAP, more time off—although all his FMLA time had been used up. Perhaps use of the sick leave pool, or PBA assistance might be considered.

____15. Solicited his input on these issues.

____16. Assured him of the confidentiality of the complaint and their discussion.

____17. Document other behaviors or actions not listed above.

____ **RATING**

MOST APPROPRIATE RELATIONSHIPS WITH OTHERS BEHAVIORS/ACTIONS

✓ Check All Behaviors That Apply

____ 1. Asked the role-player to have a seat.

____ 2. Advised him of the importance of the meeting with him, the candidate, to discuss a few issues.

____ 3. Established rapport with role-player.

____ 4. Listened attentively to the role-player's explanation of the alleged sexual harassment before responding.

____ 5. Listened to him vent about his personal problems.

_____ 6. Politely interrupted occasionally, especially when time was running short, noting that they still had not gone over all the essential issues.

_____ 7. Tried to calm him down when his monologue about his personal problems grew angry, especially when he contended that Ryan was the instigator and she was being flirtatious.

_____ 8. Empathized with him about his recent divorce, child's accident and the resulting emotional trauma.

_____ 9. Offered financial assistance (e.g., time off from the PBA sick leave pool, or ask other officers donate time to him).

_____10. Assured him that the department would investigate the complaint thoroughly and that he would not be retaliated against, that his status would not change.

_____11. Apologized that a meeting about a serious matter had to be their first encounter.

_____12. When attempting to calm him down spoke in a soft and pleasant voice.

_____13. Continued to calm the role-player down whenever he was complaining that Ryan was the instigator and is known for flirting with the guys.

_____14. Maintained a pleasant but firm demeanor.

_____15. Tactfully and effectively handled the situation.

_____16. Document other behaviors or actions not listed above.

_____ **RATING**

Exhibit 16 293

MOST APPROPRIATE PLANNING AND ORGANIZING BEHAVIORS/ACTIONS

✓ Check All Behaviors That Apply

_____ 1. Explained the complaint to the role-player and told him why he was asked to come to the meeting.

_____ 2. Explained the procedures regarding investigating sexual harassment complaints.

_____ 3. Reviewed items in the role-player's personnel file (a commendation, one unsustained citizen complaint, his divorce) and showed the items to the role player.

_____ 4. Explained to role-player what type of behavior was expected of him based on internal G.O.s and other city policies and procedures.

_____ 5. Did not fidget or shuffle papers during meeting.

_____ 6. Completed meeting in the time allotted for the exercise.

_____ 7. Did not allow role player to dominate the meeting, while allowing him to vent and express his concerns, but interrupted him and responded in an organized manner).

_____ 8. Demonstrated an appropriate level of assertiveness without being aggressive.

_____ 9. Accomplished all goals of the meeting within the time allotted.

_____ 10. Set a date and time for a follow-up meeting to assess the need for more time off as result of investigation.

_____ 11. Document other behaviors or actions not listed above.

_____ **RATING**

MOST APPROPRIATE LEADERSHIP
BEHAVIORS/ACTIONS

✓ Check All Behaviors That Apply

_____   1. Asked role player if he knew that a female officer had filed a sexual harassment complaint against him and gave him the opportunity to respond.

_____   2. Told him directly about the complaint and thus the purpose of meeting.

_____   3. Acknowledged to him that he was aware of his personal problems and would provide whatever support and assistance he could.

_____   4. Told him of the seriousness of the offense if substantiated, that it was a violation of current G.O. and personnel policies and of federal law.

_____   5. Asked him for his side of story, listened, and solicited his comments on it.

_____   6. Directed him not to engage in this kind of behavior in future, especially after when role-player admits to doing what he was accused of doing.

_____   7. Told role-player the possible disciplinary actions that may be taken against him.

_____   8. Explained to them the reasons for such disciplinary action.

_____   9. Explained possible courses of action, that IA or the Human Resources department will investigate and determine the appropriate disciplinary action.

_____ 10. Explained to him that retaliation against his accuser was illegal, and in violation of current policy and the law.

Exhibit 16 295

____11. Told him importance of all officers following policies and procedures.

____12. Told role-player that their behavior would be monitored.

____13. Informed him that he or she would be writing a memo about their meeting as documentation for the record.

____14. Directed him to read all G.O.s and personnel policies and procedures pertinent to sexual harassment.

____15. Document other behaviors or actions not listed above.

____ **RATING**

MOST APPROPRIATE ORAL COMMUNICATION (VERBAL APTITUDE) BEHAVIORS/ACTIONS

✓ Check All Behaviors That Apply

____ 1. Maintained eye contact with role player.

____ 2. Spoke at a moderate volume, neither too loud or too soft.

____ 3. Spoke with poise and confidence.

____ 4. Listened attentively when role player was speaking.

____ 5. Used changes in voice inflection when appropriate.

____ 6. Document other behaviors or actions not listed above.

____ **RATING**

Exhibit 17

ABC POLICE DEPARTMENT
SUBORDINATE COUNSELING EXERCISE
SERGEANT
ROLE PLAYER SCRIPT

Today is May 30th. You are to assume the role of police Officer Alec Baldwin. You have been called to a meeting with your supervisor, Sgt. Kevin Spacey. When he tells you what the meeting is about, you act surprised and irritated. Throughout the exercise you are to assume an ***angry, stressed out, and belligerent attitude***.

Your demeanor is based on the following negative events that have recently occurred in your life:

- You just completed your divorce proceedings.
- Your wife is trying to clean you out financially and obtain full custody of your son.
- Your wife is marrying a police officer from another agency.
- Your son was recently in a fairly serious car accident and spent some time in the hospital and has still not fully recovered.
- You have used up most of your allowed FMLA leave and won't be able to take more time off to be with him unless the department approves it.
- His accident cost you and your ex-wife a lot of money. The department's insurance policy did not cover up all those costs—and you are angry about that, too.

You are angry at all female officers in the department, which is the result of their unwavering support of Officer Meg Ryan, the complainant. You knew that she was going to make a formal complaint about

Exhibit 17 297

you—that you sexually harassed her—but you believe she is to blame because she is a big flirt and asks for it. But you do not think your behavior was sexual harassment. You know the charges are unfounded. On the other hand, you have never bothered to read the department's general order regarding sexual harassment.

Although the aforementioned events are the cause of your negative demeanor, do not admit this to Sgt. Spacey unless he probes for details or provides moral support.

Note: The candidate should be aware of all of these events as all of the information has been provided to them.

Initial Statements During First Few Minutes of Exercise

You are to act irritated and speak in an ***angry, belligerent manner and in a stressed tone of voice***. You are also to look around the room and maintain eye contact with the candidate only occasionally. Overall, do not speak unless the candidate asks for specific information, for your input, or how things are affecting you. Otherwise, just nod your head, sit there and keep glancing at your watch.

If the candidate attempts to establish rapport with you, asks you how you are doing, or how everything is going, show some interest and say something like, "I am fine, considering all I have been through. These past few months have been horrendous. I've had very little sleep if any, my wife has taken me to the cleaners, my son is still out of commission and the insurance companies stink. Hell, right now, life stinks!"

If the candidate probes for specifics about your personal life (how your son is doing, how you are doing after the divorce, say), say something like, "Just fine, considering. But, I am still worried about my son and hope my wife doesn't get total custody."

If the candidate shows empathy and concern for your recent problems, become a little less angry and say, "Thanks for your concern, Sarge. I didn't think anyone in the department cares. The insurance people certainly don't give a damn. Let me tell you, the last few months have been just terrible for me."

If the candidate explores the issue of your comment about insurance, tell him, "They won't cover all my son's medical bills and now I have no more leave time left. I wish I could get some help here."

If the candidate offers financial assistance or other services, back down a bit, be more laid back and less belligerent.

If the candidate indicates that considering the situation with your son's health, an exception might be made to allow you extra time off or suggests that other officers might be able to donate sick time, say, "Gee, thanks. What a shock." But say it in a cooperative way.

If the candidate commends you on your good work record or mention the commendation, say, "Thanks, it's no big deal. I'm glad someone around here recognizes the good stuff."

If the candidate suggests that you see someone with EAP, say, "Do you think I really need this?"

Statements and Demeanor During Next Few Minutes of Exercise (If/After Rapport Has Been Established)

When the candidate brings up the issue of Officer Ryan's complaint of sexual harassment, which is the main reason the meeting was called, laugh and then say, "I knew she was going to do this. What a joke. She's the instigator and she loves it. What a troublemaker she is. She will never be accepted now."

When the candidate asks you for specific details about what happened, say, "I made a few comments to her, and touched her around the waist and looked at her. I told you, she loved it."

If the candidate asks you about the specific comments you made say, "I don't recall exactly, but they had something to do with her body and the way she walks."

When the candidate mentions anything like there will be a formal investigation, or that you violated department and city policies, or that you could be disciplined for this, reply: "Why? I didn't do anything wrong. She asked for it and started it. Everyone who has worked here for a while knows that she is the troublemaker. She is blowing everything out of proportion and, she incites the other women officers." In other words, at this point you do see or understand the "big picture."

Overall, you are to repeat the aforementioned statements when the candidate brings up anything related to disciplinary actions. Only when and if the candidate becomes more assertive, direct or authoritative with you about the harassment complaint are you to <u>back down</u> and start to accept that what you did to Officer Ryan was wrong and violated policy. You may say, **"Okay, I understand, Sarge, I won't**

Exhibit 17 299

bother her again." But, do tell the candidate that there will be witnesses who can attest to the fact that, **"It was a two-way street,"** with you and Officer Ryan.

Examples of comments the candidate may make which are more authoritative, direct and specific are: **"Officer Baldwin, I understand that you say she started it, but based on the information I have and what you just told me, what you did violated the policy. Officer Baldwin, based on a formal investigation, you may be disciplined and you must take this complaint seriously. And, Officer Baldwin, neither you nor anyone in the organization is to retaliate against anyone who filed any kind of discrimination or harassment charge."**

If the candidate brings up the recent citizen complaint for alleged harassment, deny it and say that you don't recall doing any such thing. If the candidate says that even if the complaint turns out to be unfounded, there might be a relationship between this and officer Ryan's complaint, act puzzled and say, **"I'd probably had a bad day, and I remember the citizen now. It was a bad week for me—and I knew Ryan was going to file charges."**

If and when the candidate directs you to cease any contact with officer Ryan, state, **"Okay, I'll do whatever you say."** If and when the candidate sets up a follow-up meeting with you, say, **"Whenever you want to meet, Sarge, is fine with me."**

If the candidate suggests strongly that you see someone in EAP, accept the suggestion and say, **"I will make an appointment as soon as I can."**

Throughout the rest of the exercise, just respond to the candidate's questions and comments with the same information. Do not add anything different and just sit there and listen to what is said. However, if the candidate never becomes assertive or authoritative with you, just continue to act like the whole situation is Officer Ryan's fault and that she caused it. Also, do not accept blame and keep asserting that she started everything. Also, continue to be belligerent, keep looking at your watch, and say whenever there is a lull in the conversation or the candidate is not making any decisions, say, **"I have a few things to take care of. When is this meeting going to end?"**

Overall, throughout the exercise repeat the aforementioned responses whenever the candidate is:

✓ Not addressing the harassment complaint and just sits there and listens,
✓ Shuffling papers,
✓ Looking irritated,
✓ Acting defensive,
✓ Apparently uninterested in you, does not ask you about any of your recent personal problems,
✓ Not responding to your position that Officer Ryan was the instigator,
✓ Raising their voice and acting nasty, or
✓ Not looking at you and seems distracted.

Otherwise, follow the script as indicated. Do not stray from your position about Officer Ryan, but that you have been very stressed out and angry over the past few months, and be *consistent* throughout with all the candidates. It would be best to memorize verbatim what you are going to say to the candidate.

Exhibit 18

ABC POLICE DEPARTMENT
PROBLEM ANALYSIS
ORAL PRESENTATION EXERCISE
LIEUTENANT
ASSESSOR GUIDE

Candidate #:_____ Assessor Name #:_____

Date:_____

RATING TABULATION MATRIX

Skill Dimension	Tentative Score	Final Score
Planning and Organization		
Analytical Thinking/ Problem-Solving		
Strategic Thinking/Innovation		
Oral Communication		
FINAL OVERALL RATING:		

MOST APPROPRIATE PLANNING AND ORGANIZING BEHAVIORS/ACTIONS

✓ Check All Behaviors That Apply

_____ 1. Completes the entire presentation within the allotted time; addresses all issues mentioned in instructions.

_____ 2. Identifies and clearly allocates manpower needed to solve problems.

_____ 3. Starts presentation by outlining what will be covered.

_____ 4. Arranges for financial and other resources needed to achieve goals and objectives (puts staff on overtime, solicits ideas and assistance from city departments, community groups etc.).

_____ 5. Indicates that staff will be informed as to what is expected of them to accomplish goals and objectives.

_____ 6. Provides timelines for completion of goals and objectives.

_____ 7. Establishes and reviews personal schedule for accomplishing goals and objectives listed in plan.

_____ 8. Indicates need to ensure that sergeants, officers and other personnel understand what is expected of them in order to implement the strategies.

_____ 9. Indicates need to ensure duplication of effort is avoided.

_____ 10. Summarizes presentation before time is called.

_____ 11. Document other behaviors or actions not listed above.

_____ **RATING**

Exhibit 18 303

MOST APPROPRIATE PROBLEM
SOLVING BEHAVIORS/ACTIONS

✓ Check All Behaviors That Apply

_____ 1. Utilizes the zone map or draws a picture on the paper which is on the easel or describes a global picture of the problems.

_____ 2. Uses best practices (SARA model or other accepted practices) to identify problem's causes.

_____ 3. Considers the problems from the perspectives of various stakeholders: parishioners, elderly residents, university staff, city commissioners, city staff, etc. (Considers how stakeholders would view the various strategies for solving the problems).

_____ 4. Maps out the process they use to solve the problems.

_____ 5. Considers issue from a political perspective, considering how the changes might affect citizens, employees, own staff, and senior management.

_____ 6. Considers that strategies outlined to solve the problems may or may not work based on all components in the system: university issues, church issues, funding, etc.

_____ 7. Notes that they would incorporate other viewpoints, such as when and how they will be affected, what their perceptions would be to each proposed solution and the result.

_____ 8. Builds on experience. Asks questions, such as: Has the department faced similar issues in the past? How can I find out? Who was involved and how was it handled? What were the results? What has changed since then for the city? How have other police departments handled similar issues?

_____ 9. Outlines how, where, and when they will gather the information for the analysis, other than that provided in the instructions.

_____10. Notes that they will obtain information needed from staff, peers, or bosses.

_____11. Identifies the criteria they will use for possible solutions.

_____12. Outlines specifically how they will deal with the employee who has not met the assigned deadline.

_____13. Document other behaviors or actions not listed above.

_____ **RATING**

MOST APPROPRIATE STRATEGIC THINKING AND INNOVATION BEHAVIORS/ACTIONS

✓ Check All Behaviors That Apply

_____ 1. Redefines the key problems to the assessors (the university, Walmart, traffic congestion, elderly citizen concerns, problem employee, etc.).

_____ 2. Uses the W questions (why, where, what, who, when and how) in approaching the problems.

_____ 3. Identifies available resources for strategy implementation in presentation.

_____ 4. Convinces assessor panel that his or her proposal will be a significant improvement.

_____ 5. Notes that teams will be formed to include cross-cultural teams, where applicable.

_____ 6. Notes that knowledge-sharing and learning will occur with teams.

_____ 7. Indicates that they will solicit help from other staff and experts who may be able to help implement the strategies.

Exhibit 18 305

_____ 8. Considers the implications of their plans, and weighs the benefits and risks associated with suggested actions.

_____ 9. Notes that they will continually look for alternative ways to work with people that will create better results and better working relationships—and perhaps have ancillary affects such as reducing citizen complaints to the department and then media, reducing fear in the elderly, and improved traffic flow.

_____ 10. Defines the problems from the perspectives of the various stakeholders (the elderly, other residents, employees, the mayor, the department command staff, council members and others).

_____ 11. Identifies and lists for the assessors, work processes that will be involved in dealing with the problems.

_____ 12. Indicates whether they think that the actions being presented will help achieve the goals of the organization.

_____ 13. Identifies the staff, citizens and other people responsible for each part of the process.

_____ 14. Maps out the entire process across all departments, agencies, functional areas and citizen groups that influence the problems.

_____ 15. Document other behaviors or actions not listed above.

_____ **RATING**

Exhibit 19

ABC POLICE DEPARTMENT
CRITICAL INCIDENT EXERCISE
LIEUTENANT
ASSESSOR GUIDE

Candidate #:_____ Assessor Name #:_____

Date:_____

RATING TABULATION MATRIX

Skill Dimension	Tentative Score	Final Score
Judgment/Decision-Making		
Planning and Organization		
Oral Communication		
FINAL OVERALL RATING:		

MOST APPROPRIATE JUDGMENT AND
DECISION-MAKING BEHAVIORS/ACTIONS

✓ Check All Behaviors That Apply

_____ 1. Call in the SWAT team because of the growing crowd and the possibility of a riot and injuries.

_____ 2. Ask sergeant what they have decided to do.

_____ 3. Make sure a perimeter has been established around the bank.

_____ 4. Make sure an outer perimeter has been established and a command post set up.

_____ 5. Make sure Fire Rescue is on alert and ready to respond.

_____ 6. Speak with a few of the officers who arrived on scene first to discuss strategy, while others manage crowd.

_____ 7. Send some officers to the school and have it locked down or evacuated due to shots fired nearby.

_____ 8. Have sergeant and others find the origin of shots.

_____ 9. When SWAT arrives, turn scene over to them to handle, if necessary.

_____10. Speak to the crowd with a bullhorn and urge calm.

_____11. Have officers: separate groups of people who are shoving each other; break up any fistfights; check for injuries; if anyone is injured send them to the EMT trucks.

_____12. If needed, summon a bi-lingual officer to the scene.

_____13. Have officers take pots and anything that can be used as a weapon away from the people.

_____14. Have officers suit up in protective gear once SWAT arrives, if necessary.

_____15. Have officers search out any weapons and perpetrators involved in the shots fired.

_____16. Keep captain informed throughout entire incident.

_____17. Have some officers remove any children from scene to protect them from injury.

_____18. Assigns sergeant to monitor and assist the police officers.

_____19. Consider calling in counselor to sit down with families who are making ethnic and racial slurs to one another.

_____20. Call for more backup if all 8-10 officers are all fully engaged.

_____21. Document other behaviors or actions not listed above.

____   **RATING**

MOST APPROPRIATE PLANNING AND ORGANIZING BEHAVIORS/ACTIONS

✓ Check All Behaviors That Apply

____   1. Immediately find out if anyone has been injured.

____   2. Do a quick assessment of the entire scene. Determine the number of officers needed for crowd control, potential for a riot, etc.

____   3. Ask sergeant specifics on what their plan is now; listen to and assist them, assign them some of my tasks if appropriate.

____   4. Continue to keep dispatch informed while I am in command.

_____ 5. Organize officers into small groups to deal with different aspects of scene; and when back-up officers arrive, assign them to crowd control.

_____ 6. If not enough sergeants available to supervise, ask officers to work in teams or assign someone as the lead decision-maker or call in for another, keep a sergeant on OT, or call someone in early.

_____ 7. Follow-up with officers assigned to the school; continue lock-down of school because of armed robbery.

_____ 8. Follow-up with officers to determine status.

_____ 9. Continue to keep captain informed throughout incident.

_____10. Make plans to meet with all supervisors after incident to discuss what we did right, what we did wrong, what we can do better.

_____11. Assign completing of After-Action Report to sergeants.

_____12. Document other behaviors or actions not listed above.

_____ **RATING**

MOST APPROPRIATE ORAL
COMMUNICATION BEHAVIORS/ACTIONS

✓ Check All Behaviors That Apply

_____ 1. Had effective delivery (vivid, organized, concise, passionate, direct; neither a halting, or caustic).

_____ 2. Used gestures effectively (positive, supportive, and varied).

_____ 3. Maintained eye contact while speaking and listening.

_____ 4. Used appropriate nonverbal communication that facilitated rather than distracted from the presentation.

_____ 5. Spoke clearly at an appropriate rate, enunciated well, avoided speaking in a monotone.

_____ 6. Used appropriate vocabulary, without using jargon, slang, or profanity.

_____ 7. Spoke appropriately and to the point and did not run on before getting to the subject at hand.

_____ 8. Used appropriate changes in voice inflection,

_____ 9. Document other behaviors or actions not listed above.

The candidates are to be rated on the overall quality of their oral communication, rather than looking at the extent to which each behavior listed above was or was not effectively covered. The above behaviors are to be used as guidelines but are not intended to be used to simply tally the number of check marks and compute anyone's score, nor should the number of check marks be used to compare candidates to determine overall ratings for this category.

_____   **RATING**

Exhibit 20

ABC POLICE DEPARTMENT
PROGRAM DEVELOPMENT WRITTEN
AND ORAL PRESENTATION EXERCISE
CAPTAIN
ASSESSOR GUIDE

Candidate #:_____ Assessor Name #:_____

Date:_____

RATING TABULATION MATRIX

Skill Dimension	Tentative Score	Final Score
Problem Analysis/Decision Making		
Planning and Organization		
Interpersonal Relations		
Oral Communication		
Written Communication		
FINAL OVERALL RATING:		

MOST APPROPRIATE PROBLEM ANALYSIS
DECISION-MAKING BEHAVIORS/ACTIONS

✓ Check All Behaviors That Apply

_____ 1. Make social services and other help available for those willing to leave the street and build a new life is covered in the report.

_____ 2. Bring together law enforcement and other organizations, partners and researchers, to address crime problems is covered in report.

_____ 3. Create partnerships among federal, state and local prosecutors, law enforcement, researchers, community leaders and media and outreach specialists, is covered.

_____ 4. Tailor intervention strategies to the needs of gun problems in each district.

_____ 5. Draw on principles of Operation Ceasefire and other programs to not only stop gun violence, but also to shut down open-air drug markets and the chaos that comes with them: street sales, crack houses, drive-through buyers, prostitution, gunplay, and the struggles for control of public space.

_____ 6. Create comprehensive anti-gang initiative programs to address gang membership.

_____ 7. Create a "Gang Resistance Education and Training" (G.R.E.A.T.) program which can be a partnership between the police department and the Bureau of Alcohol, Tobacco, Firearms and Explosives (ATF).

_____ 8. Use the G.R.E.A.T. program to make our young people aware of the consequences if they choose to become involved with gangs or in criminal activity. It will provide them with positive alternatives and ways to avoid involvement. The goal is to decrease gang and youth violence.

_____ 9. Have the police department's police gang officers interact with teenage students and explore alternatives to the perils of gang involvement.

_____10. Help train the city's school resource officers and safe passage volunteers in recognition of signs of gang membership and gang identifiers.

_____11. Host a safe communities' peer exchange, which will laud unusual transparency, authenticity, and integrity as another way to reduce gang and youth violence in city.

_____12. Equip staff members with a set of skills they can apply when engaging with gang members or dealing with the many complexities of the street. We cannot just tell people to stop fighting.

_____13. Use crime data to predict city's hot spots and follow the patterns that develop; find a better system of tracking gangs and gang associates, and employ a crime analyst to help prevent and investigate crimes.

_____14. Have everyone on the force—detectives and patrol officers—gather information about gang members: who members associate with, the kind of vehicle they drive, and places they frequent.

_____15. Have the analyst collect the information and disseminate it to everyone on the job to help police make connections faster when crimes are committed.

_____16. Make life uncomfortable on the gangs' turf with more patrols and arrests, down to violations as minor as blocking a sidewalk.

_____17. Assign the school resource officers to schools with the most, or the most serious, incidents.

_____18. Have gang officers conduct home visits with gang members' families; talk to parents about what their children were doing; visit schools for the same purpose.

_____19. Talk to the kids, call the parents in, and also look for ways to prevent the kids from joining gangs.

_____20. Apply for federal grants from the Project Safe Neighborhoods program to help reduce gun and gang violence. Funding will be used to increase targeted enforcement patrols and identify the gangs' "impact players" who are driving violence in high-crime neighborhoods, and to gather and analyze data on anti-crime and anti-violence programs, and evaluate strategies and best practices.

_____21. Document other behaviors or actions not listed above.

_____   **RATING**

MOST APPROPRIATE PLANNING AND ORGANIZING BEHAVIORS/ACTIONS

✓ Check All Behaviors That Apply

_____ 1. Report included an outline or table of contents.

_____ 2. Outline was prepared in an appropriate format.

_____ 3. Written report was organized; there was a beginning, middle and end.

_____ 4. Report included an introductory statement.

_____ 5. Report included a summary statement.

_____ 6. Report followed the sequence of the outline.

_____ 7. Report did not recap case components or include any extraneous comments.

_____ 8. Written report was no longer than seven pages, was double spaced, and had one-inch margins on all four sides.

_____ 9. Document other behaviors or actions not listed above.

_____ **RATING**

MOST APPROPRIATE DEALING WITH PEOPLE BEHAVIORS/ACTIONS

✓ Check All Behaviors That Apply

_____ 1. Report includes offering valuable programs, lectures, displays, seminars, crime prevention and safety tips to all citizens and community groups free of charge.

_____ 2. Notes that a spirit of cooperation between the public and the police should be fostered which inevitably will lead to a safer environment for everyone.

_____ 3. Make sure gang awareness program informs parents, teachers, community organizations, and other adult groups, on what to look for in our children that may indicate their inclination to join a gang. This program defines what a gang is and how and why it attracts our children.

_____ 4. Make sure program addresses prevention and seeks to eliminate the gang's most precious asset – members; concentrates on marginalized youngsters, potential members, and strives to direct the youths toward positive alternatives, and away from gangs.

_____ 5. Have instructors work together to realize a common goal of protecting our children. Also, conduct a summer component where we mix the curriculum with life skills, self-esteem-building, sports, and other social activities to reinforce the programs.

_____ 6. Have gang officers assigned to the team voluntarily visit and meet with students who are seeking a way out of gangs or want to express their concerns about becoming victims.

_____ 7. Make sure the program reiterates that gang membership is a lifestyle choice that doesn't offer great benefits for the participants—they end up either dead or in prison.

_____ 8. Make sure that the PD is strongly involved in innovative crime prevention work, to connect and reinforce the idea that change can be easy but that sustaining change is really hard, and sustain change by building on strong relationships, both within and among the agencies involved in the work.

_____ 9. Make sure that Victim's Services follows up on any shooting or stabbing the next day, offering victims and their families mental health counseling, support groups, advocacy, and assistance dealing with the state's victim compensation board.

_____10. Schedule weekly gatherings at a recreation center that attracts youths and provide further opportunities to build relationships, learn about and intervene in any simmering feuds, and demonstrate to young men and women how potentially violent situations can be addressed and resolved by nonviolent means.

_____11. Consider offering recreational programs; soccer, baseball, basketball; for children in community; redirect behavior and foster teamwork, one of the most positive values.

_____12. Develop programs especially for teenage women run by female police personnel.

_____13. Consider tapping into former community heroes, such as former or current high school, college or professional sports stars from the area, as well as military vets and others. Strong lessons can be learned from former gang members who have served time in prison but have changed their ways.

_____14. Document other behaviors or actions not listed above.

_____ **RATING**

MOST APPROPRIATE WRITTEN COMMUNICATION BEHAVIORS/ACTIONS

✓ Check All Behaviors That Apply

_____ 1. Used correct grammar.

_____ 2. Used correct spelling.

_____ 3. Used appropriate sentence and paragraph construction, neither too long nor too short; did not overuse bullet points or lists.

_____ 4. Used appropriate punctuation.

_____ 5. Writing was clear and succinct.

_____ 6. Writing was well organized, with a beginning, middle and end.

_____ 7. Wrote appropriately for the audience: police officials, court system, general public, etc.

_____ 8. Outline was prepared in an appropriate format.

_____ 9. Cited references from Internet at end of report.

_____10. Document other behaviors or actions not listed above.

The candidates are rated on the overall quality of their written communication rather than looking at the extent to which each action listed above was or was not covered. The list above is a guide, but it is not in- tended to be tallied and used to compute a score, nor should the number of check marks it be used to compare candidates to determine anyone's overall rating for this category.

_____   **RATING**

Exhibit 21

ABC POLICE DEPARTMENT
LEADERLESS GROUP DISCUSSION EXERCISE
LIEUTENANT
ASSESSOR GUIDE

Candidate #:_____ Assessor Name #:_____

Date:_____

RATING TABULATION MATRIX

Skill Dimension	Tentative Score	Final Score
Planning and Organizing		
Interpersonal Relations		
Perception and Analysis		
Leadership		
Oral Communication		
FINAL OVERALL RATING:		

MOST APPROPRIATE PLANNING AND
ORGANIZING BEHAVIORS/ACTIONS

✓ Check All Behaviors That Apply

_____ 1. Suggests that everyone jot down their ideas and then one person serves as scribe to transfer the information to the easel paper on the stand.

_____ 2. Suggests that meetings be set up.

_____ 3. Indicates the need for sergeants and officers responsible for Zones 2 and 5 collaborate and assist one another as necessary when dealing with Zone 13 calls or issues.

_____ 4. Emphasizes importance of staying on time to get plan prepared before end of the forty-five-minute period.

_____ 5. Indicates need to set up follow-up meetings with this group to monitor plan.

_____ 6. Indicates need to set up follow-up meetings with sergeants on a regular basis for updates to ensure goals and objectives are met.

_____ 7. Indicates need to ensure staff understands what will be expected of them in order to provide police services in Zone 13.

_____ 8. Indicates need to avoid duplication of effort.

_____ 9. When time was running short, suggests that group finalize list and review.

_____10. Asks specific participants to commit to gathering additional information or conducting additional analyses that may be needed in preparation for follow-up meeting to put together a complete plan.

Exhibit 21 321

____11. Document other behaviors or actions not listed above.

____ **RATING**

MOST APPROPRIATE INTERPERSONAL RELATIONSHIPS BEHAVIORS/ACTIONS

✓ Check All Behaviors That Apply

____ 1. Solicits ideas from other participants.

____ 2. Acknowledges contributions made by other participants.

____ 3. Does not interrupt other participants when they are speaking.

____ 4. Shows interests in other participants' ideas by nodding head, looking at the person, showing a positive facial expression.

____ 5. Notes importance of everyone present working together as team to make sure plan is executed.

____ 6. Notes importance of sergeants and police officers working together as a team to make sure plan is executed.

____ 7. Allows others to speak; does not dominate the conversation.

____ 8. Notes that everyone needs to consider suggestions made by others.

____ 9. Indicates need to assure visibility of patrols to engender trust by citizens in the annexed area.

____10. Emphasizes importance of communicating with, and reassuring citizens in the annexed area of our commitment to protecting life and property.

____11. Notes importance of sharing the plan with subordinates who will be involved in implementation.

_____12. Document other behaviors or actions not listed above.

_____ **RATING**

MOST APPROPRIATE PERCEPTION
AND ANALYSIS BEHAVIORS/ACTIONS

✓ Check All Behaviors That Apply

_____ 1. Indicates need to increase patrols on the afternoon and evening shifts.

_____ 2. Suggests stricter code enforcement so landlords who violate codes can be fined for violations more promptly.

_____ 3. Indicates need to increase staffing by at least three officers.

_____ 4. Suggests adding Community Policing, CID, and Traffic Enforcement positions to plan for future needs of annexed area.

_____ 5. Notes that with increased staff comes the need for more vehicles, equipment and other resources, such as firearms, uniforms, and bulletproof vests.

_____ 6. Sees the current problem of having so many types of crimes occurring in the area without additional staffing.

_____ 7. Sees the need to ensure the police department works cooperatively with the sheriff's office.

_____ 8. Points out during discussion that Boutwell Street was not included in the annexed area and that the city cannot enforce traffic laws or any crime on that road (even though the department may still get calls for service from residents there).

_____ 9. Notes that any plan requires persistence and dedication.

Exhibit 21 323

_____10. Perceives that the student housing is not within annexed area but will still create some spillover problems in the city.

_____11. Document other behaviors or actions not listed above.

_____ **RATING**

MOST APPROPRIATE LEADERSHIP BEHAVIORS/ACTIONS

✓ Check All Behaviors That Apply

_____ 1. Suggests the need to identify more specifically the details surrounding Part 1 Crimes to enable specific targeting of police patrols and actions.

_____ 2. Demonstrates enthusiasm to influence and guide others toward the establishment of goals and objectives for the plan.

_____ 3. Comments on other candidates' ideas that may not be workable and notes why.

_____ 4. Maintains a reasonable balance between the more reticent candidates and the more dominant members by redirecting communication as appropriate.

_____ 5. Suggests that part of plan should be to include business owners' interests in any strategies, and to solicit their buy-in and cooperation.

_____ 6. Suggests that group members each take on some detail work for the plan research, information-gathering and the like—to bring to a future meeting to finalize the plan.

_____ 7. Suggests need for that follow-up meeting to put together final details including the budget impact of the additional officers and equipment.

_____ 8. Suggests that police departments of other cities with similar experiences be contacted for their solutions to such a problem, perhaps even some novel, "out of the box" approaches.

_____ 9. Notes that sergeants and police officers need to be included in formulating ideas for the plan in order to obtain their buy-in.

_____ 10. Notes that strategies should focus on things that the department has control over, not related issues over which the department has no control.

_____ 11. Shows support for completing plan, is open to change.

_____ 12. Notes importance of ensuring clear and open communications with subordinates and others involved.

_____ 13. Document other behaviors or actions not listed above.

_____ **RATING**

MOST APPROPRIATE ORAL
COMMUNICATION BEHAVIORS/ACTIONS

✓ Check All Behaviors That Apply

_____ 1. Had an effective delivery (vivid, organized, concise, passionate, direct, and fluent, neither awkward, halting or caustic).

_____ 2. Used gestures effectively (positive, supportive, varied).

_____ 3. Maintained eye contact while speaking *and* listening.

_____ 4. Used appropriate nonverbal communication and other body language that facilitated rather than distracted; didn't tap a pen, shuffle papers, stare at the panel, look around the room, or gaze down at the floor during the presentation.

Exhibit 21   325

_____ 5. Was clear in speaking, talked at an appropriate rate, enunciated well, avoided speaking a monotone.

_____ 6. Used appropriate vocabulary, used no jargon, slang, or profanity.

_____ 7. Spoke appropriately to the point, without excessive wordiness or excessive digression.

_____ 8. Used changes in voice inflection when necessary.

_____ 9. Document other behaviors or actions not listed above.

The candidates are rated on their overall quality of their oral communication, rather than looking at whether the actions listed above were or were not effectively covered. The information above is a guide, but it is not intended to be used to tally the number of checks to compute a score, nor should the count be used to compare candidates to determine their overall rating for this category.

_____   **RATING**

Exhibit 22

ABC POLICE DEPARTMENT
BIAS IN POLICING PROBLEM ANALYSIS
ORAL PRESENTATION EXERCISE
SERGEANT ASSESSOR GUIDE

Candidate #:_____ Assessor Name #:_____

Date:_____

RATING TABULATION MATRIX

Skill Dimension	Tentative Score	Final Score
Planning and Organizing		
Perception and Analysis		
Judgment/Decision Making		
Adaptability		
Oral Communication (Verbal Aptitude)		
FINAL OVERALL RATING:		

Exhibit 22 327

MOST APPROPRIATE PLANNING AND ORGANIZING BEHAVIORS/ACTIONS

✓ Check All Behaviors That Apply

_____ 1. Outlines purpose of presentation and what will be covered without recapping entire set of instructions.

_____ 2. Covers the three topics (analysis, elaborating and describing) included in the instructions.

_____ 3. Indicates how he/she will arrange for any resources needed to achieve goals and objectives (e.g., ideas and assistance from officers, community groups, training materials, etc.).

_____ 4. Indicates that staff will be informed of what is expected of them to reduce bias.

_____ 5. Includes a timeline for dealing with the three issues (i.e., #3 is contingent upon the complaint).

_____ 6. Summarizes each topic covered.

_____ 7. Saves time for questions from audience (i.e., the assessors).

_____ 8. Summarizes presentation before time is called (including time left to respond to questions).

_____ 9. Document other behaviors or actions not listed above.

_____ **RATING**

MOST APPROPRIATE PERCEPTION AND ANALYSIS BEHAVIORS/ACTIONS

✓ Check All Behaviors That Apply

_____ 1. Provides analysis about some of the research findings; (i.e., could/should be used in officer training on bias in policing).

_____ 2. Comments reflect knowledge and awareness of the issue.

_____ 3. Notes that he/she would like to have more information on some of the studies (i.e., not sure how the information can be utilized when dealing with subordinates).

_____ 4. Will use the information to conduct group and one-on-one training sessions with each officer, when necessary.

_____ 5. References importance of monitoring and holding officers accountable.

_____ 6. Recognizes that the research reinforces what has happened in some police departments around the U.S. and is therefore relevant to the police department for which he/she works.

_____ 7. Comments on what he/she knows and has experienced regarding stereotyping; and this topic can be discussed with officers in terms of dealing with citizens.

_____ 8. Notes that the information is important from a political and societal perspective and why.

_____ 9. Comments made reflected that he/she carefully read the research summaries.

_____10. Document other behaviors or actions not listed above.

_____   **RATING**

MOST APPROPRIATE JUDGMENT/DECISION MAKING BEHAVIORS/ACTIONS

✓ Check All Behaviors That Apply

_____ 1. Obtain and review all documentation about the complaint.

_____ 2. Make sure the officers know when a complaint or complaints have been filed against them.

Exhibit 22 329

____ 3. Follow all standard operating procedures (SOPs) applicable to the complaint (e.g., the IAB will be handing the investigation, union, other).

____ 4. Make sure that officers know that all SOPs will be followed regarding their rights.

____ 5. Advise officers that I am there to support them at all times.

____ 6. Make sure the officers understand that if a complaint against them is founded they will be disciplined accordingly.

____ 7. Advise officers that I will not treat them differently during the investigation; e.g., no retaliation.

____ 8. Review each officer's personnel file.

____ 9. Based on nature of complaint may need to provide further reinforcement to officers about biased based complaints.

____10. Assure officers that I will maintain confidentiality of anything we discuss.

____11. Keep my supervisor informed.

____12. Monitor all officers on the job daily or intermittently to ensure they are dealing with citizens and offenders in an appropriate manner and per policies and procedures.

____13. Meet individually with any officer who did not handle a citizen or offender encounter in an acceptable manner (e.g., was rude, raised his/her voice when situation did not call for it, used aggressive or threatening body language, other).

____14. Provide one-on-one coaching with feedback about specific encounter.

_____15. Indicates that each officer must be fully aware of the consequences of engaging in biased-based policing. If not, he or she will be required to receive additional training.

_____16. Document other behaviors or actions not listed above.

_____ **RATING**

MOST APPROPRIATE ADAPTABILITY BEHAVIORS/ACTIONS

✓ Check All Behaviors That Apply

_____ 1. Solicit input and ideas from officers during roll call or individually and on a regular basis.

_____ 2. Ask each officer to provide his/her opinion about why it is important not to engage in bias.

_____ 3. Ask each officer to provide a time when they engaged in biased behavior, what happened and what they would do differently in the future.

_____ 4. Ensure all officers that no one is being singled out or being accused of engaging in bias but the topic must be discussed.

_____ 5. Facilitate after-action meetings with officers to discuss any cases which could have ended in a bias complaint.

_____ 6. Listen for understanding and then allow the officer to present his/her views without prejudice.

_____ 7. Stress that I do not want any officer to be disciplined or possibly lose his/her job based on an unfounded citizen complaint.

_____ 8. Ensure that all officers know that I am there for them (e.g., "I am available to discuss any concerns or recent problems they have had when dealing with citizens").

Exhibit 22 331

____ 9. Make sure they know that my door is always open for them.

____10. Be honest with officers by telling them that we all need to admit that each one of us have biases and used some stereotypes in past.

____11. Emphasize that we need to help one another to not engage in bias, think before we act, ask partner or other officer for input, etc.

____12. Tell all officers that we must be aware of how other's feel about our behaviors and actions and adjust our behavior accordingly.

____13. Reinforces the need for each officer to understand the different perspectives of citizens, offenders, victims, others and adapt to the differences.

____14. Tell officers that we need to focus on how to manage ourselves and recognize that any bad behavior could result in problems for the entire police department.

____15. Document other behaviors or actions not listed above.

____ **RATING**

MOST APPROPRIATE ORAL COMMUNICATION (VERBAL APTITUDE) BEHAVIORS/ACTIONS

✓ Check All Behaviors That Apply

____ 1. Had effective delivery (vivid, organized, concise, passionate, direct; neither a halting nor caustic).

____ 2. Used gestures effectively (positive, supportive, and varied).

____ 3. Maintained eye contact while speaking and listening.

_____ 4. Used appropriate nonverbal communication that facilitated rather than distracted from the presentation.

_____ 5. Spoke clearly at an appropriate rate, enunciated well, avoided speaking in a monotone.

_____ 6. Used appropriate vocabulary, without using jargon, slang, or profanity.

_____ 7. Spoke appropriately and to the point and did not run on before getting to the subject at hand.

_____ 8. Used appropriate changes in voice inflection,

_____ 9. Document other behaviors or actions not listed above.

The candidates are to be rated on the overall quality of their oral communication rather than looking at the extent to which each behavior listed above was or was not effectively covered. The above behaviors are to be used as guidelines but are not intended to be used to simply tally the number of check marks and compute anyone's score, nor should the number of check marks be used to compare candidates to determine overall ratings for this category.

_____ **RATING**

Exhibit 23

ABC POLICE DEPARTMENT
NON-LETHAL USE OF FORCE
TRAINING EXERCISE
SERGEANT
ASSESSOR GUIDE

Candidate #:_____ Assessor Name #:_____

Date:_____

RATING TABULATION MATRIX

Skill Dimension	Tentative Score	Final Score
Planning and Organizing		
Perception and Analysis		
Judgment/Decision Making		
Oral Communication (Verbal Aptitude)		
FINAL OVERALL RATING:		

MOST APPROPRIATE PLANNING AND ORGANIZING BEHAVIORS/ACTIONS

✓ Check All Behaviors That Apply

_____ 1. Outlines purpose of training session and what will be covered without recapping entire set of instructions.

_____ 2. Summarizes the key topics that will be included in the training.

_____ 3. Indicates how he/she will arrange for any resources needed to conduct training for all officers during roll call or other times.

_____ 4. Indicates that staff will be informed of what is expected of them to reduce bias.

_____ 5. Includes a timeline for conducting the training for all officers (e.g., 1 or more months based on size of squad).

_____ 6. Includes number of hours/sessions for the training session.

_____ 7. Summarizes presentation before time is called (including time left to respond to audience questions).

_____ 8. Document other behaviors or actions not listed above.

_____ **RATING**

MOST APPROPRIATE PERCEPTION AND ANALYSIS BEHAVIORS/ACTIONS

✓ Check All Behaviors That Apply

_____ 1. Includes each section of the rule.

_____ 2. Comments reflect knowledge and awareness of the issues.

Exhibit 23 335

____ 3. Recognizes importance of using examples in each section.

____ 4. Recognizes importance of allowing officers to actively participate in the training.

____ 5. References importance of monitoring officer's adherence to the rule and includes in training outline.

____ 6. Recognizes importance of including a question-and-answer session.

____ 7. Recognizes importance of obtaining sample policies and procedures (aka standard operating procedures, directives, etc.) from other departments) to compare and discuss during training.

____ 8. Document other behaviors or actions not listed above.

____ **RATING**

MOST APPROPRIATE JUDGMENT/DECISION MAKING BEHAVIORS/ACTIONS

✓ Check All Behaviors That Apply

____ 1. Outline included open discussions.

____ 2. Outline included videos.

____ 3. Outline included examples of misuse of force and discussions about.

____ 4. Outline included role play exercises.

____ 5. Outline included demonstrations (e.g., use of equipment).

____ 6. Outline included a pre and post quizzes.

_____ 7. Outline included time for question/answer session.

_____ 8. Outline included an evaluation form to a section for open-ended comments.

_____ 9. Document other behaviors or actions not listed above.

_____ **RATING**

MOST APPROPRIATE ORAL COMMUNICATION (VERBAL APTITUDE) BEHAVIORS/ACTIONS

✓ Check All Behaviors That Apply

_____ 1. Had effective delivery (vivid, organized, concise, passionate, direct; neither a halting nor caustic).

_____ 2. Used gestures effectively (positive, supportive, and varied).

_____ 3. Maintained eye contact while speaking and listening.

_____ 4. Used appropriate nonverbal communication that facilitated rather than distracted from the presentation.

_____ 5. Spoke clearly at an appropriate rate, enunciated well, avoided speaking in a monotone.

_____ 6. Used appropriate vocabulary, without using jargon, slang, or profanity.

_____ 7. Spoke appropriately and to the point and did not run on before getting to the subject at hand.

_____ 8. Used appropriate changes in voice inflection,

_____ 9. Document other behaviors or actions not listed above.

Exhibit 23 337

The candidates are to be rated on the overall quality of their oral communication rather than looking at the extent to which each behavior listed above was or was not effectively covered. The above behaviors are to be used as guidelines but are not intended to be used to simply tally the number of check marks and compute anyone's score, nor should the number of check marks be used to compare candidates to determine overall ratings for this category.

____ **RATING**

Exhibit 24

ABC POLICE DEPARTMENT
BODY CAMERAS PROBLEM ANALYSIS ORAL
PRESENTATION AND WRITTEN EXERCISE
LIEUTENANT ASSESSOR GUIDE

Candidate #:_____   Assessor Name #:_____

Date:_____

RATING TABULATION MATRIX

Skill Dimension	Tentative Score	Final Score
Planning and Organizing		
Judgment/Decision Making		
Interpersonal Relationships/ Human Relations		
Oral Communication (Verbal Aptitude)		
Written Communication		
FINAL OVERALL RATING:		

Exhibit 24 339

MOST APPROPRIATE PLANNING AND ORGANIZING BEHAVIORS/ACTIONS

✓ Check All Behaviors That Apply

_____ 1. Identifies specific goals and objectives for the presentation.

_____ 2. Outlines purpose of presentation and what will be covered without recapping entire set of instructions.

_____ 3. Indicates who will be involved in accomplishing the goals and objectives.

_____ 4. Includes a timeline for implementing and using the measurement and evaluation criteria.

_____ 5. Includes a timeline for training of police officers.

_____ 6. Includes plan for storage and retrieval of video feed.

_____ 7. Indicates need to have regular meetings with stakeholders to assess progress.

_____ 8. Indicates need to keep captain informed.

_____ 9. Saves time for questions from audience (i.e., the assessors).

_____ 10. Summarizes presentation before time is called (including time left to respond to questions).

_____ 11. Document other behaviors or actions not listed above.

_____ **RATING**

MOST APPROPRIATE JUDGMENT AND
DECISION MAKING BEHAVIORS/ACTIONS

✓ Check All Behaviors That Apply

_____ 1. Covered all issues included in instructions in presentation.

_____ 2. Pros covered included what is already known nationally about the use of body cameras (i.e., candidate covered some of the research).

_____ 3. Cons covered included what is already known nationally about the use of body cameras (i.e., candidate covered some of the research).

_____ 4. Storage and retrieval part of presentation included currently accepted practices based on national research (i.e., candidate provided some examples of how this is done by other departments).

_____ 5. Covered the state of usage of body cameras around U.S.A. and cites some specific examples of success.

_____ 6. Fully and clearly explained the measurement and evaluation criteria when using body cameras and what it might be for the police department; and made other related comments.

_____ 7. Perceives importance of communicating/sharing ongoing updates regarding implementation of body cameras usage in department.

_____ 8. Perceives importance of comprehensive training for all police officers on how to use body cameras.

_____ 9. Stated his/her opinion concerning the pros and cons of using body cameras.

Exhibit 24   341

_____10. Document other behaviors or actions not listed above.

_____   **RATING**

MOST APPROPRIATE INTERPERSONAL RELATIONSHIPS/
HUMAN RELATIONS BEHAVIORS/ACTIONS

✓ Check All Behaviors That Apply

_____   1. Solicits questions from audience in a tactful manner.

_____   2. Tactfully answers questions from audience, if applicable.

_____   3. References negative impact on community when a police shooting or other incident happens and community has perception that misuse of force took place; may also reference some national cases.

_____   4. Indicates need to assure visibility of the police department in the area to ensure the laws are enforced, etc. regardless of what the perceptions may be.

_____   5. References importance of training of police officers; and that they follow the policies and procedures regarding use of body cameras.

_____   6. Covers the cons of using body cameras with respect to what has occurred nationally; that citizens take their own videos; concern for citizen bystanders, family members and other community stakeholders.

_____   7. Suggests that police department should deliver citizen training overview on how cameras are used, etc. to limit and/or reduce their suspicions.

_____   8. Suggests possible membership (e.g., community stakeholders, police officers, university measurement and evaluation experts, etc.) in committee to develop measurement and evaluation criteria.

____ 9. Notes importance of sharing updates and progress with all stakeholders regarding implementation of using body cameras in department.

____ 10. Document other behaviors or actions not listed above.

____   **RATING**

MOST APPROPRIATE ORAL COMMUNICATION (VERBAL APTITUDE) BEHAVIORS/ACTIONS

✓ Check All Behaviors That Apply

____ 1. Had effective delivery (vivid, organized, concise, passionate, direct; neither a halting nor caustic).

____ 2. Used gestures effectively (positive, supportive, and varied).

____ 3. Maintained eye contact while speaking and listening.

____ 4. Used appropriate nonverbal communication that facilitated rather than distracted from the presentation.

____ 5. Spoke clearly at an appropriate rate, enunciated well, avoided speaking in a monotone.

____ 6. Used appropriate vocabulary, without using jargon, slang, or profanity.

____ 7. Spoke appropriately and to the point and did not run on before getting to the subject at hand.

____ 8. Used appropriate changes in voice inflection,

____ 9. Document other behaviors or actions not listed above.

The candidates are to be rated on the overall quality of their oral communication, rather than looking at the extent to which each behavior

Exhibit 24 343

listed above was or was not effectively covered. The above behaviors are to be used as guidelines but are not intended to be used to simply tally the number of check marks and compute anyone's score, nor should the number of check marks be used to compare candidates to determine overall ratings for this category.

_____ **RATING**

MOST APPROPRIATE WRITTEN COMMUNICATION BEHAVIORS/ACTIONS

✓ Check All Behaviors That Apply

_____ 1. Used correct grammar.

_____ 2. Used correct spelling.

_____ 3. Used appropriate sentence and paragraph construction, neither too long nor too short; did not overuse bullet points or lists.

_____ 4. Used appropriate punctuation.

_____ 5. Writing was clear and succinct.

_____ 6. Writing was well organized, with a beginning, middle and end.

_____ 7. Wrote appropriately for the audience: police officials, court system, general public, etc.

_____ 8. Outline was prepared in an appropriate format.

_____ 9. Document other behaviors or actions not listed above.

The candidates are rated on the overall quality of their written communication rather than looking at the extent to which each action listed above was or was not covered. The list above is a guide, but it is not intended to be tallied and used to compute a score, nor should the number of check marks it be used to compare candidates to determine anyone's overall rating for this category.

____ **RATING**

Exhibit 25

ABC POLICE DEPARTMENT
PRESIDENT'S TASK FORCE ON 21st CENTURY
POLICING WRITTEN AND ORAL
PRESENTATION EXERCISE
CAPTAIN OR DEPUTY CHIEF ASSESSOR GUIDE

Candidate #:_____ Assessor Name #:_____

Date:_____

RATING TABULATION MATRIX

Skill Dimension	Tentative Score	Final Score
Planning and Organizing		
Perception and Analysis		
Adaptability		
Judgment/Decision Making		
Oral Communication (Verbal Aptitude)		
Written Communication		
FINAL OVERALL RATING:		

MOST APPROPRIATE PLANNING AND ORGANIZING BEHAVIORS/ACTIONS

✓ Check All Behaviors That Apply

_____ 1. Outlines purpose of presentation (i.e., the two pillars and sub-components will be covered).

_____ 2. Provides written and oral comments on the two pillars and each subsection.

_____ 3. Summarizes sections of action plan(s) to implement the two pillars.

_____ 4. Summarizes each pillar before moving on to next.

_____ 5. Includes strategies (i.e., action steps) that will help the department to strive to have a diverse workforce with respect to race, gender, religion, and sexual orientation as possible.

_____ 6. Includes strategies (i.e., action steps) that will work to build trust in immigrant communities.

_____ 7. Includes strategies (i.e., action steps) that involve community policing to include cascading it throughout the culture, evaluating officers' efforts to engage members of the community, evaluate the efficacy of team-oriented crisis prevention and work with and collaborate with community residents to achieve meaningful results.

_____ 8. Includes a timeline for preparing and implementing the 2 pillars and sub-components.

_____ 9. Saves time for questions from audience (i.e., the assessors).

_____10. Summarizes presentation before time is called.

_____11. Document other behaviors or actions not listed above.

_____   **RATING**

MOST APPROPRIATE JUDGMENT/DECISION-MAKING BEHAVIORS/ACTIONS

✓ Check All Behaviors That Apply

_____   1. Indicates that a survey should be developed and use to gauge the community's level of trust.

_____   2. Indicates that data can also be collected via re: focus group meetings to determine degree of low morale, why people are leaving the department, and other.

_____   3. Emphasizes importance of obtaining and correctly analyzing data in order to make implement the pillars.

_____   4. Provides comments on his/her experience with similar projects.

_____   5. Notes what department is currently doing to diversify the workforce.

_____   6. Acknowledges that he/she will collaborate with the HR department to facilitate this process as required and/or allowed.

_____   7. Notes that he/she will find out what other departments have done to build trust in their immigrant communities; will borrow some of their best practices.

_____   8. Notes what the department is already doing with regard to non-enforcement activities.

_____   9. Outlines some ways trust can be built with an emphasis on non-enforcement community activities.

_____10. Outlines some strategies he/she will use to cascade community policing throughout the organization.

_____11. Will ensure that subordinate officers document what they are doing to engage members of the community.

_____12. Provides suggestions on how team-oriented crisis intervention can be evaluated.

_____13. Noted that he/she will personally work with and collaborate with residents to identify problems and meaningful results for the community; i.e., attend meetings, speak to residents, support staff with their efforts.

_____14. Articulate his or her support for all community policing efforts on regular basis.

_____15. During change process maintain open lines of communication with staff and ensure that they do the same; the same applies for superiors.

_____16. Identify and endure that implementation of the pillars is continually monitored to sustain engagement.

_____17. Document other behaviors or actions not listed above.

_____ **RATING**

MOST APPROPRIATE ADAPTABILITY BEHAVIORS/ACTIONS

✓ Check All Behaviors That Apply

_____ 1. Solicit input and ideas from officers during roll call or individually and on a regular ongoing basis.

_____ 2. Ask each officer to provide their ideas regarding each pillar.

_____ 3. Notes that he/she will provide support for all subordinates who express their concerns (e.g., are an LGBT person, is an immigrant, lives in an immigrant community).

_____ 4. References importance of making sure that Mayor, city council members, community watch groups, leaders of the clergy and citizens living in the lower economic sections of the city know that he/she and his/her staff will do their best to implement each pillar.

_____ 5. Ensure that all officers know that as their leader, I am there for them (e.g., "I am available to discuss any concerns or recent problems they have had when dealing with citizens who distrust them"; "I will coach them as much as is necessary"; "My door is always open for them").

_____ 6. Will advise officers that "we are in this together" and need to focus on how to implement the pillars.

_____ 7. Document other behaviors or actions not listed above.

_____ **RATING**

MOST APPROPRIATE ORAL COMMUNICATION (VERBAL APTITUDE) BEHAVIORS/ACTIONS

✓ Check All Behaviors That Apply

_____ 1. Had effective delivery (vivid, organized, concise, passionate, direct; neither a halting nor caustic).

_____ 2. Used gestures effectively (positive, supportive, and varied).

_____ 3. Maintained eye contact while speaking and listening.

_____ 4. Used appropriate nonverbal communication that facilitated rather than distracted from the presentation.

_____ 5. Spoke clearly at an appropriate rate, enunciated well, avoided speaking in a monotone.

_____ 6. Used appropriate vocabulary, without using jargon, slang, or profanity.

_____ 7. Spoke appropriately and to the point and did not run on before getting to the subject at hand.

_____ 8. Used appropriate changes in voice inflection,

_____ 9. Document other behaviors or actions not listed above.

The candidates are to be rated on the overall quality of their oral communication, rather than looking at the extent to which each behavior listed above was or was not effectively covered. The above behaviors are to be used as guidelines but are not intended to be used to simply tally the number of check marks and compute anyone's score, nor should the number of check marks be used to compare candidates to determine overall ratings for this category.

_____ **RATING**

MOST APPROPRIATE WRITTEN
COMMUNICATION BEHAVIORS/ACTIONS

✓ Check All Behaviors That Apply

_____ 1. Utilized notes or memos to convey information to people.

_____ 2. Utilized appropriate grammar.

_____ 3. Utilized appropriate spelling.

_____ 4. Utilized appropriate punctuation.

_____ 5. Utilized appropriate word usage.

____ 6. Wrote legibly.

Note: Remember that written communication is evaluated across entire IB on a 1–5 scale for all items.

____ **RATING**

Exhibit 26

ABC POLICE DEPARTMENT
CULTURE CHANGE WRITTEN AND
ORAL PRESENTATION EXERCISE
POLICE CHIEF
ASSESSOR GUIDE

Candidate #:_____   Assessor Name #:_____

Date:_____

RATING TABULATION MATRIX

Skill Dimension	Tentative Score	Final Score
Planning and Organizing		
Perception and Analysis		
Adaptability		
Judgment/Decision Making		
Oral Communication (Verbal Aptitude)		
Written Communication		
FINAL OVERALL RATING:		

MOST APPROPRIATE PLANNING AND
ORGANIZING BEHAVIORS/ACTIONS

✓ Check All Behaviors That Apply

_____ 1. Outlines purpose of presentation and what will be covered without recapping entire set of instructions.

_____ 2. Covers the four topics included in the instructions in the presentation and paper.

_____ 3. Outlines plans for cascading the culture changes throughout the department.

_____ 4. Includes plans for resolving the turnover and recruitment problems (e.g., recognition, regular feedback, support, find out what other departments are doing to recruit (e.g., sign-on bonuses, moving expenses other out of the box ideas) and other.

_____ 5. Includes a timeline for preparing and implementing a strategic plan.

_____ 6. Includes a timeline for completing different sections of plan.

_____ 7. Summarizes each topic before moving on to next topic.

_____ 8. Saves time for questions from audience (i.e., the assessors).

_____ 9. Summarizes presentation before time is called (including time left to respond to questions).

_____10. Document other behaviors or actions not listed above.

_____ **RATING**

MOST APPROPRIATE JUDGMENT/DECISION MAKING BEHAVIORS/ACTIONS

✓ Check All Behaviors That Apply

_____ 1. Indicates that data will be collected via a survey (i.e., employee opinion survey) to determine degree of low morale, why people are leaving the department, and other.

_____ 2. Indicates that data can also be collected via re: focus group meetings to determine degree of low morale, why people are leaving the department, and other.

_____ 3. Emphasizes importance of obtaining and correctly analyzing data in order to make evidence-based culture change decisions.

_____ 4. Provides comments on his/her experience with similar projects.

_____ 5. Will ensure that representatives from all ranks and departments participate in ideas for changes; continually reinforce this; their input is critical – they need to own the changes that they have supported.

_____ 6. Recognizes importance and problem with officers who have resigned.

_____ 7. Plan includes retention strategies (e.g., bonuses, job enlargement/enrichment, empowerment, other).

_____ 8. Recognizes importance of dealing with bias problems and taking all actions necessary to prevent it.

_____ 9. Will ensure that officers who have engaged in excessive force receive more training, discipline or other interventions as appropriate.

____10. Reinforce my continual commitment ensuring change takes place.

____11. Will ensure that training includes relevant, up-to-date and valid scenarios; time to practice, other.

____12. Make sure early-warning system identifies problem officers who are beginning to display unprofessional or unethical behavior.

____13. Share my vision for department with all staff, my superiors and city officials where and when appropriate.

____14. During change process maintain open lines of communication with staff and ensure that they do the same; the same applies for superiors.

____15. Identify and endure that implementation of change process is continually monitored to sustain engagement.

____16. Document other behaviors or actions not listed above.

____ **RATING**

MOST APPROPRIATE ADAPTABILITY BEHAVIORS/ACTIONS

✓ Check All Behaviors That Apply

____ 1. Ensure that command staff solicit input and ideas from officers during roll call or individually and on a regular on-going basis.

____ 2. Ask each officer to provide opinions about why it is important not to engage in bias.

____ 3. Indicates that change doesn't come easy for most law enforcement agencies; notes whether introducing new policies, procedures, or technology, most law enforcers are culturally resistant to change.

_____ 4. Notes that he/she needs to deal any employee concerns about how their relationship(s) may change because of the changes taking place (e.g., new job responsibilities, union contract, change in organizational structure, other).

_____ 5. References importance of making sure that Mayor, city council members, community watch groups, leaders of the clergy and citizens living in the lower economic sections of the city know that he/she and his/her staff will do their best to make changes which will address everyone's concerns.

_____ 6. Recognizes that his/her and the employee's expectations change and grow over time and subsequently he/she will adapt to this accordingly.

_____ 7. Will reinforce to employees that it is important that they find meaning and purpose in their work.

_____ 8. Ensure that all staff know that as their leader, I am there for them (e.g., "I am available to discuss any concerns or recent problems they have had when dealing with citizens"; "I will coach them as much as is necessary"; "My door is always open for them").

_____ 9. Will make to be transparent and honest with officers by telling them that we all need to admit that we have been biased and used stereotypes in past; no one is perfect; we need to help one another to not engage in bias, think before we act, ask partner or other officer for input, etc.

_____10. Provides the concept of a sense of shared destiny and makes efforts to enroll others so they can see their own interests as being aligned with the organization.

_____11. Will advise officers that "we are in this together" and need to focus on how to manage ourselves and recognize any inappropriate behavior could result in problems for the entire police department.

____12. Document other behaviors or actions not listed above.

____ **RATING**

MOST APPROPRIATE ORAL COMMUNICATION (VERBAL APTITUDE) BEHAVIORS/ACTIONS

✓ Check All Behaviors That Apply

____ 1. Had effective delivery (vivid, organized, concise, passionate, direct; neither halting nor caustic).

____ 2. Used gestures effectively (positive, supportive, and varied).

____ 3. Maintained eye contact while speaking and listening.

____ 4. Used appropriate nonverbal communication that facilitated rather than distracted from the presentation.

____ 5. Spoke clearly at an appropriate rate, enunciated well, avoided speaking in a monotone.

____ 6. Used appropriate vocabulary, without using jargon, slang, or profanity.

____ 7. Spoke appropriately and to the point and did not run on before getting to the subject at hand.

____ 8. Used appropriate changes in voice inflection.

____ 9. Document other behaviors or actions not listed above.

____ **RATING**

The candidates are to be rated on the overall quality of their oral communication, rather than looking at the extent to which each behavior listed above was or was not effectively covered. The above behaviors are to be used as guidelines but are not intended to be used to simply tally the number of check marks and compute anyone's score, nor should the number of check marks be used to compare candidates to determine overall ratings for this category.

MOST APPROPRIATE WRITTEN COMMUNICATION

✓ Check All Behaviors That Apply

____ 1. Utilized notes or memos to convey information to people.

____ 2. Utilized appropriate grammar.

____ 3. Utilized appropriate spelling.

____ 4. Utilized appropriate punctuation.

____ 5. Utilized appropriate word usage.

____ 6. Wrote legibly.

Note: Remember that written communication is evaluated across entire IB on a 1–5 scale for all items.

____ **RATING**

REFERENCES

Albright, A. (with) Wasson, E., Varghese, R., & Mosendz, P. (June 15, 2020). Better cops? Or fewer cops? *Bloomberg Businessweek*, pp. 32–33.

Ansbacher, H. L. (1951). History of the leaderless group discussion technique. *Psychological Bulletin, 48*(5), 383–391.

Armacost, B. (2016). The organizational reasons police departments don't change, *Harvard Business Review.*

Associated Press, (2020). Police funding, officer job cuts. *Wall Street Journal,* July 3, 2020, p. A2.

Bargh, J. A., Chen, M., & Burrows, L. (1996). Automaticity of social behavior: Direct effects of trait construct and stereotype activation on action. *Journal of Personality and Social Psychology, 71,* 230–244.

Bass, B. M. (1954). The leaderless group discussion. *Psychological Bulletin, 51*(5), 465–492.

Barrett, G. V., & Depinet, R. L. (1991). A reconsideration of testing for competence rather than for intelligence. *American Psychologist, 46*(10), 1012–1024.

Bledow, R., & Frese, M. (2009). A situational judgment test of personal initiative and its relationship to performance. *Personnel Psychology, 62*(2), 229–258.

Boyatzis, R. E. (1982). *The competent manager: A model for effective performance.* New York, NY: John Wiley & Sons.

Bracken, D. T. Jr. (1989). *Assessment center exercise performance: An examination of the trainability of the leaderless group discussion.* Unpublished doctoral dissertation, University of Georgia, Athens, GA.

Brannick, M. T., Michaels, C. E., & Baker, D. P. (1989). Construct validity of in-basket scores. *Journal of Applied Psychology, 74,* 957–963.

Bray, D. W. (1964). The management progress study. *American Psychologist, 19,* 419–420.

Bray, D. W., & Grant, D. L. (1966). The assessment center in the measurement of potential for business management. *Psychological Monographs, 80*(17), 1–27.

Bray, D. W., Campbell, R. J., & Grant, D. L. (1974). *Formative years in business. A long-term AT&T study of managerial lives.* Robert E. Krieger Publishing Company.

Brostoff, M., & Meyer, H. H. (1984). The effects of coaching on in-basket performance. *Journal of Assessment Center Technology, 7,* 17–21.

Byham, W. C. (1970). Assessment centers for spotting future managers. *Harvard Business Review, 48*(4), 150–160.

Carter, S. L. (June 8, 2020). The wrong reach of the law. *Bloomberg Businessweek,* p. 38–39.

CBS News. (2020, June, 17). *Atlanta police officer fired after fatally shooting black man Rayshard Brooks.*

Chan, D., & Schmitt, N. (1997). Video-based versus paper-and-pencil method of assessment in situational judgment tests: Subgroup differences in test performance and face validity perceptions. *Journal of Applied Psychology, 82*(1), 143–159.

Christian, M. S., Edwards, B. D., & Bradley, J. C. (2010). Situational judgment tests: constructs assessed and a meta-analysis of their criterion-related validities. *Personnel Psychology, 63*(1), 83–117.

Correll, J., Park, B., Judd, C. M., Wittenbrink, B., Sadler, M. S., & Keesee, T. (2007). Across the thin blue line: Police officers and racial bias in the decision to shoot. *Journal of Personality & Social Psychology, 92*(6), 1006–1023.

Correll, J., Hudson, S. M., Guillermo, S., & Ma, D. S. (2014). The Police officer's dilemma: A decade of research on racial bias in the decision to shoot. *Social & Personality Psychology Compass, 8,* 201–213.

Coy, P. (June 8, 2020). Mainstream economics has many ideas about getting beyond racism. Which lessons apply in real life? *Bloomberg Businessweek,* pp. 7–8.

Devine, P. G. (1989). Stereotypes and prejudice: Their automatic and controlled components. *Journal of Personality and Social Psychology, 56,* 5–18.

Devine, P. G., & Baker, S. M. (1991). Measurement of racial subtyping. *Journal of Personality and Social Psychology, 17,* 44–50.

Devine, P. G., & Elliot, A. J. (1995). Are racial stereotypes really fading? The Princeton trilogy revisited. *Personality and Social Psychology Bulletin, 11,* 1139–1150.

Donovan-Smith, O., & Epstein, K. (2019, June 2). 72 Philadelphia police officers pulled off the street amid probe into racist Facebook posts. *Washington Post.*

Dovidio, J. F., Evans, N., & Tyler, R. B. (1986). Racial stereotypes: The contents of their cognitive representations. *Journal of Experimental Social Psychology, 22,* 22–37.

Duncan, B. L. (1976). Differential social perception and attribution of intergroup violence: Testing the lower limits of stereotyping of blacks. *Journal of Personality and Social Psychology, 34,* 590–598.

Eberhardt, J. L., Goff, P. A., Purdie, V. J., & Davies, P. G. (2004). Seeing black: Race, crime, and visual processing. *Journal of Personality and Social Psychology, 87*(6), 876–893.

Eurich, T. L., Krause, D. E., Cigularov, K., Konstantin, C., & Thornton, G. C. (2009). Assessment centers: Current practices in the United States. *Journal of Business and Psychology, 24*(4), 387–407.

Fairchild, H. H., & Cozens, J. A. (1981). Chicano, Hispanic, or Mexican American: What's in a name? *Hispanic Journal of Behavioral Sciences, 3,* 191–198.

Fetzer, M., & Tuzinsky, K. (Eds.). (2013). *Simulations for personnel selection.* New York: Springer.

Fleishman, E. A., Wetrogan, L. I., Uhlman, C. E., & Marshall-Mies, J. C. (1995). Knowledge. In N. G. Peterson, M. D. Mumford, W. C. Borman, P. R. Jeanneret,

& E. A. Fleishman (Eds.), *Development of prototype occupational information network content model.* 1, 1–10. Salt Lake City: Utah Department of Employment Security (Contract Number 94-542).

Frese, M., Fay D., Hilburger T., & Leng, K. (1997). The concept of personal initiative: Operationalization, reliability and validity of two German samples. *Journal of Occupational & Organizational Psychology, 70,* 139–161.

Friedman, B. (June 13-14, 2020). Amid calls to "defund" how to rethink policing. *The Wall Street Journal,* pp. C2–C4.

Gill, R. W. T. (1982). A trainability concept for management potential and an empirical study of its relationship with intelligence for two managerial skills. *Journal of Occupational Psychology, 52,* 185–197.

Glaser, J., & Knowles, E. D. (2008). Implicit motivation to control prejudice. *Journal of Experimental Social Psychology, 44,* 164–172.

Goldstein, I. L., & Ford, J. K. (2002). *Training in organizations.* Belmont, CA: Thomson Learning.

Harvey, R. J. (1991). Job analysis. In M. D. Dunnette & L. H. Hough (Eds.), *Handbook of industrial and organizational psychology* (Vol. 2, 2nd ed., pp. 71–163). Palo Alto, CA: Consulting Psychologists Press.

Henry, V. E. (2003). *The compstat paradigm management accountability in policing.* New York: Looseleaf Law Publications.

Holcombe, M., McLaughlin, E. C., & Henderson, J. (2020, August 5). DA wants bond revoked after ex-officer charged with murder in Rayshard Brooks case takes Florida trip. CNN. https://www.cnn.com/2020/08/05/us/rayshard-brooks -garrett-rolfe-bond-revoke-request/index.html

Holder, S. (June 8, 2020). The city that remade its police department. *Bloomberg Businessweek,* pp. 37–38.

Howard, A., & Bray, D. (1988). *Managerial lives in transition, advancing age and changing times.* New York, London: The Guilford Press.

InjusticeWatch. (n.d.). *Cops around the country are posting racist and violent comments on Facebook.*

International Task Force on Assessment Center Guidelines. (2009). Guidelines and ethical considerations for assessment center operations. *International Journal of Selection and Assessment, 17*(3), 243–250.

Jackson, L. A. (1995). Stereotypes, Emotions, Behavior, and Overall Attitudes toward Hispanics by Anglos. *Research Report No. 10.* East Lansing, MI: Julian Samora Research Institute.

Kotter, J. (1990). What leaders really do. Reprinted in 2001 by *Harvard Business Review, Breakthrough Leadership,* 85–96.

Kurecka, P. M., Austin, J. M., Johnson, W., & Mendoza, J. L. (1982). Full and errant coaching effects on assigned role leaderless group discussion performance. *Personnel Psychology, 35,* 805–812.

Li, W., & Lodhi, H. (2020. The states taking on police reform after the death of George Floyd. *The Marshall Project,* p. 1. https://fivethirtyeight.com/features /which-states-are-taking-on-police-reform-after-george-floyd/

Lievens, F. (2002), Trying to understand the different pieces of the construct validity puzzle of assessment centers: An examination of assessor and assessee effects. *Journal of Applied Psychology, 87,* 675–686.

Lievens, F. (2002). An examination of the accuracy of slogans related to assessment centres. *Personnel Review, 31*(1), 86–102.

Lievens, F., Peeters, H., & Schollaert, E. (2008). Situational judgment tests: A review of recent research. *Personnel Review, 37*(4), 426–441.

Lievens, F., Buyse, T., Sackett, P. R., & Connelly, B. S. (September 2012). The effects of coaching on situational judgment tests in high-stakes selection. *International Journal of Selection and Assessment, 20*(3), 272–282.

MacKinnon, D. W. (1977). From selecting spies to selecting managers. In J. J. Moses & W. C. Byham (Eds.), *Applying the assessment center method.* New York: Pergamon Press, p. 91.

Marin, G. (1984). Stereotyping Hispanics: The differential effect of research method, label, and degree of contact. *International Journal of Intercultural Relations, 8,* 17–27.

McDaniel, M. A., Morgeson, F. P., Finnegan, E. B., Campion, M. A., & Braverman, E. P. (2001). Predicting job performance using situational judgment tests: A clarification of the literature. *Journal of Applied Psychology, 86,* 730–740.

Morgeson, F. P., & Campion, M. A. (2000). Accuracy in job analysis: Toward an inference-based model. *Journal of Organizational Behavior, 21,* 819–827.

Motowidlo, S. J., Dunnette, M. D., & Carter, G.W. (December 1990). An alternative selection procedure: the low-fidelity simulation. *Journal of Applied Psychology, 75*(6), 640–647.

Motowidlo, S. J., Borman, W. C. and Schmit, M. J. 1997. A theory of individual differences in task and contextual performance. *Human Performance, 10,* 71–83.

Niemann, Y. F., Jennings, L., Rozelle, R. M., Baxter, J. C., & Sullivan, E. (1994). Use of free responses and cluster analysis to determine stereotypes of eight groups. *Personality and Social Psychology Bulletin, 20,* 379–390.

Offices of Strategic Services (OSS) Assessment Staff. (1948). *Assessment of men.* New York: Rinehart.

Park, J., & Banaji, M. R. (2000). Mood and heuristics: The influence of happy and sad states on sensitivity and bias in stereotyping. *Journal of Personality and Social Psychology, 78,* 1005–1023.

Peruche, B. M., & Plant, E. A. (2006). The correlates of law enforcement officers' automatic and controlled race-based responses to criminal suspects. *Basic & Applied Social Psychology, 28,* 193–199.

Peterson, N. G., Mumford, M. D., Borman, W. C., Jeanneret, P. R., Fleishman, E. A., & Campion, M. A., et al. (2001). Understanding work using the Occupational Information Network (O*NET): Implications for practice and research. *Personnel Psychology, 54,* 1–51.

Petty, M. M. (1974). A multivariate analysis of the effects of experience and training upon performance in a leaderless group discussion. *Personnel Psychology, 27,* 271–282.

Plant, E. A., & Peruche, B. M. (2005). The consequences of race for police officers' responses to criminal suspects. *Psychological Science, 16,* 180–183.

Ployhart, R. E., Weekley, J. A., Holtz, B. C., & Kemp, C. (2003). Web-based and pencil-and-paper testing of applicants in a proctored setting: Are personality, biodata, and situational judgment tests comparable? *Personnel Psychology, 56,* 733–752.

Sagar, H. A., & Schofield, J. W. (1980). Racial and behavioral cues in Black and White children's perceptions of ambiguously aggressive acts. *Journal of Personality and Social Psychology, 39,* 590–598.

Schaller, M., Park, J. H., & Mueller, A. (2003). Fear of the dark: Interactive effects of beliefs about danger and ambient darkness on ethnic stereotypes. *Personality and Social Psychology Bulletin, 29,* 637–649.

Shippmann, J. S., Ash, R. A., Battista, M., Carr, L., Eyde, L. D., Hesketh, B., & Sanchez, I. et al. (2000). The practice of competency modeling. *Personnel Psychology, 53,* 703–740.

Siddiqui, S. & Gersham, J. (June 19, 2020). Atlanta police prosecution is a "tough case." *The Wall Street Journal,* p. A6.

Siddiqui, S. (2020, Jun 17). Atlanta police officer who shot Rayshard Brooks charged with felony murder; second officer, Devin Brosnan, charged with aggravated assault; he also is cooperating with prosecutors. *Wall Street Journal* (Online) Retrieved from https://login.ezproxy.fau.edu/login?url=https://search-proquest-com.ezproxy.fau.edu/docview/2414051377?accountid=10902

Smith, K. C. (1996). A situational judgment test: Criterion and construct validity evidence. Paper presented at the annual meeting of the *International Personnel Management Association Assessment Council,* Boston, MA.

Smither, J. W., Reilly, R. R., Millsap, R. E., Pearlman, K., & Stoffey, R. W. (1993). Applicant reactions to selection procedures. *Personnel Psychology, 46*(1), 1–49.

Spencer, K. B., Charbonneau, A. K., & Glaser, J. (2016). Implicit bias and policing. *Social and Personality Psychology Compass, 1,* 50.

Sternberg, R. J., Wagner, R. K., & Okagaski, L. (1993). Practical intelligence: The nature and role of tacit knowledge in work and at school. In Puckett J. M., Reese, H. W. (Eds.), *Advances in lifespan development.* Hillsdale, NJ: Erlbaum.

Thornton, G. C., III, & Byham, W. C. (1982). *Assessment centers and managerial performance.* New York: Academic.

Thornton, E. G., III., & Gibbons, A.M. (1982). Validity of assessment centers for personnel selection. *HR Management Review, 19*(3), 169–187.

Thornton, G. C., III, & Mueller-Hanson, R. A. (2004). *Developing organizational simulations: A guide for practitioners and students.* Mahwah, NJ: Lawrence Erlbaum Associates, Inc.

Thornton, G. C., & Rupp, D. E. (2006). *Assessment centers in human resource management: Strategies for prediction, diagnosis, and development.* Mahwah, NJ: Lawrence Erlbaum Associates, Inc.

Tuzinsky, K., & Fetzer, M. (Eds.). (2013). *Simulations for personnel selection an introduction.* New York: Springer.

Ulrich, D., Brockbank, W., Yeung, A. K., & Lake, D. G. (1995). Human resource competencies: An empirical assessment. *Human Resource Management, 34,* 473–495.

Vasilopoulos, N. L., Reilly, R. R., & Leaman, J. A. (2000). The influence of job familiarity and impression management on self-report measure scale scores and response latencies. *Journal of Applied Psychology, 85*(1), 50–64.

Vallas, P. G. (2020, July 18-19). Police reform wasn't the only big change in Camden. *The Wall Street Journal,* p. A11.

Walsh, W., Banaji, M. R., & Greenwald, A. G. (1995, May). A failure to eliminate race bias in judgments of criminals. Paper presented at the *7th Annual Convention of the American Psychological Society,* New York.

Weekley, J. A., & Ployhart, R. E. (2005). Situational judgment: antecedents and relationships with performance. *Human Performance, 18*(1), 81–104.

White, V., & Robinson, S. (2014). Leading change in policing: Police culture and the psychological contract. *Police Journal, 87*(4), 258–269. https://doi-org.ezproxy.fau.edu/10.1350/pojo.2014.87.4.675

SUGGESTED READING

Bennis, W. G. & Thomas, R. J. (2002). *Geeks and geezers: how era, values, and defining moments shape leaders.* Harvard Business School Press.

Blanchard, K., Carlos, J. P., & Randolph, A. (1999, 2001). *The 3 keys to empowerment.* San Francisco: Berrett-Koehler Publishers, Inc.

Blanchard, K., & Bowles, S. (1998). *Gung ho! Turn on the people in any organization.* New York: William Morrow and Company, Inc.

Block, P. (1993). *Stewardship: Choosing service over self-interest.* San Francisco: Berrett-Koehler Publishers, Inc.

Bolman, L. G., & Deal, T. E. (2001). *Leading with soul.* Jossey-Bass.

Boyatzis, R., & McKee, A. (2005). *Resonant leadership: Sustaining yourself and connecting with others through mindfulness, hope, and compassion.* Boston, MA: Harvard Business School Press.

Byham, W. C. with Cox, J. (1988). *Zapp! The lightning of empowerment: How to improve productivity, quality and employee satisfaction.* New York: Harmony Books.

Goleman, D. (1997). *Emotional intelligence.* New York: Bantam.

Goleman, D. (1998). *Working with emotional intelligence.* Bantam Books, New York.

Goleman, D., Boyatzis, R. E., & McKee, A. (2002). *Primal leadership: Realizing the power of emotional intelligence.* Boston, MA: Harvard Business School Press.

Heifetz, R. A. (1994). *Leadership without easy answers.* Cambridge, MA and London, England: The Belknap Press of Harvard University Press.

Heifetz, R. A., & Linsky, M. (2002). *Leadership on the line staying alive through the dangers of leading.* Boston, MA: Harvard Business School Press.

Kotter, J. P. (1996). *Leading change.* Boston, MA: Harvard Business School Press.
Kotter, J. P. (1988). *The leadership challenge.* Free Press, New York.

Kouzes, J. M., & Posner, B. Z. (2002). *The leadership challenge* (3rd ed.). Jossey-Bass.

Kouzes, J. M., & Posner, B. Z. (1993). *Credibility: How leaders gain and lose it, why people demand it.* San Francisco: Jossey-Bass Publishers.

Kouzes, J. M., & Posner, B. Z. (1999). *Encouraging the heart: A leader's guide to rewarding and recognizing others.* San Francisco: Jossey-Bass Publishers.

INDEX